The Rest of Us Catholics

The Loyal Opposition

Dedication

To the late Dr Gerry McGarry,
founder and editor of The Furrow, *Maynooth,*
who was the first to encourage me
and many of my generation to try to write
– and to have the courage on occasion
to stick our necks out,
even when we might have preferred
to remain part of the crowd.

The Rest of Us Catholics

The Loyal Opposition

by
Joseph Dunn

Templegate Publishers
Springfield, Illinois

Copyright © 1994, Joseph Dunn

First published in the Republic of Ireland in 1994 as

No Lions in the Hierarchy

by

The Columba Press
93 The Rise, Mount Merrion
Blackrock, Co Dublin

First published in the United States in 1994 by

Templegate Publishers
302 East Adams Street
P.O. Box 5152
Springfield Illinois
62705-5152

ISBN 0-87243-208-4

Acknowledgements

Anyone who reads more than a few pages will see that I am indebted to my favourite weekly reading matter, *The Tablet*. Also to a few friends who made suggestions about the text – Peter Kelly who was involved in making many of the programmes, Dr Jim Byrne and some others who might prefer not to be identified. And to RTÉ for making the whole experience possible.

Contents

Each chapter heading (except the last) is the title of a Radharc/RTÉ television programme.

Introduction

Joe Dunn, as he always introduces himself (the "Father Joseph" is a conclusion to which others come) is one of a vanishing breed of priests. He is first of all a product of an era which, in the finest traditions of the priesthood, believed that some priests could represent God and the Church by performing with the highest degree of professional excellence in the professional world. Archbishop McQuaid of Dublin, no flaming radical by any stretch of the imagination, knew enough of the history of the priesthood to comprehend this truth, and sent many of his most gifted priests off for training in the various disciplines which he thought might be important and permitted others to acquire professional skills which might somehow be useful to the Church and its mission. Thus Joe Dunn became a TV cameraman and director. In the tradition of the search for excellence which was part of the ideology of that era just before the Second Vatican Council he became an extraordinarily skillful cameraman, if not the best in Ireland or even the best in the world as some of his close friends claim, certainly the best it has ever been my privilege to see at work.

This notion of the priest as secular professional has fallen into disfavor today. The current ideology says that the lay person can represent the Church just as well as if not better than the priest, a theoretical and naïve conviction that shows not even the most elementary understanding of what a Catholic priest stands for in the minds of those who live and work in the secular world. The Catholic layman may be a better Christian than a priest, but sociologically he can not represent the presence and concern of the official Church the way a priest can. Like so many other insights of our past, we Catholics will rediscover this one, only after most of the priest professionals are dead.

Like so many others of his generation, Joe Dunn also represents those of us who were excited and exhilarated by the promise of Pope John and the Council and have lived since to see our bright hopes smashed by the ecclesiastical power structure and those leaders for whom the preservation of their own power and prestige is more important than listening to and responding to the needs and the experiences of the Catholic laity.

The work of the Council can never be undone, not among ordinary Catholics. Those curialists who are trying to undo the Council are in power just now and they can persuade themselves that they have won. Even in the short run, however, they have been unable to turn back the wave of history and have in fact succeeded only in destroying their own credibility.

Priests like Joe Dunn who have lived through the years of hope and frustration, of glowing expectations and bitter disappointments, know that they are on the side of history. As Finley Peter Dunne's Mr. Dooley once remarked, "Histhry, Hennessey, always vindy-cates the Dimmycrats, but only after they're dead. Nothing is ever officially true till the Raypooblicans admit it and by that time all the Dimmycrats are dead."

Be that as it may, it has not always been easy for what I would call the Conciliar generation of priests to believe that the Holy Spirit is still at work in the Church, still blowing whither She will, especially in recent years. That Joe Dunn still believes in Her and Her ways, this usually gentle, sometimes acerbic, and always perceptive book is persuasive proof. It is the story of one man's life in the priesthood, of a generation's torment in the priesthood, and of a Church which suddenly, almost without warning, changed and which no one is ever going to change back again.

Andrew Greeley
Grand Beach
June 1994

Author's Explanation and Preface

The chapter headings in this book recall the titles of a selection of programmes made for Irish television by Radharc Films, an independent TV production unit working in the socio-religious field, which I helped to found, and now direct. (RADHARC is an Irish word which may be roughly translated as 'Vision' and pronounced RYE–ARK).

Each chapter is complete in itself, so one can dip in at any point.

The whole is part travel book and part autobiography, but it is mostly about the issues raised by the experience of making the particular programmes. For this reason the subheadings may sometimes give a better indication of what the chapter is about than the actual programme title itself.

It is said that people write books because they are conceited, because they want to set the record – as they see it – straight, or because they hope to earn money. This last cannot be true in my case. The first and second maybe – although I would like to deny it; the reader will judge. But there are other reasons for writing. In this case I would like to think that I am deeply motivated by a love for my church, and concern for its future; concern too for the future of my own country.

There is this selfish reason as well. There are enormous areas of human experience where I feel unsure because I don't know what I think. And I don't like not knowing what I think. In the past I have found that the only way to clarify my thoughts on any subject is to write about them. As the old lady quoted by E.M. Forster said: 'How can I know what I think till I see what I say.'

One of my core beliefs is that television broadcasting – the area to which I have given most of my working life – has been a very significant agent of change; change to which society in general and the church in particular have so far found great difficulty in adapting. Radharc programmes have inevitably helped to chronicle some of these changes.

In the making of a television programme, one is privileged to meet interesting people in interesting places at interesting times, and to be able to say to them, 'Tell me everything you know – who, why, what, when, where?'

And even after thirty years I am still amazed at the fact that when one comes into town with a camera and mentions television, one can reasonably expect that princes, presidents and prime ministers, cardinals and archbishops will try to make time for you to interview them, and invite you to functions and occasions where you would normally not have access.

Over the years I have been involved in making over 350 television programmes, mainly on church-related topics, in over seventy different countries. In the course of that work I have met and interviewed many interesting people. I've had afternoon tea with Jomo Kenyatta, and supper with Lech Walesa, and interviewed Archbishop Romero and spent a night in the jungle with Burmese freedom fighters. So I have a range of experiences which provides matter for reflection.

I think too that, because of my work, I am probably freer than most priests to look at different sides of a problem – as well as to express my own views for whatever they are worth. Because while I am a priest in good standing, I am neither a professional theologian nor a practising parish priest. Nor indeed a writer who has to please editors or publishers to earn a living.

Much of the time I am only quoting other people. But in so far as I express my views, some will appear theologically conservative, some radical, some rash, some stupid. I would like them to be judged by one criterion alone – do they make sense, common sense? Because if they do they might be true. The mark of God's world is intelligibility, and human knowledge has only progressed because those who push forward the frontiers of knowledge take it for granted that this is so. Einstein said once that the only incomprehensible thing about the universe is that it is comprehensible. He himself made some extraordinary predictions on the basis of mathematical calculations alone, others provided the experimental proof.

To continue living as a human being requires one to believe that the world makes some sense, be it in art, in science or in religion. At the same time a modicum of intellectual honesty is all one requires to admit that what one believes to be true may conceivably be false. I express some opinions in this book which I believe to be sensible and true, while accepting that any or all may be false. That is all that is possible in the human condition.

I know at least one relative of mine who will criticise the book as being mainly about church politics, whereas what's really important is Christian living. Agreed. But the two are related. If we believe Christ wanted leaders to guide us in Christian living, then one of the essential purposes of his church must be to continue this leadership function. And do it well.

So it is right to be interested in, and concerned about how leaders are appointed, and how they carry out their mandate. The process has to be carried on by frail human beings, and is therefore a fitting subject of critical concern.

But I believe in the church and I love the church, and I would be deeply grieved if I felt that anything I say here would do anything to weaken anyone else's love or belief. Christ supported by word and action the religious institution of his day, while at the same time offering the most withering criticism of its leadership.

When he criticised the functionaries of his day, he used images that would certainly cause eyebrows to rise if anyone were to use them today – phrases like 'brood of poisonous snakes', 'blind guides straining out gnats and swallowing camels', 'shutting up the kingdom of heaven in men's faces'. The powerful invective in chapter 23 of Matthew is unique in the gospels, and awesome, coming from the gentle Master. 'Alas for you, scribes and Pharisees, you hypocrites! You who are like whitewashed tombs that look handsome on the outside but inside are full of dead men's bones and every kind of corruption. In the same way you appear to people from the outside like good honest men, but inside you are full of hypocrisy and lawlessness.'

I once came across a story in a sermon book about a passenger who was critical of the way the captain was running the ship. So he jumped overboard in protest! Christianity would be far stronger today if in the past, those who had rows with the skipper and crew of the Barque of Peter had stayed aboard and kept reminding both sailors and passengers that there were other possible directions in which to navigate.

So if I am sometimes critical of the captain and crew, it's my ship as well, and I am sticking with it.

Countries in which the author has directed film

(The number refers to separate occasions.)

AFRICA: Kenya (3), Mozambique, Sierra Leone, South Africa, The Gambia, Zambia, Zimbabwe.

ASIA: Bali, Hong Kong, (2) India, Indonesia, Japan, Korea, Macao, Myanmar, Sri Lanka, Taiwan, Thailand, The Philippines (2), Vietnam.

AUSTRALASIA: Australia (2), Kiribati, Nauru, New Hebrides, Tasmania, Tonga.

EUROPE: Austria (2), Belgium, Czech Republic, Denmark , England (4), France (3), Germany (3), Greece, Iceland, Ireland, Italy (5), Luxembourg, Malta, The Netherlands, Norway, Poland, Portugal, Russia, Scotland (2), Sicily, Switzerland, Spain (3), Sweden, The Vatican (3), Yugoslavia.

MIDDLE EAST: Israel.

CANADA: Ontario, Quebec.

CARIBBEAN: Antigua, Barbados, Cuba, Dominica, Grenada, Haiti, Montserrat, St Vincent, Trinidad.

CENTRAL AMERICA: Guatemala, Mexico, Nicaragua (2), El Salvador.

NORTH AMERICA: Arizona, California (2), Florida, Iowa, Maryland, Michigan, Missouri, Montana, New Jersey, New York, Ohio, Virginia, Washington State, Washington DC.

SOUTH AMERICA: Argentina, Bolivia (2), Brazil (2), Chile, Columbia, Ecuador, Peru.

1
THE FORMATION OF PRIESTS
Seminary life in the 1950s & 60s. The fall in vocations

Vocations to the priesthood and religious life are much more infrequent nowadays than when I took the shilling. I am not too depressed by that – presumably God has his reasons. Neither am I surprised, given the changes that have taken place in society over the last forty years. Nor do I expect there will be any sudden upturn in the descending graph.

When I was a teenager, nearly three times as many teenagers chose to be priests and nuns as do today. My own views of how and why this change came about inevitably arise from my own experience of vocation, so it is necessary to analyse that experience to arrive at any conclusions.

People call it a 'vocation' or 'calling', because it is part of the culture that no one chooses to be a priest unless called by God. That calling is only confirmed when one receives the grace of ordination. 'You have not chosen me but I have chosen you' – Christ's words to his apostles.

At the moment of being called to ordination or religious profession, 'vocation' has some reality. But up to that point it is easy to talk about and impossible to define. If it were to mean that God spoke to one in the night or appeared with finger pointing like Lord Kitchener, it might be definable. But I never met anyone who got such a call. And I certainly didn't.

In an ideal world, a vocation would be based on the love of God and somehow be a response to it. But the average young person in his or her teens hasn't had much time or opportunity to grow in the love of

God. Not enough anyway to give up joyfully all that one is required to give up to become a priest or a nun.

And there is a lot to give up. Sex for instance, and all that little word encompasses – a basic human experience, pleasure, the tenderness of a shared love, a close relationship – physical and intellectual, a kind of sharing which is not possible in any other state, the deep yearning in all of us to pass on our genes, the joy of children.

Other important things too – like the freedom to determine one's own destiny. I was locked up, regimented, forbidden to read newspapers, or smoke, or be seen in public talking to women. Forced to wear a stupid hat, to cycle in all weathers to the university, to study subjects that didn't interest me. Forbidden to attend the theatre, or have a drink in a pub, and so on and so on.

Do young people think of these things when they join up? I did, and I dreaded them.

So why did I become a priest? It certainly was not because I felt any attraction, in fact I hated the whole idea. My teens were not a happy time: I felt much as a young person must feel who contracts leukemia and has to try and come to terms with the prospect of an early death. I prayed hard that I would get some sign from the Lord saying he didn't want me. I hoped I might be rejected by the seminary. And in all this I am sure I was not that unusual. Colm Murphy, a classmate at school and now a Columban priest, told me that he felt the same way.

Entering the Seminary

Almost everything in seminary life, I found out later – my seminary was Holy Cross College, Clonliffe – was determined by what was called 'seniority', and seniority in the diocese was decided for ever by the order in which the new aspirants arrived on the very first day.

The second day was spent getting to know the place. I remember meeting one group of more senior students – including a deacon who was only one year from ordination. In my innocence I expected clerical students to talk about holy things, or at least serious things. This deacon talked mostly about football, and laced his conversation with what in seminary jargon is called 'the broad f'. I was amazed.

15

(My mother was brought up a Protestant, and she was very strict about profanity.)

The other thing that surprised me was that half my fellow students were not even Dubliners, but came, complete with their varied provincial accents, from so-called diocesan colleges around the country. I walked for a while with a chap from St Brendan's, Killarney and North Kerry, Con O'Keeffe – later a colleague in the early days of Radharc. Long afterwards he remembered that first meeting, saying he hardly understood one word I said. So far as I remember the incomprehension was mutual.

Some of these students from outside the diocese chose to be in Dublin, others came because the quota for their own diocese had been filled in Maynooth, the National Seminary, and it was either Dublin or the foreign missions. This was not to say that their academic standard fell below that of Dublin students. On the contrary, academic requirements were perhaps lower for native Dubliners because there were never anything like enough applicants from the diocese itself.

Seminary Life

Clonliffe was a dull claustrophobic place. One never got out except to attend lectures in the University or Mass in the Pro-Cathedral. Recreation consisted in the main in walking around the grounds of the college. What walking space there was had to be divided between Junior and Senior House, who inhabited the same building but were always kept apart – with no intercommunication during class or recreation. The available walking space was therefore effectively halved, with use of back and front walks alternating between Juniors and Seniors. The back walk was one way round and round a very small football pitch, completely overlooked by the main building. The front walk brought one down by an early Georgian house where the French Sisters of Charity lived. A right angle bend at the house led one across the front of the main building and down towards the main gate. The main driveway which would have completed a circle was out of bounds – so the student traffic moved both ways on relatively narrow paths. Because of this dearth of walking space, everyone was on top of everyone else at recreation time; and one

16

could never escape the presence of the high featureless grey limestone building, and prying eyes of prefects and deans of discipline. Perhaps it was part of a plan to keep everyone under continuous observation. It certainly was unnecessary because there were fields going down to the Tolka river which were only used occasionally for football. With a little imagination, a president or bursar might have built extended walks round these pitches and along by the river, and thereby contributed mightily to the psychological wellbeing of the student body.

The college itself consisted of four long straight corridors, one on top of the other with a stairway in the middle (a new wing was added later). There was a choir room and church tacked on one end and a library over the kitchen at the other. But otherwise it was featureless inside and out. The building boasted an antique central heating system whose antiquity was dignified by a brass plaque in the corridor inscribed in Latin. It spoke of *aqua calida per tubos.* The *aqua calida,* if and when it flowed in the *tubos,* was adequate to warm the building in mild spring or autumn weather. In winter it didn't seem to make any apparent difference.

We had visitors once a month. I remember my father sitting in the visitors' room wrapped up in rugs with only a little of his face showing. I remember too getting up in the morning without heat, shaving in icy cold water, going down to a cold oratory and then, when the seventy or so bodies had heated it up after half an hour of meditation, parading out and down the corridor to Mass in an unheated church. I suffered agony in winter from chilblains. On Saturday mornings we were confined to our rooms to study. When the bell sounded after eleven for a mid-morning cup of tea, the lower corridor rapidly filled with figures dancing on the tiled floor trying to restore blood circulation. One tip I learnt from an older student was to bury my stocking feet in a cardboard box filled with blankets.

The holy rule said, 'The students shall observe strict silence except at times when speaking is permitted.' Most of the time speaking was not permitted. Going up the stairs to study at five in the evening, one knew one would not enjoy any human company or discourse until the half hour of recreation after supper (meals were eaten in silence).

Going to one's room after evening recreation was the loneliest time of the day. There was nothing to look forward to except a study period followed by night prayer and bed and sleep and rise with the 6 o'clock bell, wash in cold water and get down in time for morning prayer and a half hour of meditation and community Mass and breakfast. Only after breakfast was speaking again permitted.

Did some people break the rules and occasionally visit a fellow student in his room? Very few. To be caught was a serious offence. To be caught in a room after night prayer was immediate expulsion. I know, because I know somebody it happened to. Now maybe there were other things wrong that I wasn't aware of, but anyway he was sent packing the following morning before we had time to miss him. He joined an English diocese.

I found Clonliffe difficult. I got what the doctor called a threatened duodenal ulcer, which could be painful at times. It was probably psychosomatic in origin, reflecting something of my mental state at the time: according to the contemporary medical fashion I was given tripe, ground rice and milk.

And why did I put up with all this? And worse. Well ... because it was all part of the mysterious process called 'having a vocation.'

Having a Vocation

Looking back after forty something years, I think that there were five factors involved in my vocation. Leaving aside the providence of God and the way he orders things, these factors were the prevailing view of the priesthood at the time, fear of rejecting a genuine call, awareness of death, the experience of prayer, and the logic of belief.

Exalted view of priesthood

I remember a Jesuit scholastic telling us that if a young man were to spend fourteen years studying to be a priest, and if he fell dead after his first Mass, it would all have been worthwhile.

Fear

I hate to admit it, but my experience of myself and others tells me that fear is the most powerful of all human motivation. Why do children study hour after hour for an exam? Because they love the subject matter? Maybe we'd like to think so, but realistically we know the emotion is not so much love as fear — fear of not living up to parental expectations; fear of not living up to one's own hopes for oneself; fear of reducing one's options to choose a desirable career.

I went to school with the Jesuits who in those days were big into fear. Every class had its yearly retreat, and there would always be talks on vocation. One could be called to be a doctor or lawyer or businessman or all sorts of things. But the real vocation of vocations was to become a (Jesuit) priest, although there were other sorts of (lesser) priests as well.

And how did one know one had a vocation? Here things became much more vague. The retreat master, of course, would be glad to give individuals advice. But what happened if one had a vocation and was too selfish, too obsessed with the pleasures of this world to accept it? How would one feel when the day eventually came to meet one's Maker? Would it be like the apostles who were able to say to the Lord, 'We have left all things to follow you, what reward shall we have?' – and were promised an exalted position in the life to come? Or like the young man in the gospel to whom Our Lord said, 'Come follow me', and who went away because the sacrifice was too great?

It was thus I was caught in the net. As I suppose were many others. James Joyce of course escaped.

Awareness of death

My paternal grandfather died when I was fifteen and he was one hundred and four. He was born five years before the Great Famine; and yet I knew him well. My father knew his own paternal grandfather who was born in 1800 and died at the age of ninety-three. The Dunns were long lived – when they got the chance – but like all Victorian and Edwardian families they were frequent victims of killer diseases which nowadays no longer pose a threat.

In 1905 my grandfather bought Roslyn Park in Sandymount, an old Gandon house with later additions, and four and a half acres. He was a gambler – my father used say that he would gamble on two flies going up a wall – and some of his property gambles clearly paid off. I think my family background was relevant to my vocation. As children we spent most of our free time playing with cousins in

Roslyn Park. With orchards and fields and trees and animals and lumber rooms and endless corridors it was a paradise for children. But from an early age I sensed great sadness in the house as well. We heard stories of absent uncles and aunts who had died young and sometimes far away and saw their pictures on the mantelpiece. Kathy who died of pneumonia, aged fifteen, George and Nan and Betty who died in their twenties of TB. Jack who was killed in a mining accident. The shortness of life was something I didn't need to hear about in a sermon. Why bother becoming rich and famous when it could all be over so quickly, and nothing left but a picture on the mantelpiece?

The experience of family prayer

My mother was brought up in the Church of Ireland, and learnt there the habit of prayer. After marriage when she embraced Catholicism, she accepted what for her were new devotions like the rosary and novenas, retaining a love for the bible, a strict view of Sunday observance and a horror of taking the Lord's name in vain. My father was pious as well, and kept an assortment of leather bound prayer books on a little table beside his bed – along with the packet of Goldflake, box of matches and ashtray. He is the only man I've ever seen smoking while shaving with soap and water. With such parents it was natural to have grace before meals, the rosary most nights, and family prayers. Prayer was a constant reminder of God, and our relationship with him.

The logic of belief

Faith in God, they say, is a gift of God. It is a gift I seem to have had from my earliest years, and am thankful to retain. As I see it, my belief is based on reason to the extent that I would find it an irrational act to disbelieve. I find intelligence everywhere and in everything, and I relate that to God. I find matter hard to comprehend while the immaterial seems part of my normal experience. The concept of eternity on reflection seems to me no more difficult to comprehend than time. Given that cast of mind, logic would perhaps suggest some choices rather than others. Or to put that in simple terms, given the shortness of life and the length (so to speak) of eternity, it would seem less than logical to spend most of one's energies for that three score and ten playing with stocks and shares, accumulating estates, and breeding racehorses. All of which I might have been good at.

Perhaps I have been a bit self indulgent in analysing my own motivation for becoming a priest. At the same time I find the exercise is a help towards understanding why fewer young people come forward today. In 1955, twenty-one other priests were ordained with me for the Dublin archdiocese. In 1993, when the population of Dublin was half as large again, there were only seven.

Diminished view of priesthood

For good and solid reasons, theologians in the second half of this century have emphasised the important role of the laity in the church. They even speak of 'the priesthood of the laity'. The ordained priest acts in an essential ministerial role, but all the People of God share in offering the Holy Sacrifice. At the same time the holiness of the married state — modelled according to St Paul, on the union between Christ and his church — is seen in a new light. When I was a seminarian marriage was more often referred to as 'a remedy for concupiscence', while the text quoted from Paul was more likely to to be 'better to marry than to burn!'

Decline of the motive of fear

Liam Ryan, Professor of Sociology in Maynooth, once made the point to us in an interview that at different times in the church there has been, now a pessimistic, now an optimistic attitude to salvation. Both can be sustained from the New Testament. The present phase is an optimistic one — God wills all men to be saved, and God's will is not likely to be thwarted. There are no hellfire sermons anymore, or mention of the primrose path that leads to the everlasting bonfire. Love has taken the place of fear. But if we are all going to be saved that easily, then it is hard to find the motivation to put ourselves out too much on the way. Or to use another image, if everybody will pass the exam automatically, why bother with the inconvenient and painful study?

Hidden death

Young people today are insulated from death in a way that was impossible for former generations. Medical progress has meant that the young rarely die except by accident. Old people die, but at a distance — in hospital or old people's homes. One can easily live into middle age without ever seeing a real dead body. 'Today for me, tomorrow for thee' is a phrase one doesn't often hear in today's world.

Family prayer

Where does it exist?

The logic of belief

In the end, I think the basic reason why fewer young people are willing in the old phrase 'to give their lives to God' is that they don't share the certainties that their parents and grandparents shared about the scope and importance of revelation through Christ, and the need for an institutional church to carry that revelation through history.

Young people today are born into a world dominated by the broadcast media whose characteristic role is to question, even undermine all certainties. A world too where biblical scholarship – in my opinion incorrectly presented and incorrectly understood – has tended to reduce the credibility of the bible in young peoples' minds to that of a folk tale, admirable and beautiful, but more the work of man rather than the work of God. Every few years as far back as I can remember there seemed to be another stupid TV programme on the Dead Sea Scrolls suggesting that new findings somehow invalidated the gospels. Now the gospels may not be written in the way we write history, but without ignoring massive evidence, it is impossible to contradict the historical truth of Christ's message; not anyway without throwing out all of the rest of ancient history. That is a position which, I believe, can be supported with the most rigorous scholarship. But I don't think that is what is communicated through the media today, and that is where the young pick up their ideas and attitudes. Without a greater measure of certainty among young people about the historicity of the gospels, and the importance of the revelation through Christ, one can't expect to find as many as in the past saying 'yes' to poverty, 'yes' to celibate chastity, 'yes' to humble obedience.

There are other factors also at work today. Because sexual imagery is so pervasive in modern society more and more young people seem to feel that perpetual celibacy is an impossible commitment. (This idea is developed in Chapter 2.)

Lack of parental support

Few parents today, I believe, encourage children who may be considering a religious vocation. They see the priesthood and religious life as being unstable in the sense that nowadays many do not persevere. Fathers and mothers, good people, don't want to face the trauma that often accompanies priests leaving the ministry. Being the mother or father of a priest may traditionally have been an honoured position. But mother or father of an ex-priest can be a troublesome role to play, and is not honoured in the same way.

Failure of priests to recruit

Priests and nuns, as one might expect, were once the great recruiting agents for their order. No more! Fr Andrew Greeley the sociologist gave his own view as to why when we interviewed him in 1992:

> The church isn't engaged in any vigorous recruiting campaigns: if the Navy was short on jet pilots there'd be a crash programme – there is no crash programme for vocations in this country. And finally I think there is a sort of a general malaise in the church that is being created by the sense that everything that was accomplished at the Vatican Council is being slowly taken away and that discourages everyone, lay people, priests and young men.

Concern about the fall in vocations

The fact that there are fewer and fewer vocations and that old established orders are going out of existence doesn't keep me awake at night. The change in European Christendom is so significant and seemingly so irreversible, one must presume that the providence of God has a part in it. And one can see reasons. Perhaps the reason why the laity never played a responsible role in the church was that a superfluity of clergy in the past made it unnecessary. Fr Timothy Radcliffe, Master General of the Dominicans, pointed out recently that while the thirteenth century saw the death of some of the older religious orders, new mendicant orders like the Dominicans and the Franciscans came to take their place. Our age has seen the growth and development of lay organizations like Opus Dei, Communione e Liberazione, the St Egidio Community, Dorothy Day's Catholic Worker, the Christian Family Movement, the Legion of Mary, the Focolare and Museum movements. Some have come under strong and valid criticism, some will not last more than a few generations. But by and large these lay organisations are more related to the spirit of this age than some of the older religious orders now fading away.

But one aspect of the decline in traditional vocations does concern me, and that is a drop in moral and intellectual quality. It is said that some of the many abuses current in the church in the century before the Reformation were related to the Black Death. The plagues that then ravaged Europe hit the clergy harder than others, simply because the clergy were heavily engaged in the corporal works of mercy. So their numbers were severely depleted. When the plagues had passed, churches, hospitals, alms houses and schools were crying out for personnel, and so the standards for entry to the clergy were lowered. Unfortunately the same factor seems to be at work today. In my day no one was accepted for the Dublin seminary without the matriculation needed to get into university. Today the clerical student attending the university is the odd exception. Now I don't want to be snobbish about university education, but if on average the clergy are less well educated than those in other professions, then the whole credibility of the group to which I belong is affected. And that hurts.

Summary thoughts

Since my time at Clonliffe, the regime has become much less strict – university students for instance are now allowed to attend societies in University College Dublin. We hadn't been even allowed to talk to lay students at the university in our day. However, one is aware of how many now go on to ordination, and shortly after abandon the priesthood. Whereas comparing with my own class who entered in 1948, one left in the seminary, the rest – twenty-two in all – went on to ordination, and apart from one who died, remain as serving, and so far as I know, celibate priests.

So if the purpose of the exercise is to turn out men who are faithful to their vocation according to the prevailing norms of the church, then there must be something to be said for the old tough system –

though I am not going to say it here. What I will say is that I believe that the process of becoming a priest should be humanly unattractive — to help keep out unsuitable candidates. And I would take a hard look at anyone saying he would *like* to be a priest — unless his principal motive was that of following a course which he saw as God's will.

An appointment as curate or parish priest can be the beginning of a comfortable existence – salary and pension guaranteed, as much leisure time as one chooses to take, an honourable position in society, and the opportunity to be totally selfish. None of which has much to do with denying oneself, taking up one's cross daily, and following Christ.

Postscript on happiness

Looking back after nearly forty years of priesthood, have I been happy? Let me say first that the question I believe has only limited relevance. In the beginning I did not expect to be happy in the priesthood, and I never considered 'being happy' as having any relevance to staying or leaving.

I was in my parents' house when my first letter of appointment arrived. I opened it sitting on the piano stool in the front room. It said I was appointed to teach religion in a vocational school. I read it once, and once again, and then did something I have never done before or since. I brought my two fists crashing down with all my strength on the keys of the piano. I had chosen to be a secular priest to avoid teaching; I had carefully avoided any course which might have suggested academic pretensions. And now here I was being sent to teach in a school and study for a Higher Diploma in Education!

Teaching in the vocational schools turned out to be a three year sentence. I did my best; and I remember consoling myself by saying that at least I hadn't been appointed chaplain to the University, which I knew I would dislike even more. Needless to say, my second appointment was to the chaplaincy in UCD – interrupted by an interlude in Britain and the US under orders from my archbishop to study television. I hadn't even got a television set at the time. The whole idea of being involved in television frightened me and fascinated me. It doesn't frighten me any more, but the fascination remains. Since those far off days I have had a full life and an interesting one, but quite untypical of your average secular priest. Has it been a happy life? I would have to say 'Yes'. But then the statistics, according to Andrew Greeley, show that priests are generally happy in their vocation – as happy as married men and happier than single men. So maybe I just conform to the norm.

Loneliness

If priests as a whole don't seem to be as lonely as one might expect them to be, then I think that fact is due to the special relationship that often exists between a priest and his immediate family, and sometimes even families of close friends. I call it special because I think that family and friends, aware that a priest has foregone the joy and privilege of having children are often willing to let him share in their own family in a more intimate way than they would permit others, even another unmarried brother or sister. Be that as it may, I know that belonging to an extended family, (with forty-eight members at last count, leaving out cousins) was and is important to my own well being. Not that I see that much of any of them, but I know that they are there, and in a special way, always welcoming.

2
VOCATIONS WORKSHOP
Thinking about celibacy

I'm writing this sitting alone on a little-frequented beach in Greece. Perhaps that requires a little explanation. I have been suffering for the past three years from an ailment picked up in the tropics, and doctors so far haven't been of much help. Having been through the usual course of antibiotics and various negative hospital tests, the symptoms remain. Could it be a psychosomatic illness brought on by stress, to be cured by psychological means rather than medicines? I hadn't taken a holiday in two years. In a fit of mild desperation, I suddenly decided to try the sun and sea rest cure à la package holiday. And so I find myself here, sitting in the sun, bored and lonely, trying to write something to pass the time.

The beach is about two hundred yards from my *pensione,* along a narrow walk, down very rudimentary steps cut in the side of a cliff. There was a man and a woman here when I came, joined later by two other pairs. It isn't a naturist beach, but, as is often the case nowadays in the Mediterranean, women go topless. The first woman is slight and has insignificant pigeon breasts. The second has big floppy breasts, and an ample body to carry them. The third has a meagre shapeless body, with large pointed breasts. Body and breasts are unbalanced; I don't feel they go together. All in all, it seems as suitable a place as any to write about celibacy.

Twenty or thirty years ago perhaps I could not have looked on a scene like this with such equanimity. Firstly, because it would have been much more unusual and, therefore, more sexually stimulating. Secondly, the sexual thing becomes less insistent when one passes sixty. But the human body doesn't cease to be beautiful, beautiful as defined by St Thomas Aquinas as *Quod visum placet.*

The Swedish lady has a gentle swim, removes the remaining scrap of costume and lies down. I don't know if she is Swedish, but in my mind I decide that is what she must be. Her boyfriend, perhaps her husband, rubs oil into her breasts, her navel, and the soft inside of her legs.

I reflect to myself that in sixty-one years, I have never touched a woman with sexual intent; or for that matter child, man, or beast. And yet I have, or had, sex drives as strong as the next. How did I do it? It wasn't lack of natural desire. How I quietly envied relatives going off on their honeymoon!

Apart from what one had to learn from the moral theology textbooks, and the fact that so-called special friendships were strongly dealt with in the seminary, the thought of homosexual acts never entered my ken. I think the male body is interesting and beautiful like all God's creation, but the range of sexual activity possible between two men seems to me rather less beautiful and interesting – leaving aside any question of morality.

But that was a digression. I put to myself a question – why am I still virgin and celibate? I love the variety of human experience, and like to try everything at least once. Anything worth doing is worth doing badly, I often like to say, paraphrasing Chesterton. Of course one tries to do everything well, but that isn't always possible.

I used to dream that maybe the Lord would be forgiving and perhaps permit me one tryst. Just for the experience – and then absolution. But I never went further than to dream, and it's nearly too late now to do anything else. And why didn't I? Just once. The Lord would have forgiven, and maybe he might even have understood.

I think I didn't for four reasons. The first is because I feared, and deep down knew that if I once broke the habit of celibacy I would be starting something I couldn't stop. Which would mean choosing between leaving the priesthood or living a double life – a living lie. The second reason is that I am prepared to accept the traditional teaching, based on scripture, that celibacy can have value as a sign, permitting a certain freedom among those (supposedly anyway) committed to working for God. The third reason is that I think fidelity to promises is important in life – after all it is the basis on which the

28

institution of Christian marriage also depends. When a man, after at least seven years preparation and consideration, takes a vow of celibacy, it doesn't seem to me sufficient to say a few years later, 'I've changed my mind'.

But the fourth reason may be the strongest. One needs to feel that one has achieved some part of what one set out to be in life. For whatever reason, I set out to be a Roman Catholic priest – by definition celibate. And when I set out I naturally wanted to be a good example of what I intended to be. So I had high ideals: I would pray a lot, and well. I would be of service to people. I would be poor in spirit and in fact. Well, I offer Mass and say the breviary daily, but after that I don't pray that much, and when I do I am often bored by it. I haven't really been of service to anyone, or available to help anyone because for that you need to have time, and for most of my life I seem to have been in administrative positions where I have been short of time. I believe in the particular job I am doing and that it is something right and fitting for a priest to do, but I couldn't honestly say I do it for that reason. I do it because I like doing it, and because it has worked out in such a way that, subject to my archbishop's tolerant acceptance, I am my own boss. I have a tiny income, but everything, nearly everything I want to do – play with machinery, visit interesting places, meet interesting people – all comes in the line of work. So I really have nothing much to offer the Lord in the end. I didn't fight any good fight. All has been selfish, or if not, it's not measurable. Except for one thing: I could still say in my defence on the judgement day that despite all the temptations, I am still virgin and celibate. It may not be much but it's measurable: and in the absence of something better to offer, I hope it will be enough.

The arguments for celibacy

Celibacy is something I have had to think about several times in life, so I am prepared to speak about it. I have satisfied my mind on certain aspects, while on others I keep an open mind. I have also thought about marriage, but am less happy to put my thoughts on paper. Marriage involves such complex relationships that only those with experience can have much of value to say about it.

With regard to celibacy, there is one aspect about which I am very clear. In the Roman church celibacy is attached to eucharistic ministry – one can't have one without the other. Where there are enough clergy to provide a eucharistic service one may argue about the pros and cons of this church law. But where, as in certain parts of the world, there are nothing like enough celibate clergy to provide an adequate eucharistic service, and never have been, and so far as one can humanly foretell never will be, then to refuse to ordain married men because of a purely church law seems to me to risk Divine vengeance.

How Jesus saw celibacy

Celibacy involves three forms of denial: denying oneself the loving companionship of a partner in marriage, denying oneself the joy of children, denying oneself any legitimate sexual activity. All the evidence in scripture points to Jesus being celibate, and encouraging the notion in others:

> There are eunuchs born that way from their mother's womb, there are eunuchs made so by men and there are eunuchs who have made themselves that way for the sake of the kingdom of heaven. Let anyone accept this who can. (Mt 19:12)

In the light of other sayings of Christ, it seems reasonable to believe that celibacy also has a symbolic value. It points to the fact that the kingdom of God is worth giving up things for – the pearl of great price which a man sold everything he had to be able to purchase. It can also be a sign of the detachment from the things of this world which the gospel proposes as an ideal.

Training in self denial

Service to others requires self denial. When a needy parishioner calls at the door and the priest is watching his favourite television series, it can be very convenient to have his housekeeper say, 'He is out' (to visitors!). Self denial is a habit formed by training, and avoiding sexual thoughts and deeds for life is as tough a form of training in self denial as any.

A long tradition

The impression is sometimes given that celibacy first appeared in the church in the Middle Ages. The weight of evidence seems to argue the contrary. Galen, for instance, the Greek physician writing in the latter half of the second century, referred in passing to Christians:

> Their contempt of death is patent to us every day, and likewise their restraint from intercourse. For they include not only men but also women who refrain from intercourse all through their lives.

Justin, explaining Christianity to the Roman elite in the middle second century:

> Many, both men and women of the age of sixty and seventy years who have been disciples of Christ from their youth, continue in immaculate purity ... It is our boast to be able to display such persons before the human race.

Athenagoras wrote to the Emperor Marcus Aurelius around 177:

> You would find among us, both men and women, growing old unmarried, in the hope of living in closer communion with God. (For) remaining in virginity and in the state of a eunuch brings one nearer to God.

Those who would like to see a change in the law will argue that, while there was great respect for celibacy in the early church, it was not bound up with ministry. There were two ways to God for ministers as for ordinary Christians. Some of the apostles were married, and many holy priests and bishops.

One way or another, it is clear that celibacy was a much esteemed Christian tradition from the earliest times, and one must respect the church which has fought long and hard to maintain the tradition. Admittedly this has been for a complex of reasons – some more cogent in yesteryear. Some, but not all.

Avoiding nepotism

One of the lessons of history which the church is still very conscious of is that, in periods when celibacy was lax, clerics worked morally and immorally to secure their children's future as best they could and, like all fathers, were happiest to be able to offer career prospects to their children in their own chosen profession. So priests tried to get parishes for their sons, and bishops to get bishoprics, and this was a source of great scandal to the church. One writer said of the Franciscan friar Miler MacGrath, who became Archbishop of Cashel in the turbulent sixteenth century, that he was 'the principal means under God to prevent the growth of Protestantism in Munster, for he so enriched himself and his children with the spoil of the dioceses of Cashel, Lismore, Emly and Waterford.' Whether Miler was Protestant or Catholic, or whether he was interested in knowing the difference when it didn't suit him, is a moot point. The question is how relevant this argument about nepotism is today. Married or unmarried, I think Miler might find it a lot more difficult to get away with such double-dealing nowadays, even if the basic instinct of parents to do the best for their children will always remain the same.

Control of human resources

From the point of view of the institution, celibacy allows enormous flexibility in the distribution of human resources – an advantage which of course can lead to abuse. One contemporary of mine was moved around five different posts in fourteen months. Just suppose he was married! So while it is clear that celibacy assures flexibility for clerical personnel managers, it's not so clear that such flexibility is always in the best interests of the clergy – or the church.

The Roman church has always favoured strict control of its clergy, and still does – even if it is more difficult to exact today . When I was ordained we could be reprimanded for smoking in public, or being seen on the street without a hat. We were forbidden to be seen at the theatre, and forbidden to own a car. We were never to travel alone with a woman – some priests I know are meticulous about that rule to this day. Many parish priests laid down the hour before midnight when the curate was expected to be in his bed. That sort of thing would never work with a married clergy!

For those who dream of a different kind of church, one less clerical, less authoritarian, less pyramidical in structure, a celibate clergy is part of the obstacle. But for those who sit in their offices in Rome and make the laws for the rest of us, a celibate priesthood is essential to the only structure in which they can operate, and probably the only structure which they can even imagine. Which is why we must presume they will never contemplate change. It would have to be imposed by pope or ecumenical council – against the curia's most resolute opposition.

Financial considerations

Abandoning celibacy could have very significant financial consequences. Celibate priests don't have to provide for the present and future needs of a wife and family. My feeling is that in the Roman church, a married clergy would tend to become a part time clergy, where the main family income would come from a secular job or profession. Otherwise, the laity would have to double, maybe triple, their contributions. Germaine Greer commented on this aspect of celibacy in connection with the Bishop Eamonn Casey affair:

> Marriage itself is a demanding rule of life that most people break in thought, word and deed; should the marriage vow be therefore abolished?

> The rationale of the vow of celibacy is not simply that the Catholic Church places a high value on abstention from sexual activity; it is the same rationale that until this century denied the right to marry to soldiers, apprentices, domestics and scholars, namely that the governing institution could not afford to support wives and families, and would not countenance the dividing of the employee's attention from his primary duty to the institution.

A father for all

Another argument sometimes put forward in support of celibacy is that the celibate, in committing his love to no particular person, is free to love everyone. He is indeed a 'father' to all. I was never fully convinced by this argument because it seems to contradict the experience of love, namely that love is not a rationed thing, and that learning to love one person deeply can help one to love others more deeply.

Availability

It is argued too that the celibate is more available – better able to give himself to those in need because he is not tied down by a family. In theory that is always true, but in some cases there is a practice which seems to deny it. Freedom from the need to care for wife and child can mean freedom to care only for oneself, and become committed to idleness and personal comfort. It depends on the character type and on the available work. My work is varied and interesting, and if I think I work as hard as any, it's because I want to. Some priests I know have not found their work congenial and have settled quietly into lives of non-performance. There is a clerical story about a parish priest describing his day: 'I get up about eight, and have my breakfast. Mass is at ten. Then I go and get the paper and have a good read. Lunch is at one, and after that I am feeling a bit tired so I have a siesta ...'

In my experience, however, a high proportion of celibates are workaholic. That isn't necessarily a bad thing – Jesus, we read, didn't have time to eat. It is a way of sublimating sexual energy I have been told, and I am sure that's true – whatever it means. Work certainly helps to keep one's mind off sex if that's all they are trying to say. In my experience, a really dedicated priest or sister will do the work of two people for half the cost. Which is why when nowadays they retire from church concerns or activities, they are often too expensive to replace with laypeople.

Freedom from care

I think very few, cleric or lay, pause to reflect on the extraordinary freedom from worry and care enjoyed by a Roman cleric. I have never had to think about mortgages, or about paying for my own or anyone else's education. I am guaranteed work. I am guaranteed a place to live. I don't have family sickness to worry about and my own health insurance is paid for me. Good provision is made for retirement. Much of the pain of living is thereby removed.

I am very conscious, too, of the many sorrows and cares which only the married may be called upon to face. Above all the untimely death of a beloved spouse or child, the worry of sick or handicapped or drug dependent children, the tensions between being a responsible parent and pursuing a career. And, above all, the fact that in some marriages love dies.

Many clerics who left the priesthood in a hurry in the 1970s saw marriage as a solution to personal problems, and found out too late that this wasn't so. A surprising number of these sudden marriages ended up in separation or divorce.

The right to be a priest

Some question the church's right to attach celibacy to priesthood, as if there was an infringement of human rights – either the right of a priest to marry or of a married person to become a priest. I am not sure that anyone has a right to be a priest, or that the church infringes human rights by laying down conditions. In Old Testament times, priesthood was reserved to the members of one Jewish tribe. Even today, circumcision is not optional for an orthodox male Jew. Nor is celibacy optional for a Buddhist who feels called to be a monk. Priesthood is not something for oneself but for others. If others are helped by priests being celibate, then that is sufficient justification for the church to demand it of them. But that is the essential question: If one could argue cogently that people would be helped more if there were married clergy, then that would be the most telling argument against mandatory celibacy.

Celibacy and social research

Based on his sociological research, Fr Andrew Greeley has given the celibacy argument a few new twists:

> We discovered that if a married woman has a *confidante* relationship with a priest, it not only facilitates her marital happiness, but also the marital happiness of her husband. And indeed it correlates with higher levels of sexual satisfaction in the marriage for both the woman who has the *confidante* relationship, and for her husband. It doesn't work the other way around. If a man has a *confidante* relationship with a priest it has no impact on the spouse or on the marriage. Now there are two conclusions you can draw from that. One is that the theory behind celibacy may well have inadvertently been validated – that it does give a man a special perspective for dealing with human problems that he might not have if he had a family of his own. The second conclusion is there ought to be women priests so men could have a similar *confidante* relationship with a priest, and that would benefit not only them, but, if the theory is right, their spouses too. I also looked at the same thing for Protestants and found no trace of the same

phenomenon. Protestant married ministers had no such impact on either a woman or her husband in a marriage.

I think this is because it is a relationship with a male in which the woman can be reasonably trusting and confident. I mean one can share a lot of yourself with this man, and yet be at least reasonably safe from him taking advantage of you because you've been so vulnerable to him. Celibacy in other words provides a relationship in which at least some women can be more vulnerable, profitably vulnerable in terms of their emotional life. I think it is also good that there be some men in the world who demonstrate by the way they live that they can find women enormously attractive and appealing without having to hit on them, as the saying goes, or much less having to jump into bed with them. You know I am not absolutely opposed to the ordination of married men or to married priests, and I think there should be room for that too, just as there should be room for women priests. But I don't want to see the celibate witness which has been so powerful in the church for a thousand years and more, dismissed with arguments that are little better than pop psychology.

Binding oneself for life

Many question the capacity of a young man of twenty-four to make a decision binding himself to celibacy for life. One friend of mine explained his decision to quit the priesthood. 'Quite simply I've changed,' he said. 'I now know more about myself than when I made the vow.' I didn't find that a compelling argument. All vows are made to a greater or lesser extent in the dark. For vowing is an act of profound trust, a giving your word before God that you will accept the vowed life with the good and evil that vowing may involve. My friend might argue that such a promise is impossible. But if it is impossible for celibates to vow, then it must be even more impossible for young couples to pledge themselves in marriage. Two young people starting out together must also expect to change, and to learn more about themselves and each other. If what they find is not entirely to their liking, is that a sufficient reason to kick the marriage vows? (I don't want to get into an argument about divorce, but only to make clear the comparison).

Optional celibacy

Despite what Andrew Greeley says, I have always felt that there are special problems about optional celibacy. Young men don't normally put on clerical collars to become celibates but to become priests. In the present dispensation, the Roman church makes celibacy part of the job specification – there is no option. If celibacy were to become optional I find it hard to imagine many candidates for the priesthood choosing such a tough option for a good reason – that is unless they were very, very detached and saintly to a rare degree. Your average candidate will normally want to marry. Therefore the presumption may well be that those few who don't choose to marry are either afraid of the intimacy involved in marriage, or are too selfish to be bothered by the trouble of living with another person, or don't want to be saddled with children, or are simply homosexual. None of which qualifications could normally be considered as specially fitting in a candidate for the pastoral ministry. So the social pressure will be strongly in favour of marriage.

The Orthodox Church of course provides us with experience and example of the married priest. But the model here – which would appear to be the only model available – is that of a two-tiered clergy. Priests working in parishes normally marry, although oddly enough, they may only do so before ordination. Priests who are monks are presumed to be aiming at a higher state of sanctity and must remain celibate. The leaders of the Orthodox Church are only chosen from the ranks of the celibate. Which means that there are lower class married priests with no prospects of promotion, and detached, holy celibates, worthy to be bishops!

But one thing the Orthodox experience of a married clergy does seem to make clear is that taking a vow of permanent celibacy is a very radical choice which is best situated in an ascetic, prayerful and protected context. In Roman terms that would suggest a normally married secular clergy and celibate monks and religious.

Instead of speaking of optional celibacy, I would prefer to speak of optional marriage, which approximates more to the normal human experience. Not all lay people are married – some may marry in future, some may not. Among secular priests there could also be married and unmarried. Among the unmarried, some who may not wish to marry, some who may not happen to have met the right partner yet, some who may choose to be celibate for a spiritual motive; but whatever way it is, it is a private affair. There would be no public vows of celibacy, (except among monks and religious) because that would seem to institutionalise a more perfect and less perfect way to God, and inevitably lead to a two-tier secular priesthood.

Homosexuality in the priesthood

Of the three hundred or more priests I would have known from seminary days in Clonliffe College and Maynooth, I can only think of two who got into trouble afterwards on grounds of homosexual activity, and one who got cashiered in the seminary for taking too much interest in good-looking younger students. However that is not a survey, but an impression.

I think it is reasonable to presume that a cross section of the clergy may be more homosexual in orientation than a cross section of the whole community. Firstly, because it is said that homosexuals are more caring and service oriented, and are therefore more likely to enter a caring profession. Secondly, because a person tempted towards homosexual acts which he believed seriously sinful, might well see the priestly life as protecting him from his own sinful inclinations. (Presumably seminary directors try to screen out such candidates, but they may not be always successful.) Thirdly, in embracing the celibate state, the heterosexual has more to give up than the homosexual, and lastly, in every country, but particularly perhaps in the United States, the large numbers of presumably heterosexual priests who left the priesthood to marry must have affected the percentages.

With regard to percentages, figures are bandied about, but there are no remotely reliable statistics, and every reason to be careful. When there were no reliable statistics for the percentage of homosexuals in the general population, everybody accepted the results of Kinsey's flawed research, which was 10%. There is even, I believe, a West Coast magazine for gays called *The 10%*. However, when the first reliable statistics were published in the United States in 1993, they confirmed similar surveys in France and Britain, and the 10% dropped to a little over 1%!

One important fact – which seems often overlooked when people talk about homosexuality, is that there appears to be no rigid division between homosexual and heterosexual. Only a tiny portion of the population feel no attraction to the opposite sex. After that there is a scale as it were, and different people occupy different places in the scale. And for many there may be a certain choice as to where they put themselves on the scale, either temporarily or permanently. It is well known, for instance, that normally heterosexual men may become temporary sodomites in prison when there is no opportunity for heterosexual activity. Among clerics who were trained to avoid all female company, as indeed my generation was, a priest who engaged in homosexual activity may not be presumed to be homosexual in basic orientation. As with the prisoners, homosexuality may have been the only reasonably available outlet. A recent survey conducted in Mexico, Columbia and Peru in connection with AIDs, concludes that 22% of married men and 30% of all normally heterosexual men also engage in homosexual activity. It seems that in the Latin culture there is a widely held notion that sexually penetrating another man is evidence of virility, and those who engage in this activity – often with male prostitutes – don't even consider themselves bi-sexual.

The fact that the world population of homosexuals now appears to be one tenth of what it was said to be last year is a warning to all against pontificating about homosexuality at this stage of human knowledge. Clearly very little is known with certainty – there is still no agreement as to whether sexual orientation is determined mainly by genetic or environmental factors. But quite apart from theories and statistics, a homosexual man or woman may clearly be called to the priesthood or religious life at least as easily as a hetero-sexual. And so long as he or she remain true to their vows, then it can make no difference to their worthiness. On the other hand, if the priesthood were ever generally perceived to be weighed in favour of homosexual types, as certain other professions appear to be, that might well affect its credibility.

Child abuse

The church in America has been rocked with stories of clerics involved in child abuse, and countless millions of dollars have been spent settling cases in and out of court. And there have been cases in Ireland and there will be more. I heard that the US lawyers, having cleaned up in America, now have their eyes on Europe.

Fifteen years ago, paedophilia was hardly mentioned in the psychiatric literature. Now there's hardly talk of anything else. Although there are indications that the interest has already peaked.

I have no wish to get involved in developing controversies in this field, but only to comment on its relevance to celibacy. The naïve assumption is that celibates, having no lawful sexual outlet, are more likely subjects of paedophilia. In so far as there are facts – statistics from the US – the facts deny it. Parents and married people are the most likely to abuse children. Among clerics, married clerics are more likely to abuse children than celibates.

Paedophilia is an evil business, and more evil when committed by people who supposedly have vows of chastity. But we should keep it in perspective. It's always been with us, and given sinful human nature it always will be – it's just that people didn't talk about it before outside the family. My own mother told me she had to flee from the advances of her stepfather.

A temporary celibate priesthood

Some fifteen years ago I wrote an article called 'Why Forever?' It suggested the setting up of religious orders where people could give a commitment to serve God in religious life for a (renewable) period, after which they could retire in dignity and honour and, if they so wish, marry. I am still in favour of that solution, and if extended to the secular clergy I think it would be a lot less traumatic than optional celibacy. Some secular priests in their late fifties have begun to take the option already in so far as they are announcing at the same time their retirement from active ministry and decision to marry. What is more, they seem to expect their congregations to approve, and give them a joyful send-off! My own training makes me unsympathetic to what amounts to taking the law into one's own hands. But all my instincts are that the law should be changed to permit one to give 10,

20, or 30 years of one's life to the ministry, and then leave with honour, free to marry.

But these are all old arguments: there are other new factors which must be considered in the celibacy debate. There is the demise of the traditional closed seminary (though there have been efforts to revive it). Then there is the changing relationships between men and women, and the new dominant role played by television in the latter half of this century

New factors relevant to the celibacy debate

The demise of the traditional seminary

Before the 1960s it was rare for a priest to leave the ministry to get married. This was a time when aspirants were formed in a seminary environment where contact with women was largely excluded, and sexual imagery rigidly controlled. When I was in the seminary we were denied newspapers, magazines, books – apart from what was needed for our studies – and of course there was no radio or TV. It is not unreasonable to presume that this harsh regime helped to condition men for the celibate life.

This wasn't simply Victorian mores spilling into the twentieth century – the tradition was much older than that. Some of the early Celtic monasteries went so far as to exclude female animals – cows for instance – from the environment of the monastery. Even today no woman is allowed visit the famous monastery of Mount Athos in Greece. I once interviewed a young Buddhist monk of English/Irish origin whom I met by chance in a Bangkok temple. His name was Shaun and he came from a monastery up at the Laotian border. He told me he was out for the day from the hospital where he had been treated for typhoid. The Buddhists monks have a special hospital for themselves in Bangkok where all the nursing staff are male!

I remember as if it were yesterday the scene when, shortly after we entered the seminary, the Dean briefed us on the conduct expected from us at the university. Before leaving every morning in twos on our bicycles, the senior of each pair was instructed to say *'Averte, Domine, oculos meos'*, to which the junior replied, *'Ne videant vanitatem'*. (A rough translation might be 'Cast down my eyes, O Lord, lest they see this world's vanities.') At coffee time in the

41

university we were to proceed as a group to the canteen where we would be served at special tables. (This last arrangement caused a lot of resentment among lay students who had to queue up and wait while the staff served the mass of clerics all dressed in black.) But the most important rule came at the end. No Clonliffe student at the university should ever be seen talking to a girl. We were generally prepared for a strict regime, but this seemed a little over the top. A classmate raised his hand and asked a question: 'What if one happened to meet one's sister?' The reply was delivered only half in jest: 'You may talk with your sister, Mr X, if you put a placard round her neck stating clearly "this is my sister".'

How were such rules enforced? For that there was the prefect system. One among us was appointed a prefect. His duty, understood by all, was to report to the Dean regularly on any aberrant behaviour that came to his notice at seminary or university. It was a dirty job, which one wasn't free to refuse, and must have caused those who were given it much trouble and anxiety.

It may seem odd now, but I accepted the prefect system, and had nothing but sympathy for my colleague who went up in the evening to tell tales about us to the Dean. And that for three reasons. Firstly, the spirituality we were taught encouraged acceptance of such things. Secondly, the prefect was only doing what he had to do, and thank God it wasn't me that had been appointed. Thirdly, it must be important to weed out unsuitable types from among those being prepared for a celibate priesthood. If a lad couldn't keep away from the girls at the university, well maybe celibacy was not an attainable goal for him, and the earlier the authorities discussed the matter with him the better.

During the holidays, of course, we were relatively freer. But we were warned always to wear clerical dress, never to go out without a black clerical hat, and above all never to be seen *solus cum sola,* best translated, perhaps, as 'alone with a woman'. And these admonitions were enforced. I remember being quite upset when our family car passed one driven by the Clonliffe Dean one day in Ballsbridge, because he of course was wearing his hat and I wasn't. Whatever about the hat, if one were seen or reported as not wearing clerical dress, or being seen *solus cum sola,* then certainly a very serious view would be taken.

That having been said, the holidays inevitably meant more normal relationships with humanity. Most students had sisters, and female family friends. But certain standards were expected of a cleric by family and community. Dancing was certainly out for the neophyte cleric, and where a cleric indulged, it was taken to be an indication that he was making up his mind to leave.

It was a tough regime. It could not be brought back today, even if someone wanted to. It had its disadvantages, which no doubt my generation of priests make manifest. But to give the system its due, it achieved at the time the limited defined results it was seeking. None of my class of twenty-two who entered Clonliffe left the priesthood to marry. Ten years later there were classes where nearly half of those ordained are now married.

Such a regime, possible forty years ago, is no longer possible because relations between the sexes are generally much freer than they used to be. And because the Christian community seems to consider that it can be psychologically damaging for candidates to the priesthood to be totally deprived of female company. And because normal young people are not nowadays prepared to accept that level of restriction on their freedom.

The emancipation of women

I was chaplain to a convent when I was first ordained. I never ate with the sisters – it was forbidden – and I rarely talked to them except from the altar. Now I have lunch every day in a convent refectory.

It is not that long ago since the only women to appear on television were the ones who spun the wheel on game shows.

I grew up in a world where men decided nearly everything. That may still be true of the church, but it is no longer true of the rest of society, and it will be even less true in the future.

I well remember the furore in senior clerical circles when *Intercom*, the magazine distributed to all clergy in Ireland by the Communications Institute, which I had begun and was ultimately responsible for, published an article in 1975 called 'In Praise of Women'. Gerry

43

Reynolds CSsR, the editor, put together a feature where seven priests reflected (anonymously) on friendship with women, and seven women – three sisters, two married and two single women – commented from their experience. One quote from a priest in his late thirties may give a flavour of the content:

> ... my instinct, and my experiences, (and now even my theology) teach me that I as a priest, like any other man, am made to love and be loved in a very human way. And I know now there is no companion like a lady companion, and that I need such companionship if I am to survive as a man and priest. This lesson has not come easy but it has been a very enjoyable one to learn.

Many years later, when I proposed Gerry Reynolds for another job, I was told that he would not be acceptable to the bishops because of this one article. But it was part of the beginning of a movement throughout the church at the time towards an acceptance that men and women need each other, and that some way must be found for celibates to have meaningful relationships with the opposite sex, short of genital expression. Perhaps too the movement was fuelled by the realisation among women that part of their problem with the church was not only that male clerics made all the decisions, but worse still, they were male celibate clerics who lived in isolation from the other half of the human race.

Be that as it may, clerics in the nineteen-seventies began to feel happier about having women friends. It may even have become fashionable to flaunt them, and thereby witness to one's sexual normality. At the same time, it seems to me that many priests were quite naïve about the biological factors involved. Certainly the numbers of clergy leaving the priesthood to get married dramatically increased. One curate I knew stood up in the pulpit on Sunday, reminded the congregation of his work with one of the sisters on a parish project, informed them that they had now fallen in love and intended to leave the next day and get married, and hoped everyone would understand. It was a sermon to remember!

Recognition of the biological imperatives
A Dominican sister told me recently that when she was in her last year at convent school some fifty years ago, an elderly nun told them

that if they had their mind set on marriage they should not bother to wash too often. Smell, she told them, plays an important part in attraction between the sexes. Fifty years later *Time* magazine, in a cover story on 'What is Love', confirmed the old nun's intuition. Indeed I was amused to note an advertisement in a nephew's motor magazine recently which informed me that 'Pheromones, the most potent natural but undetectable female attracting scent, is now available in little bottles, price $29.95.'

The *Time* story takes a most unromantic look at the next stage in falling in love. Mutual attraction, we read, 'is revved up by phenylethylamine and possibly the neurochemicals dopamine and norepinephrine, all natural amphetamines. These produce feelings of euphoria and elation'. At a later stage 'larger amounts of endorphins, (chemicals similar to morphine) flow into the brain leaving lovers with a sense of security peace and calm.' Oxytocin ('the cuddle chemical') stimulates sensations and produces feelings of relaxed satisfaction and attachment.

A meeting of eyes, a touch of hands or a whiff of scent sets off a flood that starts in the brain, and races along the nerves and through the blood. The results are familiar ... Men can seize up youth and vitality in a glance, and studies indeed show that men fall in love quite rapidly. Women tumble more slowly, to a large degree because their requirements are more complex ...

What the *Time* magazine story in essence says is something the church has always recognised – that when men and women come together in work or play, the sexual hormones may begin to cascade. It is a biological mechanism directed towards mating over which individuals have little control – except in so far as they control or avoid situations where they know the biological mechanisms come into play.

Of course married men and women as well as celibates may find themselves physically attracted to someone of the opposite sex at work or play – it is a normal part of living. Of course – but there is this enormous difference. The married return each evening to the arms of a loving spouse, while the celibate returns to an empty house and an empty bed.

In my view, the seemingly general acceptance that men and women need each other if they are to fully develop as human beings enormously complicates the celibacy issue, and has led in recent years to much upheaval in the formation process for priests. In 1992 I attended the opening of the new seminary in the diocese of Recife in Brazil. The new seminary was in fact the old seminary perched on a hill at Olinda, a sort of seaside suburb of Recife, which was abandoned in the early seventies, and now had been completely refurbished. In the meantime students for the priesthood had been receiving their training in a theological college called ITER, founded and supported by Archbishop Helder Camara, and situated in a poor barrio area of Recife itself. ITER was open to lay students including women.

When, however, Helder Camara retired at seventy-five, his successor closed ITER and reopened the old seminary – where women will no longer be accepted as students. This is a pattern repeated in recent years in other countries, and reflects the belief in Rome, presumably based on statistics, that where men and women study theology together, fewer aspirants persevere to the celibate priesthood, and those who do may be less than firm in their commitment to celibacy.

The influence of television
Another very significant new factor influencing the celibacy problem is media, and particularly television. When I was a teenager spending a few weeks of the summer in France, I knew I could go to Paris and see naked women at the *Folies Bergères*, but it would have had to be a decision. Nowadays, as a casual and infrequent viewer of TV drama and film, I find it difficult to keep the naked ladies out of my living room.

Contrary to what most people think, most of the money and expertise in television is expended not on programmes but on the advertisements. Most advertisements use sexual images to sell. Check it for yourself.

Two researchers in California did an intensive analysis in 1986 of ten prime time television shows. They summarised the average frequency of sexual behaviour as follows:

Kissing, hugging, sexual touching, once every 4 minutes.
General allusions to sexual behaviour, once every 3.6 minutes.
Sexual intercourse suggested every 24 minutes.
Sadomasochism, exhibitionism and other discouraged sexual practices, once every 9.6 minutes.

And that was eight years ago!

The American Academy of Paediatricians' journal wrote about rock videos:

> Music videos may represent a new art form, but we believe that it is one that contains an excess of sexism, violence, substance abuse, suicide and sexual behaviour. 75% of videos contained sexually suggestive material.

I have no wish to get into arguments here about the morality or otherwise of sexual explicitness on television. I only want to point out that the changed environment brought about by television makes lifelong abstention from sex very much more difficult. Which I believe is one important reason why there are fewer vocations: and why, it is said, more younger priests have liaisons on the side, and a higher proportion of seminarians are homosexual. I say 'it is said' because for obvious reasons there is no way of compiling statistics. But there is, I believe, a tenable argument that the environment created by present day media, and particularly television, are making it increasingly difficult to maintain a celibate priesthood.

A summary and conclusion

Civilisation would be impossible without some taming of natural biological urges. Celibacy however requires a level of suppression (a conscious manoeuvre) and possibly repression (an unconscious process) which is well above the normal, and which is probably only possible when exposure to sexual stimuli is severely limited. Nowadays children are bombarded with sexual stimuli from their earliest years. The question arises as to whether one can take young people, brought up in this changed world, put them in seminary or convent and fashion a celibate being. Humanly speaking, it seems to me to be getting more and more difficult.

Whatever one may say in praise of celibacy, it is in itself a form of self-negation. Whatever value it has, it is mostly for others. For the celibates themselves there is the loneliness – inevitable for anyone who has a heart to love; and there is a permanent fast from sexual intimacy, from female companionship and from parenthood. Ideally that loneliness makes more room for God, and when it does there is a measure of sanctity which is palpable to others. One can see that in the case of a Mother Teresa, or a Francis of Assisi – celibacy in that case has succeeded, God is mediated to the community through the dedicated person. But celibacy can also lead to loneliness which leads to turning in on self; and the selfishness that results is equally recognisable, and sterile from the point of view of the community, and destructive of the personality of the celibate.

Having run through many of the questions relating to celibacy, I find the exercise illuminating, yet unsatisfying. In the end perhaps it is only belief in Christ's word as reported in the gospels that seems to me definitive in establishing that celibacy has a spiritual value. '... and there are eunuchs who have made themselves that way for the sake of the kingdom of heaven. Let anyone accept this who can.'

Those who do accept may of course be aided by the grace of God, which is not subject to our measurement.

3

DE VIVIS NIL NISI BONUM

A Portrait of Pope John Paul II

There seems to be a relatively stable Catholic tradition which places an incumbent pope on a pedestal, as if he were some quasi divine being. I was certainly brought up to revere Pius XII in this way – 'Angelic Shepherd' was his second name. And when I first saw him in the flesh at Castel Gandolfo, I cried a little as did most of the adoring crowd. That tradition to a great extent remains.

At the same time there has always been another tradition, which is to debunk the pope as soon as he passes to his reward. Pius XII was barely cold before the process of demythologising began, led in ecclesiastical circles by Domenico Tardini, who had been very close to Pius, sharing responsibility with Giovanni Montini for the work of the Secretariat of State.

The deification of leaders, and their subsequent downgrading is a noticeable feature of autocratic governments, a fact that might give us pause. China deified Mao, Germany Hitler, Russia deified Marx, Lenin, and Stalin and even to some extent, Brezhnev.

I was in Moscow in 1978, and made a point of seeing the TV News. A substantial portion of the newscast consisted of Brezhnev holding court, ministered to by worried-looking aids who stood as unobtrusively as possible in the background, but were always ready to step forward to adjust a microphone, give or take a page of a speech, whisk away some proffered gift, and whisper something in the boss's ear as the next person approached.

Brezhnev himself listened to fulsome addresses, read a little speech, received visitors from far off provinces, and gave them a medal, or some little gift carefully graded to fit the client's worldly seniority.

And when he spoke, everybody leaned slightly forward with rapt attention, and bowed and smiled in the most servile way when their turn came to embrace the great man. It all seemed so familiar, and I couldn't think why. Then it suddenly struck me. I was watching a mirror image of a papal audience.

It is important that Roman Catholics respect and honour the successor of St Peter. At the same time, it can be of little benefit to church or pope to treat him in a way that it would be inconceivable to treat St Peter himself.

Peter is anything but deified in scripture. Jesus himself, the evangelists and apostles take good care of that. In fact we seem to hear far more of Peter's failings than of his virtues – he was the one who cursed and swore that he did not even know Jesus.

I wrote the above paragraphs in 1981 as draft material for one of a series of articles in *The Furrow,* the Maynooth magazine, which were published under the general heading 'I Had an Idea'. It was meant to be the beginning of an article which would have been critical of traditional attitudes to the papacy and in particular perhaps, critical of the then and current holder of the office, John Paul II. But I didn't develop my ideas further for two reasons. In the first place, I felt that *The Furrow* wouldn't want to publish it. And secondly, I was genuinely afraid of acquiring a maverick image which might interfere with my prime interest, which was to be left working in television.

This was in fact my second attempt to express disquiet about the present papacy. The other one, which would have been mild enough, failed for different reasons.

We were filming in Rome in 1980 and had planned three films, one of which was a portrait of John Paul II. It was early in the pontificate, but I remember Fr Vincent O' Keefe, then Assistant General of the Jesuits, saying that if one could judge a pope by his first appointments, there was cause for worry. Silvio Oddi had just been appointed Prefect of the Congregation for the Clergy. Oddi was very conservative, and according to O'Keefe, would not have been remotely considered for such a post by the two previous regimes.

The film was rough cut when the assassination attempt on Pope John Paul took place. Fr Liam Swords and I were actually in Rome at the time, although working on a different programme about the Irish Colleges in foreign lands. RTÉ (the Irish national TV network) lunch time news found out where we were and got on the telephone. Our report was put together in the house of the Irish Franciscans with me on the telephone, and Liam in an adjacent room listening to the local radio and handing me bits of paper with the latest information. It was just long enough after the event to make the important educated guess that the pope would survive. That evening I heard Liam tell the Franciscans at supper how his breast swelled with pride when he heard me mention in the report that, 'I was in Rome with the Radharc team.' There were of course only the two of us, and this was the first time he had been invested with plurality!

The assassination attempt clearly posed two problems for us.

There was an emotional wave of sympathy for the person of the pope, which I understood because I experienced it myself. It was not the time to do even a mildly critical portrait – and some of the interviews we collected were mildly critical. In the second place, the events of that terrible day made much of our comment out of date. We could not now do a programme without further interviews and a whole rethink of the programme.

However, for the record, I include a taste of the interviews which were recorded when John Paul II was less than two years in office.

F.X. Murphy, a Redemptorist priest, had written well on the Vatican Council for the *New Yorker* under the pseudonym of Xavier Rynne:

In one sense I'm very happy that he has been called, *il Papa Vagabondo,* the Vagabond Pope, because I think that it really is the function of the pope to give witness to Jesus Christ all around the world, not merely to the Christian world but to the Moslem and the rest of the world. On the other hand, there's great danger in that: that little by little all the admiration and adulation can go to his head, and he begins to think after a while that the grace he receives as pope makes him omniscient, and omnicompetent and, in this sense, he creates a populist approach to his own person and to his own mind. But unfortunately with the populist approach, it doesn't last very long. He's there, people are enthused, they're mesmerised. He leaves, there's a very fine afterdraft and then all of a sudden something happens, problems come up and people begin to realise that what he said does not exactly fit their position and they just drop him, particularly the younger people.

Gerald O'Collins, an Australian Jesuit theologian in the Gregorian University in Rome:

It's worth remembering that St Peter was not only a positive character but there was a shadow side to him. He really was quite a simple person, denying his Lord during the passion three times, and that's remembered by the early church and it's remembered as something that's important for his successor. It's not just a piece of information about a person who lived a long time ago but I'm sure it's in there because it's the kind of thing that, alas, we might find coming from his successor. And then we find St Peter at Antioch letting the side down in St Paul's letter to the Galatians, and once again we find something very important in the writings of St Paul reminding us that we can't expect a perfect pope.

Good and bad popes

A lot has happened since 1980, and I have seen a lot of the church in different parts of the world since then. As a Catholic priest I hate to say it, but within that period, pretty well everything I have seen and everybody I have met in the course of my work have led me towards a negative judgement on the pontificate of John Paul II.

Now there can be different kinds of popes. Some, like the Borgias, scandalise people. Fr Vincent McNabb OP, one of the great Hyde Park Preachers, had a technique to deal with hecklers who shouted 'What about the Borgia popes?' 'Alexander VI?' McNabb would reply. 'Why he was a paragon of virtue compared to John XII. Now there was a really bad pope.'

Venal men who sought and won the papacy for worldly reasons never caused me much bother. It is the strong upright men who have often done the serious damage.

Pope Paul III was elected pope in 1534 at the age of 66, having sired three sons and a daughter when a cardinal. He carved the Duchy of Parma out of the papal states for one of his sons, who was soon murdered for his tyranny. He made his own grandsons cardinals when they were only boys. So it is stretching it a bit to call him a good *man*. Yet in many ways Paul was a good *pope*. He called together the reforming Council of Trent, and commissioned Michelangelo to paint the Last Judgement. He is remembered by humanity as the pope who issued the brief condemning slavery.

I think that John Paul II is a good saintly man who has done a lot of harm to the church in my generation. And most of the people whose opinion I value think more or less the same way (although few seem to feel in a position to say so). I wish I did not think that way. But I do. And I can't think otherwise unless I receive new and different information.

Now that his reign may be winding down, and people are beginning to wonder who will next sit in that chair, I think it is important for people to say openly – as many will say in private – that John Paul was not a good choice, and that the church urgently needs someone quite different to succeed him.

That is, of course, judging his papacy in fallible human terms: and we all know that God's ways are not defined by our little minds. In God's providence all things work for good. Yes. At the same time, he often chooses to write straight with crooked lines.

I must admit to a feeling of apprehension when I first heard that a Pole had been appointed pope. But I had been wrong before. I nearly cried at the appointment of John XXIII – a man of 77, previously unheard of. And ugly as well!

What worried me were two things. Karol Wojtyla spent all his adult life under Nazi and Communist dictatorships. He had no experience of either free broadcasting, or commercially driven media, and so he could not possibly understand the changes that media in general, and broadcasting in particular, have helped to bring about throughout much of what we used to call 'the free world'. And in that I think I was proven right – he is a pre-broadcasting era pope. (At the same time, he is of course a media star, but that is more related to acting ability.) The second fear I had, knowing the interest that the curia has in papal elections, and the general attitude of the strong Italian element to outsiders, was that the curial mind would only have accepted him if they were absolutely sure of his conservative credentials.

I never met Cardinal Wojtyla, though I knew a close friend of his in the Vatican. This was Bishop Andre Deskur, Secretary, and later President of the Mass Media Commission when I was a consultor. The Mass Media Commission was very low down in the Vatican pecking order, and Deskur had about as much power as a Vatican flunkey. We put it down to the fact that he was a Pole caught up in an Italian mafia without powerful friends or a wealthy church behind him. But whenever Wojtyla came to Rome for a short visit, Deskur spent the time with him. One of the great tragic ironies of Deskur's life was the day before his great friend became pope, he suffered a stroke from which he only made a partial recovery. John Paul made him a cardinal, but his active career had in reality ended.

The overriding image

John Paul is a distant man. Halina Bortnowska is a friend who has known him since she was a student thirty years ago in Cracow, and she is very fond and protective of him. But she will readily admit that 'he knows us thoroughly but none of us feel we really know him'.

Bishop Agnellus Andrew was functional head of the Mass Media Commission in the early days of John Paul's reign (with the incapacitated Deskur nominally in charge – though not so incapacitated as to prevent him from interfering). Agnellus told me that the pope was on occasion willing to listen to him, but never to dialogue. Agnellus found that unsettling. He made his business known to the pope; the pope listened; the decision was communicated later.

John Paul is a conservative man, whose views on most things can therefore be predicted. He wants nuns to wear their habits, and the faithful to receive communion on the tongue, and he has stopped general absolution and emphasised auricular confession and so on. Predictability is not generally a good characteristic in a leader. Nor does it fit with the gospel, where the parable of the talents shows the Lord commending the risk-takers and condemning the safesider.

54

John Paul is a pessimistic man, always seeing dangers and uttering warnings and corrections. John Paul has no concept of a loyal opposition. So he fills every post around him in his own image.

All of which fits him for authoritarian leadership. Which many feel is not what the church needs at the end of the twentieth century. In that, I say nothing original or new. The leader writer in *The Tablet* — the influential London weekly edited by Catholic laymen — wrote as long ago as June 1985:

> Even the meekest, mildest people are beginning to notice the creeping paranoia which seems to be seizing Rome. For what kind of mentality is it which sees virtually the whole church as cracking up and falling apart? Which harbours dark suspicions of all but a few hand-picked and specially certificated bishops? Which cannot trust religious orders, that have lasted centuries, to know their own business? Which sees local hierarchies as misguided muddlers who need to have their jobs done for them? What does such a view make of the role of the Holy Spirit, which appears not to admit him any activity except within the bounds of Vatican city, and only then with an official licence? What strange view of the church is it which regards most of its ordinary members as broken reeds, and steadily withdraws trust from one segment after another of the Catholic population? The ordinary Catholic in the street is not much concerned with ecclesiastical politics ... but he does register a general climate of distrust when cardinals are treated like delinquent schoolboys and religious orders like Fifth Columnists.

The wandering pope

In his first ten years, 1978 to 1988, John Paul made forty journeys outside Italy and spent the equivalent of a year taking his message to over seventy countries. And many more in the years since. They say he has been seen by more people than anyone else in human history.

He is a superstar, a great actor and people like to see him. But it is a mistake to presume that because of that they listen, and follow where he would like to lead. Nor is the image he communicates necessarily a happy one. He can look like the chairman of the corporation come to address the workers while the branch managers (the bishops) stand around hoping he won't embarrass or scold them. It might sometimes be better if the chairman let the local managers do the local management, and not try to do it himself over their heads.

The sign of unity?

The source of unity in the church is not the papacy, but the Holy Spirit in the hearts of the believers. The papacy, however, may function as a sign of unity. But to be a sign one cannot adopt partisan positions, or take the side of the minority in the church who were disappointed with Vatican II, as many feel John Paul II has done. By forcing unpopular conservative bishops on many dioceses, he has caused disunity on a scale quite new to the Roman church.

Promoter of right wing organisations

On an early visit to Rome, Cardinal Wojtyla prayed at the tomb of Mgr Escriva, founder of Opus Dei, and several sources say that Opus Dei played a key role in offering a platform to make him and his theology known in Rome, and thus could claim to have provided stepping stones to his papacy. 'The Father', as Escriva is always known within Opus Dei, has been beatified by the pope within seventeen years of his death in 1975, a feat never achieved by any other Christian in recent history. And priest members of Opus Dei worldwide seem to have a better than even chance nowadays of becoming bishops.

Pope John Paul also expresses obvious enthusiasm for another right wing organisation called *Communione e Liberazione,* which is not much liked by some senior Italian bishops, including Cardinal Martini. His enthusiasm may however have been tempered by allegations against some of its members in the recent *tangentopoli,* (city of rake-offs) scandals.

Disregarding collegiality

It has been said that while Vatican II laid emphasis on the team, John Paul lays the emphasis on the captain. For example: 98% of nearly 2,000 bishops said they didn't want the old Latin Mass reintroduced. Nonetheless, John Paul did so by personal decree.

The Synods of Bishops, originally conceived as continuing the process of collegial decision-making which distinguished Vatican II, are now organised to rubber stamp papal policy. The synods are carefully controlled in operation, and have no power to issue their own documents.

Other instruments for exercising collegiality are the Conference of Bishops in the different countries, and the regional conferences, such as the CELAM, a meeting of Latin American bishops which takes place approximately every ten years. Both have been downgraded in the present pontificate.

Downgrading the Conferences of Bishops

The pope clearly shares the view of Cardinal Ratzinger (or vice versa?) that episcopal conferences have no 'theological reality' and therefore have no *mandatum docendi* or mandate to teach. One is tempted to see behind this a fear of power slipping away from Rome to the periphery. Individual bishops have a mandate to teach, but they can be easily controlled as individuals. Episcopal conferences, like that of Brazil with over 300 members, are a different and possibly dangerous phenomenon if they were ever to challenge the powers of the Roman authorities to decide everything. By denying the bishops' mandate to teach as a conference, this danger is removed.

When the Vatican drafted a document on bishops' conferences in 1988, the US bishops rejected it as not even providing a basis for discussion. This draft, according to reports, suggested there was a danger of bishops' conferences becoming too autonomous, and setting themselves against the 'doctrinal and disciplinary directives of the Holy See'. The US bishops agreed not to publish their critical report on the document at the request of the Vatican.

The US bishops have issued pastoral letters dealing with important issues, such as peace and justice and the economy, and these have caused a lot of interest and comment even outside of the US. But Rome has never made the slightest reference to these conference documents; nor did the pope mention them on his visit to the US when many expected he might commend the bishops on their pastoral initiative. The reason why? Because to have done so would be to empower and legitimate the bishops in their common action as a bishops' conference.

In 1985 the election of a president for the Italian bishops' conference was set aside, and the pope imposed Cardinal Poletti, Vicar of Rome, on the conference. More recently he appointed Cardinal Ruini. This was a reversal of John XXIII's decision in 1962 to rewrite the Statutes of the Conference so that the bishops might be free to elect an independent leader.

At the meeting of Latin American bishops (CELAM) in 1992, John Paul imposed an unprecedented co-secretary of his own choice in addition to the Secretary General of CELAM itself. The man he appointed was a noted right winger, friend of the disgraced Chilean dictator Pinochet, and the only bishop in Chile to publicly campaign for Pinochet when he eventually put himself up for election (and lost). The pope also appointed a co-President.

At the same time, Bishop Padin, nominated to attend the conference by the Brazilian bishops, was not permitted to attend. No adequate reason was given. Observers noted that after the previous conference at Puebla, Padin had pointed out that the Vatican had changed the text voted upon by the bishops.

None of the key posts at the meeting itself were open to free election. The rules, drawn up by the Vatican, stated that no document might be published before the pope had approved it. Instead of discussion, the Vatican-appointed presidency imposed lecture sessions. Bishop Mauro Morelli from Brazil said the presidency was trying to hold a conference, not of bishops but for bishops. In the end, on the eleventh day, the conference revolted in frustration, with bishops grabbing the microphone and shouting at each other. The session had to be suspended.

150 of the press corps told the conference authorities in a signed letter that they were fed up with the way they were being manipulated in so-called press conferences by apparatchiks and non-entities, and demanded to speak to some bishops whose objectivity they trusted.

Reports in *The Tablet* of 24 and 31 October 1992 summed up this conference in Santo Domingo which was to mark five hundred years of evangelisation in the New World:

The church seeks to present itself as a defender of human rights, a promoter of 'men renewed and free, conscious of their dignity', as the pope put it in his opening address. If the church cannot allow Latin American bishops to organise their own assembly, define their own rules and elect their own officials, or if the bishops are not capable of asserting their basic human rights to freedom of speech and assembly, what contribution can they make in the name of this institution to the defence of human rights on the American continent?

The innocents have discovered what the people who run things at the top are really like. This experience may, in the long run, prove more important than the documents of Santo Domingo, and may still be fresh in the mind of the participants at the next conclave. For the Roman Catholic Church itself, the Santo Domingo conference marked a high point in the centralising trend so apparent in this papacy.

Disregarding democratic procedures in religious orders

One of the features of religious orders has always been their relative freedom to elect their leaders. Pope John Paul has repeatedly interfered in this democratic procedure and imposed his own nominees.

The first occasion was when Fr Arrupe, the much loved General of the Jesuits suffered a stroke. According to the Jesuit constitutions, Fr Vincent O'Keefe became Vicar. However, on 5 October 1981, the Secretary of State arrived unannounced at the Jesuit headquarters and read a letter to Arrupe informing him that the pope had appointed Fr Paolo Dezza as his personal legate. The inner circle around Arrupe were sent packing – Vinny O'Keefe went back to New York. It was the first time a pope had interfered in the Jesuit constitutional government since the suppression in 1773.

In 1985, the pope took the Franciscan Friars Minor to task in a sternly worded letter which spoke of a 'ruinous crisis of authority', and announced that he was appointing his own personal delegate, Archbishop Fagiolo, to preside over their General Chapter, 'to ensure that the considerations raised by his letter find adequate expression at the Chapter.'

In the middle 1980s, the Vatican proposed a constitution for thirteen thousand Carmelite Sisters in eight hundred convents around the world – which, according to reports, 80% of them opposed. In 1987, the Provincials of Spain and Portugal told the Vatican that they found the rules drawn up for them 'negative, threatening and violent'. The new rules were written in a language 'harsh without foundation', and gave the impression of having 'an obsession which runs through the whole project of upholding as valid what a normal society would reject as anachronistic.'

CLAR (the Confederation of Latin American Religious)

Throughout its thirty year history, the Confederation of Latin American Religious has freely elected its own officers, namely a President, three Vice-Presidents and a Secretary General. In 1989, they elected Sr Manuelita Charría as Secretary General. The Vatican overruled the appointment and appointed a priest of their own choice in her place, on the grounds that the doctrinal and theological qualifications required for the post were not usually held by a sister.

In February 1991, CLAR was informed that the pope was appointing a delegate to run their affairs from now on, whom they must welcome in a 'spirit of filial docility due to the Holy Father.' The religious may make nominations for other positions, from which the Vatican may or may not choose before making appointments. Any future publications of CLAR must be submitted for approval to the pope's delegate before publication.

The pessimist

Teilhard de Chardin said once that 'the world belongs to those who offer the greater hope.' Too often John Paul's thinking suggests pessimism rather than hope. Speaking to the superiors of religious orders working in Latin America, early in 1991, he told them he felt 'profound worry' about 'negative repercussions at the heart of the whole church community.' It was 'not just a few groups of religious' who were slow to show obedience, and who often promoted 'parallel initiatives'. (This is a phrase much used in Vatican documents and refers to any initiative which the conservative bishops appointed by John Paul dislike.) Parallel initiatives could not be permitted at 'such a significant moment.' 'Directives have not always been heard with a generous disposition, and this was a reason for worry and pain.'

Inconsistent attitudes to involvement in politics

Time magazine, in 1992, ran a story on how the pope and President Reagan had defeated communism together. According to *Time,* a far-reaching covert network was established by the pope and Reagan. Important decisions on funding aid to Solidarity were made by Reagan, CIA chief William Casey (who became principal policy architect within days of the declaration of martial law), and National Security Adviser, William Clarke, in consultation with the pope.

William Wilson, the first US Ambassador to the Holy See, said he met frequently with the pope and discussed a broad range of subjects including the Central American issue, 'which involved Nicaragua most of the time I was over there'. He said he had 'to explain to the Vatican what our policy was, what our concerns were and what our goals were in whatever we were doing in Central America'.

For many, this political alliance was a big surprise, but for those in the know it only gave details of what they suspected already. As early as 1985, Bruce Kent, the Brittish anti-nuclear activist, spoke at a National Conference of Priests meeting in Britain about a 'different set of standards so clearly applied to church politics in Poland and in Nicaragua,' and declared that the Vatican, as a major political agent in the world today, had interests and perspectives 'which in broad practical terms are those of the United States.'

According to one cardinal present at a meeting to prepare for the 1985 synod, Pope John Paul opened the discussion by telling Chicago's Cardinal Joseph Bernardin that he did not understand why the US hierarchy was sending bishops to visit Cuba and Nicaragua or why the bishops did not 'support your own President's policies in Central America'.

US propaganda has constantly tried to exploit the fact that policies supported by Reagan were also being supported by the pope. On one occasion when Peter Lemass – former Radharc interviewer – criticised US involvement in Nicaragua, the US embassy sent him a video of the pope's visit to Nicaragua. This showed the pope admonishing publicly the well-known Latin American poet, Fr Ernesto Cardenal, and coming close to losing his temper with the congregation at Mass who asked him to pray for victims killed by the Contras.

I have met and interviewed the four priests who were involved with the Sandinistas in Nicaragua, two of them three times. I think they are good and even holy men who were very badly treated and quite misunderstood. Fr Fernando Cardenal had the total support of his Jesuit brethren. His superior gave no reason for his removal except that the pope had demanded it. By his unsympathetic treatment of the Latin American church, Pope John Paul set himself on the side of reaction, which history I believe will prove to have been the losing side.

Critics of the pope are not slow to point to his virtual canonisation of political activists like Fr Jerzy Popieluszco in his native Poland.

The Nicaraguan bishops' pastoral letter of Easter 1984 was distributed throughout the US by the State Department, and exhorted the Sandinistas to enter into dialogue with the Contras. The Jesuits in Central America, in a public statement, described the Contras as a US invasion force which had not the slightest interest in dialogue. Pretty well all the religious I ever met in Central America were unsympathetic, to say the least, to US/papal policy.

The very political Archbishop of Managua, Obando Bravo, was made a cardinal in 1985, and celebrated Mass with the Contras on his return home via Miami. I have twice interviewed the cardinal in Managua as well as one of his auxiliary bishops. They belong to a church which I would prefer to see consigned to history.

The pope's strong antipathy to Marxism has had a profound influence on the type of episcopal appointments being made all through the Third World. Any candidate for a bishopric who believes that the dreadfully unfair social system in South and Central America needs reform is open to right-wing calumny. The Catholic right know that they have only to accuse a priest of Marxism to remove him from contention for episcopal office under the present pope's leadership.

A footnote on the demise of communism

Pope John Paul's deep distrust of the communist system was never hidden. But perhaps it has become more obvious now that it's safer for him to exult in its demise. There's no doubt that many believe that Solidarity was a principal agent, if not *the* principal agent, in its downfall, and that the pope's support was in turn crucial for Solidarity. What began in Poland proceeded, according to the domino theory, throughout Eastern Europe and even Russia itself. So the pope and Ronald Reagan can bow and take the credit.

My own view is that the demise of the communist system was due to happen anyway, and was predictable, and indeed by some predicted, and had little to do with the pope or Ronald Reagan.

The communist system was fated to continue as long as the leadership who had helped to bring it about could cling on to power. So much was sacrificed for the Revolution, the old leadership could not admit failure, even though that failure was clear for all to see. But once power passed to a new generation, immutable ideology and fidelity to the gods of Marx and Lenin, was bound to crumble before the basic human desire for freedom, and a better share of this world's goods.

There was plenty of evidence too to suggest that Soviet society was ripe for reform. In 1939 only 10% of the population had secondary education, often incomplete. By 1986 70%, and if one excludes manual workers, virtually 100% had a full secondary education. Educated masses don't tolerate authoritarian governments – not for long anyway.

So the rapid collapse of Communism in Russia should have surprised nobody. And once the chains began to loosen in Moscow, the satellites began to stir as well. Without *glasnost* and *perestroika*, Solidarity wouldn't have been around long enough to fight an election – the tanks would have moved in as they had moved in before.

A narrow view of the magisterium or teaching office

The view of the magisterium or teaching office of the church, as expressed in the 1990 *Instruction to Theologians* must be taken as reflecting John Paul's view. It is a very restricted one. Theologians are explicitly excluded from the teaching office, and there is no clear sense that local bishops are included. In practice the magisterium seems to be largely synonymous with the pope and the Roman curia in the form of the Holy Office. The recent encyclical, *Veritatis*

63

Splendor provides further confirmation that this assessment is accurate.

On the matter of conscientious intellectual dissent from the magisterium, theologians are told to suffer in silence and prayer. On no account must they express dissent in any media. If their views are investigated by the magisterium, they cannot claim a violation of human rights or expect the equivalent of a civil judicial trial because standards of conduct appropriate to civil society and of a democracy cannot be purely and simply applied to the church.

If the reader is shocked by these sentiments, theologians were even more so. 'Ecclesiastical totalitarianism' was the term one used.

During the pope's visit to the USA in 1987, an attempt was made to arrange a dialogue between the pope and the American bishops. Four bishops delivered papers on the concerns of the US church, and the pope read a prepared text in reply.

Although the church has always recognised the acceptability of dissent from official teaching (the 1968 statement of the US Catholic bishops is only one case in point) the pope in his reply took up the unprecedented position adopted by Cardinal Ratzinger in the exchange with Fr Curran (removed from his post at Catholic University in Washington), namely that dissent from any official teaching is never legitimate.

Writing of the papal visit in *The Tablet,* Richard McBrien, an American theologian, said that the pope's hard-line address on dissent before the bishops at Los Angeles nearly cancelled out completely whatever positive value his long and expensive visit may have had. Among other hard teachings, the pope said that theologians are subject always to the judgement of the hierarchical magisterium, even on matters pertaining directly to their own scholarly competence, and that no expression of dissent from any official teaching, fallible or infallible, is ever compatible with authentic Catholic faith.

The pope characterised as a grave error the view that 'dissent from the magisterium is totally compatible with being a good Catholic and poses no problems to reception of the sacraments'. On the face of it, this is incorrect historically and theologically. The question is not whether dissent is ever legitimate, but when and under what circumstances it is legitimate.

The pope's assertion that dissent of any sort was a disqualification from receiving the sacraments led to reporters asking whether this applied to Catholics using artificial contraception (80% and more of the fertile Catholic population).

The moderate bishops in the US, who still remain the majority, must have been disappointed and alarmed at the evidence that their minds still run on a different track from the pope's.

If he were alive, Cardinal Newman for one would certainly not have agreed with him. In his 'Open Letter to the Duke of Norfolk', Newman wrote: 'It is never lawful to go against our conscience ... the very moment when the church ceases to speak infallibly then private judgement of necessity starts up ... There is nothing to hinder a Catholic having his opinion and expressing it, whenever and so far as the church, the oracle of revelation, does not speak [ex cathedra, or by a doctrinal definition of an ecumenical council that has been endorsed by the pope].'

The damage to ecumenism

The growth industry in disciplining theologians and bishops has had a very negative effect on Protestant enthusiasm for *rapprochement*. A recent editorial in *The Church Times (London)* concluded, 'Anglicans have Christian reasons for refusing to submit to a power which emits whiffs of Stalinism.'

According to the Kansas-based *National Catholic Reporter,* the most recent response from Rome to the work of ARCIC, the Anglican Roman Catholic International Commission, was issued as if it were 'a blush-making guilty secret that no one wished to own up to'.

It was not met with hostility but with indifference masquerading as quiet despair. It has been received with enthusiasm only by bodies such as the Protestant Reformation Society, which welcomed its candour and says it proves that the aim of the ecumenical pilgrimage can only be submission to Rome.

Time magazine's report on Christian reunification after the Roman response to ARCIC was simply headlined, 'Let's call the whole thing off'.

The authoritarian schoolmaster

Speaking to the Roman Rota, the church's court for marriage cases, the pope said, 'To bend canon law to whim or interpretative inventiveness in the name of an ambiguous and undefined humanitarian principle' would detract from human dignity as well as the correct standard. But is it not that very 'humanitarian principle' that Christ brought to law when, for instance, he said that the Sabbath law was made for man, not man for the Sabbath?

Pope John Paul repeatedly lectures bishops as if they were schoolchildren. Beginning his tour of Latin America in 1985, he lectured the Venezuelan bishops. After denouncing 'distortions in the gospel message', he continued: 'Unfortunately there are those who, abusing the mission to teach what they received from the church, proclaim not the truth of Christ but their own theories, at times in open contradiction to the magisterium of the church.' He singled out 'erring priests who disguise the gospel message, using it at the service of ideologies and political strategies in search of an illusory earthly liberation.' It was the duty of bishops to be vigilant 'in order to remove from the flock the errors that threaten it'.

In one visit to South America, the pope used the word 'contraception' disapprovingly no less than sixty times in ten days of public speeches. In the same ten days, it is estimated that around the world three million children were born, one and a half million aborted, and four hundred thousand died in childhood.

A pope needs to speak to the next generation

In Europe particularly there is a great need to find a language of faith that speaks to the younger generation. That means, I believe, going wholeheartedly in the direction of Vatican II, understood in the maximalist sense. As the bishops of England and Wales declared in their submission to the 1985 synod, and careful research in the United States bears out, the crisis in the church does not come from Vatican II but from the non-implementation of Vatican II.

Because councils like to have unanimity when it comes to voting, council documents tend to be the result of compromises, and contain something for everyone. A conservative interpretation is possible by only quoting some paragraphs, a more liberal one from quoting others. So a minimalist and maximalist interpretation of council documents is possible. John Paul and his supporters are minimalists.

As far back as 1979 the American Catholic periodical *Commonweal* wrote about John Paul II in prophetic fashion.

It is 'his vision of the teaching church that gives us the most concern. Repeatedly John Paul invokes the image of the positive truth to be safeguarded and effectively communicated as though it were a static rarefied reality, a treasure protected and at most given a different display case for every age rather than a living and growing tradition rooted in history and experience.' The article quoted the pope when he spoke about 'the right of the faithful not to be troubled by theories and hypotheses that they are not expert in judging or that are easily simplified or manipulated by public opinion for ends that are alien to the truth.'

The writer continued, 'If such a phrase has a ring that seems more fitting to the Polish Communist Party than a dissenting Polish religious leader, it is because the institutional behaviour based on such phrases more commonly resembles that of authoritarian societies than communities of free and mature believers. In so far as it encourages a teaching church that is not equally a learning one, the huge promise of his papacy may go unfulfilled.'

Veritatis Splendor

Since writing the above, I have read *Veritatis Splendor,* John Paul's encyclical – all 45,000 words and more. It draws together the pope's thinking on moral theology, and illustrates the thought processes behind the agenda which we have all seen put into action throughout his pontificate. So in that sense there are no surprises. The document has much of value to say about the enduring basis for morality. But if I had to sum up in a sentence what the cutting edge of the message seems to be, then it might run something like this: the vast majority of the Catholic laity are living in sin, and many Catholic theologians are believing and teaching error. However, not being a theologian,

I am not qualified to judge, so I looked to see what some of the better known theologians thought about it. Bernard Häring, certainly the best known moral theologian in the Catholic Church, had this to say:

> *Veritatis Splendor* contains many beautiful things. But almost all real splendour is lost when it becomes evident that the whole document is directed above all to one goal: to total assent and submission to all utterances of the pope, and above all on one crucial point: that the use of any artificial means for regulating birth is intrinsically evil and sinful, without exception.

Some other comments from theologians:

> How can we with any credibility make the case to a pluralistic (and confused) culture that the Catholic tradition has valid insights about sex, commitment, love and parenthood, when the most current official document retrieves a male-oriented perspective...? *Professor Lisa Sowle Cahill*

> (The encyclical) has many serious weaknesses. Official teachers of the church can count on assistance from the Holy Spirit, but this does not work automatically ... it is mediated through praying, sharing, discerning and especially listening with and to the whole church. *Sean Fagan SM*

> *Humani Generis,* Pius XII's encyclical, sadly led to silencing and sackings, (Yves Congar, Henri de Lubac, Jean Daniélou, et al.) Most of the positions of these distinguished theologians were eventually accepted by the church at Vatican II. *Veritatis Splendor* at key points attributes to theologians positions that they do not hold. It will, I predict, eventually enjoy an historical status similar to *Humani Generis. Professor Richard McCormick SJ*

> *Veritatis Splendor* marks the reversion to a particular school of theology that flourished in the 1940s ... It offends against the prudent principle that the church should be ruled from the centre, not the right wing. Bishop Christopher Butler's words apply: 'An authority that does not address the conscience, will soon cease to be an authority'. *Peter Hebblethwaite*

So the war between the pope and the theologians clearly continues.

I am conscious of having drawn a negative picture of Pope John Paul II, leaving out many good things which could be fairly said about him as well. But lauding live popes in print is an industry in itself, with which I'd be hard put to compete. And there is little new to say.

I think Karol Wojtyla, like his predecessor St Peter, is a saintly man who loves his Lord, who has served him faithfully to the best of his ability, and who must earn a high place in the afterlife. And who, like his very first predecessor, was unfortunately wrong about some very fundamental issues.

> When Cephas (Peter) came to Antioch, however, I opposed him to his face, since he was manifestly in the wrong ... When I saw they were not respecting the true meaning of the Good News, I said to Cephas in front of everyone: 'In spite of being a Jew, you live like the pagans and not like the Jews. So you have no right to make the pagans copy Jewish ways.'

(Paul to the Galatians 2:11-14)

Either there are no Pauls around anymore, or Peter isn't listening.

4

JOHN XXIII – MAN OF THE CENTURY

The Pope who decided he wouldn't be infallible

I saw Pope Pius XII once at Castel Gandolfo, exchanged a few pleasantries on two or three occasions with Pope Paul VI, and filmed John Paul II near enough to get a wave from him. But I never saw John XXIII in the flesh.

I did watch a film about him. The commentary was in Italian, of which I didn't know enough to keep up with it. Yet I was deeply moved just looking at the images, and am moved even now when I remember them. For John seemed to have all the qualities that bring out love and respect and trust in human beings. You could read it in his face and his movements and his gestures, and the faces and body language of everyone who met him.

John died in 1963, which means that he died before perhaps half the people now on earth were born. Yet he belongs, I believe, more to the future than any of his successors.

John for me is proof that the papacy can work. That it can be the centre of unity. That it can inspire people to believe in the goodness of God and of his creation. That it can generate optimism. And in the end help us to love God and one another better.

So in Radharc we tried to do our little bit to help keep the memory of John alive in a programme called 'John XXIII, Man of the Century?' The title arose from the comment of an American bishop, Mark Hurley, which we put at the head of the programme. Every year *Time* magazine chooses a 'man of the year' – so far they don't seem to have got around to the other half of the human race. Anyway, for the year 2000 the bishop suggested they might chose a 'man of the century', and he offered John XXIII as his candidate.

I was disappointed when we came to make the film that we could not get our hands on more archive footage of John. RAI, (Italian television) had given all their footage to the Vatican, who were in the process of cataloguing and preserving it. So it wasn't easy to get at, at least at a price we could afford in time and money. For the most part, we had to be content to collect stories from people who knew him, and of course visit his home town of Sotto il Monte and meet his living relatives and friends.

A pope without pomposity or self importance

Bishop Hurley told a story I'd heard elsewhere, but maybe he heard it from Mrs Kennedy herself! Before the visit of any dignitary, John was advised as to how he should address them. Being the man he was, he always found titles like 'your worship', 'your holiness', 'your excellency' a bit difficult to cope with.

After rehearsing the formal options for the wife of the American president, John Kennedy, he promptly forgot them when she came in and just said, 'Ah, Jackie'!

Shortly after his appointment John was having his official photographic portrait taken, and the session went on longer than expected, so that his next visitor, Bishop Fulton Sheen had to wait. John apologised for the delay saying with a grin, 'I don't understand the Lord. He knew all the time that I would be pope some day, so why didn't he make me more photogenic?'

Every pope has to have a coat of arms. Archbishop Bruno Heim prepared one for John, and because he had come to the papacy from Venice, Heim put the Lion of St Mark into the design. 'This lion, with those teeth and claws, looks too fierce, too transalpine,' the new pope said, 'Could you not make him more human?'

A man open to dialogue

Loris Capovilla, Pope John's former secretary, is perhaps the best living witness. He now lives in Sotto il Monte.

Pope John's own extended family consisted of thirty-two people. He grew up not in isolation but in a group – and he saw that everything was best done together. So he was open to dialogue. Indeed a man who comes from the country often has a different mind-set – you don't find in him the closed mind of some city dwellers.

Cardinal Suenens tells a nice story which perhaps illustrates this point:

When the Belgian bishops first came to meet him, each one was duly introduced. Then Pope John asked for the speech that had been written for him and said, 'Now my dear bishops, I shall read you a speech that was written especially for you by the services of the Secretariat of State. It will tell you what they think of you over there. Then you must tell me whether or not it is all true, and what you think of it!'

A pope who had no interest in the monarchical side of the papacy

By the mere fact of summoning a council John shifted the axis of the church. The Petrine office remained intact and essential; but there was now a moral obligation that it should no longer be exercised as though the pope were himself the sole fount of wisdom and supreme oracle of knowledge. John was always careful to try to take the whole church with him. He never packed the curia or the episcopate with his own people – in Capovilla's words:

There were people with whom he didn't agree, but whom he allowed to collaborate with him. He didn't simply surround himself with like-minded people who held the same opinion as himself and who were his friends.

One of the people John tolerated was Cardinal Ottaviani, who opposed every kind of change and was a thorn in his side all through his papacy. He had frequent arguments with Ottaviani, of whom it was said that, if he had been alive before the world was created, he would have prayed, 'Lord conserve the chaos.'

Once when Ottaviani stood beside him as he sat on the throne in St Peter's (a picture of which we did have on film), John leaned over and whispered in Ottaviani's ear, 'Our minds don't work in the same way; but let us be one in our hearts.'

A man at peace with God and the human race

Mark Hurley describes him as 'the most relaxed man I ever met':

The night before the opening of the Vatican Council, there was a big parade here in Rome. It went from the Basilica of Santa Maria Maggiore over to the cathedral of Saint John Lateran, and Pope John waited there for the people to assemble, and he gave a talk, telling them about the Council that was opening the next morning. And then when he finished with his prepared text, he put it down and he looked at the people and he said, 'Now, everybody seems to be talking about the poor pope, the poor pope,' he said, 'Now let me tell you something about the poor pope. When I leave here I am going to go back to the Vatican, I'm going to have a fine dinner and I'm going to go to bed and I'm going to sleep the whole night and I'm going to get up refreshed in the morning. Now my dear people,' he said, 'I want you to go home, and have a very good dinner and have a very good sleep and be refreshed tomorrow.' And that was the way he really opened the Council for the people of Rome.

When Loris Capovilla, first met him after he was elected pope, and burst into tears, John calmly said to him, 'There, there, do stop crying. Who's been elected pope – you or me?'

Cardinal Suenens once had his photo taken kneeling down to kiss the pope's ring – which cardinals are not expected to do. John saw a copy, and sent it to Suenens with a big *non placet mihi* written on the back (*placet/non placet mihi* – 'it pleases/displeases me' were the terms used by bishops voting at the Council). A few words of humorous teasing about his kneeling followed in Italian.

A leader who preferred to affirm rather than condemn

At the opening of the Vatican Council, Pope John said that the church 'considers that she meets the needs of the present day by demonstrating the validity of her teaching rather than by condemnations.' How quickly have those words been forgotten! The virtual persecution of theologians with which we have become so familiar in the last twelve years would be unthinkable if John were still with us. He didn't see himself as a fussy inquisitor, striking down errors and heresies as soon as they appeared. Errors there would always be, he reasoned, but 'today people are condemning them of their own accord, and they tend to vanish as swiftly as they rise, like the morning mist before the sun'. Rather than condemnations, 'today the church prefers to use the medicine of mercy rather than severity.'

John always preferred 'to affirm rather than to deny,' believing that error was best dissipated by the force of truth and that a dialogue could not begin with recriminations. John was one of the first people to take a relaxed view of Communism. As early as 1962, he said that there was little need to condemn Communist errors, because they had produced such lethal fruits that 'nowadays men are condemning them of their own accord.'

A vote for collegiality and freedom

Pope John, as was his right to do, interfered several times in the working of the Vatican Council. But, as Bishop Mark Hurley pointed out, it was always in the interest of giving the bishops greater freedom. Wilten Wynne was correspondent for *Time* magazine in Rome in the Sixties:

> At the first meeting of the Council, the agenda had been drawn up by the arch-conservatives in the Vatican and John knew it wouldn't hold up. He called the bishops of the world in, he told them to practice holy liberty in their discussions, and he made clear to them that there would be no pressure on them from the top, that it was what we call in America, an open convention. And as the bishops realised that this in fact was the case, they carried on their debates and conducted the council in a framework that you could only call holy liberty, and they took decisions that have that will affect the church throughout the rest of its life.

Bishop Mark Hurley was present when the Council opened:

> The first man up was Cardinal Liénart of France, and he was supported by Cardinal Frings of Germany. And after three years of preparation, with thousands of bishops here, thousands of people here from the press and so on, the very first words of Cardinal Liénart were, 'I move we adjourn'. And this was like a thunderbolt in the Council, to stop right at the beginning! But the reason was quite clear. The bishops of the world felt that they should be the ones to choose the working committees, not accept the nominations of the curia. And that night when the proposal was presented to John he just said, 'Why, of course'. So the

bishops were free to caucus and then to make nominations, nation by nation, as to who would be really doing the spade work of the Council itself. John did not have a preconceived notion as to how the process would work at the Council. If this was what the bishops wanted, and it was clear that they did, then he went right along with it. And I think that was very, very significant, that he was so willing to accept the consensus of the bishops of the world.

Gerald O'Collins, a Jesuit theologian, pointed out to us how the pope encouraged freedom in discussion in another way:

Pope John inspired the Council with a number of basic ideas. For instance the idea contained in his opening speech that the content of the faith is one thing and the way we express it is another. That loosened up language a great deal, it made it a lot easier for bishops and others to realise that the ways of expressing a basic Catholic Christian faith can take different forms.

An ecumenist in deed as well as in word

Fred Corson, President of the World Council of Methodist Churches, who attended the Vatican Council as an observer, came to be on friendly terms with Pope John. He told Cardinal Suenens of his embarrassment one day when John asked him unexpectedly, 'Corson, my friend, how much longer do you think it will be before unity is restored among Christians?' The reply was somewhat hesitant, so John simply said, 'Well at any rate, between you and me – it's done!' Corson later said of John. 'He is a pope who loves men more than power.'

Once the Council got going, the observers found that they were sucked into the whole process. They were being consulted all the time and finding that their input was having a marked influence on decision-making in the Council. George Lindbeck, an observer for the Lutheran Church, spoke about his experience.

First of all you have to remember that the Roman Catholic Church was here giving non-Roman Catholics greater input into an ecumenical council than any other Christian church that I know of has ever given non-members access to its own conventions and governing bodies. And this was all within the context of a reception by a pope whose ability to project warmth and love and friendship was, I think, probably greater than of any other human being in our century. That is to say he absolutely captivated everybody that came in touch with him including the kind of Protestant who really is a pope-hater, but that simply didn't work with John the XXIII. It's hard to explain what made him so fantastically effective in dealing with an enormous range of personalities and charming them all, but it had something to do with saintliness, in addition to a very warm and effective personality – I think the two in combination.

A man who trusts

A cynic might say, alas with some justification, that the Catholic Church's activities are largely based on distrust. The Roman curia doesn't trust the pope, the pope doesn't trust the curia. Neither pope nor curia trust the bishops, while the bishops don't trust each other, or the priests or the laity. Which all could be summed up by saying that nobody trusts the Holy Spirit!

If you wanted to pinpoint the most significant difference between John and his successors (*pace* John Paul I), I think it would be that John trusted the bishops while his successors didn't. So Pope Paul wouldn't let them decide with him on the question of birth control, and withdrew any teeth from the Synod of Bishops, while John Paul II harangues bishops continually like a worried schoolmaster.

Loris Capovilla, who was Pope John's secretary in Venice as well as in Rome, tells a story which is one of my favourites, and which is first hand. When Cardinal Angelo Roncalli first came to be Patriarch of Venice, he heard of an elderly priest of the diocese who had become bitter and careless, and had given up saying Mass and his breviary. Against the advice of senior priests in the diocese, who felt the man was incorrigible, Roncalli insisted on calling at the home run by sisters where the priest was staying. The old priest raged against the church, the diocese, the way he had been treated by the former bishop, while the cardinal listened with compassion. Then he touched the old priest on the shoulder and said, 'Don Giovanni, we are both old men. And we must soon appear before the judgement seat of God. What use to dwell on these things? What use? Listen to me now. Start to say your breviary again, start to celebrate Mass.'

And the priest replied bitterly, 'They stopped me saying Mass.' 'Well I am your superior now,' the cardinal said, 'and I give you permission, and bit by bit we'll clear things up.' The cardinal called in Capovilla. 'Fr Giovanni here has lost his breviary. I want you to find a nice new one for him. And tomorrow I want you to send a tailor here to measure him for a new cassock.' Before he left, the cardinal gave the priest the equivalent of $350 'for his expenses'. After his distinguished visitor had left, the priest sent out for a few bottles of wine, got drunk, and was found later singing on the streets. The story went around the dioceses – the general consensus being that the cardinal was a fool and should have known better. Capovilla heard the criticism and passed it on to the cardinal, who replied:

'Do you really think that I believed that one visit would be enough to change that man's life? It wasn't to change his life that I went to see him, but to begin to take away the bitterness. If you can take away the bitterness, then, maybe later, the life will change. But if you don't take away the bitterness, nothing else you do is worthwhile.'

'But the other priests won't understand,' Capovilla said, 'They'll say you are weak, that you should discipline him.'

Roncalli lifted a glass in his hand.

'Whose glass is this?'

'Yours.'

'And if I let it drop on the floor, the broken fragments, whose are those?'

'Yours.'

'And I must bend over and gather them up. That priest is mine. This term mine, what does it mean? I must love. If I do not love him, my condemnation is a sign that I am not a Christian.'

Christian optimism

When John opened Vatican II he said to the bishops, 'Do not listen to the prophets of doom who announce disasters as if the end of the world were at hand. Everything, even human differences, leads to the greater good of the church.'

Fr Ralph Wiltgen, who ran a press service during the Vatican Council, summed up John for us:

> Pope John's legacy I would say was a legacy of optimism. This optimism breathed forth from him whenever you would see him communicating with people. Even if he was not saying it in so many words, he was saying to people that in the church 'we don't need any inferiority complex, we are doing something good for the world, necessary for the world. And if God is with us, what do we have to worry about? Nothing!'

Among his last recorded words were these:

To the press and to the world he said, 'My bags are packed.'

To the Cardinal Secretary of State he quoted a psalm beginning:

> 'I rejoiced when I heard them say, let us go to God's house.'

To his personal secretary, Capovilla, he said:

> 'We have worked together. We have served. We have loved. We have not stopped to gather the stones which were thrown against us from one side or the other, to throw them back.'

Pope John and infallibility

Pope John said once, 'I am not infallible. I am infallible only when I speak *ex cathedra*. But I shall never speak *ex cathedra*.'

And he never did.

Pope John's words seem to lead one to the conclusion that either he didn't really believe in papal infallibility, or at least did not believe in the wisdom of ever calling upon it, which nearly comes to the same thing.

Leaving aside the question of his belief, in judging that there could be no situation where he as pope would need to or wish to draw upon the infallible charism, John was making another implicit judgement: for him to make infallible statements was either harmful or at least useless. A claim to a charism which is of negative value or useless, is a claim that may need examination.

Apart from John, other popes have been very chary about calling upon their infallibility. In the last two centuries, there have only been two cases where it seems agreed in retrospect that the pope called upon his infallible prerogative — the definition of the Immaculate Conception in 1854 and the Assumption in 1950. Both dogmas were widely accepted in the church and defining them did little or nothing to increase belief or devotion. Both dogmas are unlikely to be questioned by any new evidence — unlike, for instance, the belief in the absolute inerrancy of the Bible which led to various anathemas being proclaimed down the ages, including the embarrassing condemnation of Galileo.

There is an old Latin tag which says that *entia non sunt multiplicanda praeter necessitatem,* which might be translated simply as 'don't make things more complicated than you need to.' The positive value of defining the infallibility of the pope seems, in retrospect, to have been small. The negative value, in terms of raising difficulties for other Christians, has been very great. So if there were ever the possibility of reviewing the doctrine, the implications for church unity would be very significant.

The basic argument for infallibility

Infallibility, by the way, is essentially a charism of the church. It belongs therefore to pope and bishops, not separately, but together. It may be called upon by the pope, but only on behalf of the church, which of course includes the other bishops.

The fundamental argument for infallibility is this: since the church is the historical presence of God's will in Jesus Christ, against which the powers of this world cannot prevail, the power of divine grace cannot allow the church as a whole to fall away from the truth of God. Consequently, when the teaching authority in the church definitively teaches a doctrine which touches the core of what God has revealed, it must be preserved from teaching anything untrue.

So the basic argument is this: things must be so, because God couldn't allow it to be any other way. Applied to papal infallibility the argument may be slightly different: Jesus gave Peter the power of binding and loosing. If that power was necessary for the church in the beginning, then it's just as necessary now for Peter's successor. But God couldn't permit Peter (or his successors) to bind people to belief or action which were untrue or immoral. Therefore God must keep the pope from error if and when he uses his full authority.

The argument has its attractions, but clearly there is one basic and questionable assumption, and that is that God must conveniently act in the way we decide he should. However, God often surprises us. There are, moreover, uncontroverted facts about the papacy which are difficult to square with this line of argument. One might have expected, for instance, that God would have made sure that only good men would become 'Vicars of Christ' – if there wasn't a historical record to disprove it. Some successors of St Peter have been the very worst types of men, selfish, venal, lustful, power crazy.

I think all Christians without exception would like to have an infallible church/pope if they could believe such were possible. It would be wonderful to have a sure source of guidance on difficult moral questions which all Christians, not just Roman Catholics, could recognise as authoritative – a sort of 'Good Housekeeping seal' on doctrinal accuracy. But the first thing anyone will want to do before accepting the concept is to look at the record, and after twenty centuries there is a long record to check!

It is very difficult for the non-specialist to evaluate historical evidence over a period of twenty centuries. And maybe just as difficult for the specialist too. History is written by biased people. Those biased in favour of building up the papacy tend to ignore evidence of theological mistakes and stupidities. Those who recorded the mistakes have usually had polemical motivation.

But even after making what they feel are reasonable allowances for bias, many sympathetic Christian historians still find substantial parts of the history of the papacy and its curial arm depressing, its teachings on occasion abhorrent, and its *dicta* contradictory. Which is perhaps why the definition of papal infallibility in 1870 was so restricted that it would appear it had only been exercised once previously – by Pius IX himself, the pope who pushed through the definition.

The circle of infallibility
One apparent weakness in the infallibility argument is that the pope is infallible because so declared by an ecumenical council, and decrees of such councils are infallible. I say apparent weakness

because the definition of papal infallibility tries to get around the problem by stating that the pope is infallible *ex sese, non autem ex consensu ecclesiae* (of himself alone, not by the agreement of the church). However it is still the council which was asked to define that he was infallible *ex sese*, so it is difficult to see how this gets around the problem. Unless of course the pope were to say, 'I'm infallible because I say so myself.' (I think Pius did actually say something like that. Or if he didn't, he certainly said, *'Io sono la tradizione* – I am tradition' when a bishop suggested to him that papal infallibility was not part of the Christian tradition.)

Then there is the further problem that not all councils are ecumenical and infallible. Council teachings in one era have been reversed in another; councils have ratified doctrines which no Christian could countenance today. So one must apply certain criteria. But who sets out the criteria, and who judges they are fulfilled? John Henry Cardinal Newman, for one, questioned the credentials of the first Vatican Council, although he did accept the infallibility definition afterwards.

Quite apart from other Christians, statistical surveys seem to indicate that a majority of Roman Catholics reject infallibility, though I doubt if many of them could express very cogent arguments for doing so. On the other hand, those who question the doctrine from a basis of scholarship, base their arguments on criticism of the historical record, criticism of the circumstances in which the actual definition was proclaimed, as well as criticism of the doctrine itself. And they will point out where very significant changes in doctrinal teachings have happened before.

A new understanding of biblical inerrancy
Perhaps the most significant change in church teaching in my lifetime relates to what is called 'inerrancy' of the bible.

The early Christians seem to have regarded the sacred writers as stenographers taking dictation from the Holy Spirit. St Augustine – an especially powerful influence – wrote that the Holy Spirit alone decided the content and the form of the scriptures and therefore they were necessarily free from errors, mistakes and contradictions. The Council of Trent in the seventeenth century speaks of the books as being 'dictated by the Holy Spirit'. This kind of view persisted to modern times – the absolute inerrancy of scripture was explicitly maintained in papal pronouncements well into the middle of this century, and was basically what I was taught in the seminary. The assumption was, of course, that if scripture was in error, God would be responsible. (Another version of the 'God couldn't permit this' argument.)

At the third session of Vatican II, Cardinal König of Vienna pointed out that the scriptures, in matters of science and history, are sometimes deficient in truth. This view was supported by other speakers and eventually spelled the death knell of the older teaching. The cardinal said that, 'On the question of inerrancy, talk should be honest, ambiguous, unequivocal, and fearless'. To pretend the bible was, in the old sense, 'inerrant' didn't make the bible more authoritative, it made it unbelievable.

This little-noticed change in church doctrine is nevertheless very significant. It came about because scientific/historical evidence showed clearly that the bible contained some human errors which could not be laid at the door of the Holy Spirit. For instance, prophets are quoted and the wrong attribution given. Matthew attributed a prophecy to Jeremiah which should have been attributed to Zechariah. Mark talks of something happening under the high priest Abiathar, whereas the First Book of Samuel said it was under Ahimelech – close enough – Ahimelech was father of Abiathar, but still a mistake.

The present almost universally accepted Catholic teaching is that the Holy Spirit acts through the sacred writer, but in accordance with the nature of the instrument, which in this case is human, unique, and liable to error. Through all the human frailty and the historical conditioning and limitation of the authors, God's call to men is truthfully heard, hopefully believed and then realised in the world.

This fundamental change in our understanding of inerrancy was acceptable to the Fathers of the council because they knew cardinal König spoke with authority — as a scholar as well as a cardinal.

At a future council, someone with similar authority could perhaps stand up and say the same about infallibility, and for the same reason, i.e. that a calm objective evaluation of church teaching (including papal teaching), leads one to the unavoidable conclusion that the popes and councils have erred on a number of important issues. The charism of infallibility whose *raison d' être* was to protect the pope and the church from serious error didn't always work in practice. To pretend otherwise didn't make the pope or the church more authoritative, it made them more unbelievable. I don't say that will happen. But I do say that if it did happen, it would not in essence be much different from the move on inerrancy, considering all the anathemas pronounced in the past against biblical scholars who might have shown sympathy to what is present day official teaching.

Other examples of change

Some of the moral questions on which teaching has changed are familiar. The condemnation of usury – which was not defined as excessive interest on money, but any interest at all – has been conveniently forgotten. It is certainly ignored by whoever handles church finances!

The teaching of Pope Honorius on christology was later judged to be heretical, and condemned by an Ecumenical Council and by several subsequent popes.

The Council of the Lateran V solemnly defined that the existence of purgatory was proven in scripture, and that anyone who doubts the efficacy of plenary indulgences is automatically excommunicated.

The doctrine that there is no salvation outside the church was taught in a strict sense, without qualification, by a line of councils and popes and described as infallible by the Holy Office. This position is no longer maintained.

The Council of Trent defined that sacramental confession is necessary for salvation, and that this was a divine law, not just a church law.

Pope Urban II, at the Synod of Delphi in 1089, imposed the penalty of enslavement on the wives of clerics who had violated the law of celibacy. A lot of women in South America will be relieved to know that penalty is no longer enforced!

The belief 'that freedom of conscience and of worship is the proper right of each man, and that this should be proclaimed and asserted in every rightly constituted society' was condemned by Pius IX but affirmed by the Second Vatican Council.

Natural family planning was first condemned in this century, then later promoted.

Pius XI in his encyclical on Christian education (1931) solemnly declared that 'co-education (boys and girls together) is erroneous and pernicious, and often based on a naturalism which denies original sin.'

When defending infallibility in particular cases, one of course can argue that the pope or council did not call on the infallibility charism, or that a particular council of the church was not a true ecumenical council or that it didn't intend to make an infallible decision. But that way one can end up finding that so little is held to be infallible beyond argument, that the charism turns into an ornament – beautiful, but useless – rather than a tool that is helpful in determining truth. And Ockham's razor could again be said to apply... *Entia non sunt multiplicanda praeter necessitatem.*

Development of doctrine, not change

It seems to me, from my reading, that a lot of theological time and effort has been spent down the ages on getting around problems raised by the concept of infallibility. Because the convention requires that one never says baldly, 'the pope or the church was wrong', one says, 'they were right, but ...' This may involve much digging around decrees and encyclicals giving benign interpretations here, stretching a meaning there, whereas the more honest approach might be to say that teaching has now changed. However, in the case of the lawfulness or non-lawfulness of artificial means of contraception, to take one example, too much had been said too recently to permit much manoeuvring. The teaching had to be re-affirmed or very serious error admitted – so serious that Paul VI apparently felt that, whatever the arguments, the traditional teaching must be true. If Paul could have been persuaded that allowing contraceptives was a development of previous teaching, and not a contradiction of it, there seems little doubt that he would not have rejected the report of his Commission in his encyclical, *Humanae Vitae.*

There is an argument, of course, that the admission of occasional errors would do nothing but strengthen the teaching authority of the church and make it more acceptable and believable. The believability of the physical sciences' view of the universe is not affected by the fact that there are periodically massive shifts in outlook and understanding.

Whatever about infallibility, all Christians believe in the abiding presence of the Holy Spirit in the church, and consequent 'indefectibility', or protection from essential error. So if the Roman church were ever to embrace this concept of indefectibility rather than infallibility, it must open the door to significant progress in Christian unity

Yves Congar, the Vatican Council theologian, made an exhaustive study of infallibility in the Middle Ages. What he found was a belief not so much in infallibility, where error can't be admitted, but indefectibility, which he explains as follows:

> The universally shared basic belief was that the church in her totality herself could not err. One part or another of the church could err, and even the bishops or the pope could: the church could be storm-tossed but in the end she remained faithful.

Papal claims have been abandoned in the past

The fact that papal prerogatives in the past were established on the basis of what later historians agreed were false foundations, might also suggest a pattern for change, and modesty in claiming prerogatives today.

In 753 Pope Stephen II presented a document to Pepin, dated 30 March 315, called the *Donation or Gift of Constantine,* the Roman Emperor. It stated the See of Peter 'shall be gloriously exalted even above our empire and earthly throne' and conveyed to the pope 'all provinces and palaces and districts of Rome and Italy and of regions West.' Adrian IV, the only English pope ever, appealed to the *Donation* when he gave the Lordship of Ireland to Henry II of England. Alexander VI also cited the *Donation* when he divided the

New World of the Americas between the Spanish and Portuguese. So enormous power was wielded on the basis of this 'Gift of Constantine'

The *Donation* was, of course, a forgery, but Rome still treated it as genuine for centuries after this was known. Eventually, of course, the claim was in practice abandoned, and no pope nowadays would dare try to emulate the generosity of Alexander or Adrian.

Papal infallibility reconsidered

No less a person than Cardinal Ratzinger once wrote:

> To impose the acceptance of Vatican I on a reluctant East (i.e. the Orthodox Church) would be tantamount to postponing Christian reunion *sine die'* (i.e. with no end in sight).

This is a very remarkable statement and would appear to admit that either (a) Vatican I was not a fully ecumenical council, and therefore not infallible in its definition of papal infallibility, or (b) that in a united church the pope would be infallible in the Western, but not in the Eastern church!

The proper norms for a truly ecumenical council

One cannot ignore the circumstances in which infallibility was proclaimed, the character of the pope who wanted it proclaimed, or the methods he used to assure that it would be proclaimed.

Infallibility itself is a peculiarly nineteenth century idea, the idea that one can have a final statement of 'the way things are' or that the truth can be caught and imprisoned forever in a proposition. These are concepts full of the false optimism of nineteenth century scientism.

The genesis of the declaration by the first Vatican Council is also relevant. The council has been well reported by such sober historians as Bishop Cuthbert Butler. I remember his work being read out during meals in the seminary, and how it made a deep impression on me. It was my first experience of ecclesiastical realpolitik.

By 1870 Pope Pius IX was in a deep depression over the loss of the Papal States. He and his curia needed something to boost their morale. Against all that was best at the council, they pushed through the infallibility declaration with scant regard for opposing views on both the truth of the doctrine and the expediency of declaring it.

Excommunication was used against those who questioned the rightness of the pope ruling the Papal States. Excommunication was also used against those who felt after the council that they could not in conscience accept the definition of infallibility. The eminent German theologian, Johann von Döllinger, Lord Acton's teacher, was excommunicated and Acton expected that he himself would be.

If Vatican I's status as an ecumenical council is ever reconsidered it will likely be for one of two reasons: a) because no Eastern Orthodox bishop was present even as an observer, and/or b) because it does not fulfil other important norms proper to an ecumenical council.

With respect to Vatican I, the norms proper to an ecumenical council which are discussed are:

1. Was it free to make its own decisions?

Several months after the council, John Henry Newman wrote to a bishop friend, 'Surely it was not a free council, if the pope *lectured each bishop* so sharply as he did.' (The emphases are Newman's.)

Bishop Strossmayer wrote later: 'My conviction, which I shall defend before the judgement seat of God just as I defended it in Rome, is firm and unwavering, namely that the Vatican Council had not the freedom necessary to make it a true council and to justify its passing resolutions that would bind the conscience of the entire Catholic world.'

A.B.Hasler, in his book on infallibility and Vatican I, has a lot of allegations to make about the lack of freedom of the council members. He says, for instance, that Propaganda, the congregation which appoints and supports 800 bishops in missionary territories, summoned the missionary bishops one by one and reminded them who paid their bills. The Armenian archbishop was personally threatened by the pope with dismissal if he did not support papal infallibility. Vatican police searched his quarters and ordered him confined. He fled instead. Pope Pius was reported at the time as denouncing opponents of infallibility as 'Donkeys, betrayers, and sick in the head'. Once in a fit of anger he put his foot on the head of a kneeling cardinal, then lifted the man by the ears. Although Pius was supposed to have outgrown youthful epilepsy, which at that time was thought to cause such aberrant behaviour, Hasler suggests that his illness was lifelong.

Hasler died shortly after publishing the book, so there are no reports of an inquisition at the Holy Office to allow one to estimate curial reaction. But presumably it was negative.

2. Was there moral unanimity among the bishops?

Catholic tradition insists that an ecumenical council cannot come to dogmatic conclusions by a mere majority vote, but requires virtual unanimity. Shortly after the promulgation of the dogma of papal infallibility, Newman wrote: 'If the fact be so that the Fathers were not unanimous, is the definition valid?'

The minority at Vatican I included bishops who, though few in number, had large or important dioceses representing, it is said, probably half the Catholics of the world.

3. Was the teaching accepted by the whole church?

Most bishops submitted, but one could argue many were obedient rather than persuaded. Some, like Cardinal Schwarzenberg of Prague, seem never to have accepted the doctrine. Anyway, once the definition was made, no man who challenged it would ever be made a bishop by Rome. To this day!

Creeping infallibility

With only one clear case of the exercise of papal infallibility since 1870, and that in a relatively uncontroverisal area, it is clear that in practice at least the definition of Papal infallibility has made very little difference to the certainty or uncertainty with which we hold to most church teachings. The angst among theologians during this present pontificate rather concerns what they call 'creeping infallibility', which amounts to an unwillingness to define something as infallible, while at the same time demanding that members of the church give a similar type of assent. The most recent example has been the Apostolic Letter "On Reserving Priestly Ordination to Men Alone", which according to Cardinal Ratzinger is "the declaration of a doctrine taught as definitive and, therefore, not reformable". Is Cardinal Ratzinger saying that possibly fallible judgments of Pope John Paul II are irreformable by any of his successors? I hope not.

Yet in the note of presentation we are told "No one, not even the supreme authority in the Church can fail to accept this teaching without contradicting the will and example of Christ himself". If this last statement means anything, it would appear to rule out the possibility that even a future pope or ecumenical council could reverse the judgement being made in this papal letter. So either this new teaching about the impossibility of ordaining women is really infallible, or a new category has been created, teaching which may be fallible, (that is — which may be wrong), but which a future pope or a council may never change.

The critical nature of the infallibility question

I think any theologian would agree that the most dangerous area of all for them to begin asking questions in is infallibility. Hans Küng was one of the first to find this out in my generation. I am told his little book, *Infallible*, caused more anger in Rome than anything else he has written since.

But whether anyone wishes it or not, as long as Christian unity is still mentioned as a desirable goal – and everybody still pays at least lip service to it – the question of infallibility, and particularly papal infallibility, must also be on the agenda. Why? Because no other Christians, Protestant or Orthodox, find papal infallibility as determined by Vatican I acceptable in terms of scripture, church history, or theological agrument.

One way or another, no one, not even the severest critics of infallibility, suggests that popes and councils are less than worthy guides to Christian living. On the contrary, they have been very excellent ones. But where danger may lie is in taking any one decree, however clear and defined, and saying this *must* be true. In fact, the long haul may be our only sure guide to orthodoxy, given the occasional contradictions. Perhaps one day the declaration of Vatican I on papal infallibility will be regarded the same way as we now regard the teaching of Pope Honorius on slavery: that is, as a falling away from orthodoxy, eventually righted in the light of criticism by people like Hans Küng or A.B. Hasler, who appeared for a while to be dissidents. Perhaps. But certainly not soon.

5
THE MAKING OF A BISHOP
How bishops become bishops

In 1963 I was asked to set up a communications office for the Irish Hierarchy. This grew into a media training, press and information, and religious research unit under the guidance of an energetic and highly motivated largely lay committee. It came to be called The Catholic Communications Institute.

Working with and for the bishops for fourteen years, I got to know the culture. And though I may at times have been critical of individuals, I found very much to admire in their unselfish dedication, and their determination to do whatever seemed good and right, whatever the personal cost. But because I got to know the culture I could often make an educated guess as to who would be appointed to bishoprics. Sometimes too, I would be helped by snippets of information I picked up. For instance: I was once dining with Thomas Morris, Archbishop of Cashel, in the Montrose Hotel, when he said suddenly to me, 'There is no one I would like more to see a bishop than Joe Dunn.' I looked at him with surprise. Then a mild expression of horror came on his face. 'I mean Eamonn Casey,' he said hurriedly. So I had a fair idea then that Eamonn would make it and I wouldn't! (cf. The Epilogue, pg 309)

How are the candidates selected?

Well it's a human process, like all other methods of appointing people to leadership positions. Basically bishops appoint bishops, with different bishops having more or less input, and the Bishop of Rome having final say.

The process begins every three years when the bishops of a province draw up a list of names of priests whom they consider suitable to become bishops. These names are sent to Rome where they are filed for later scrutiny. When a diocese becomes vacant, the papal legate is responsible for consultation prior to the proposal of a list (or *ternus* as it is called), to the Holy See. As well as seeking the suggestions of bishops, the legate may seek the opinion, individually and secretly of selected priests 'and of lay persons of outstanding wisdom' (Canon 377). The aim of this process is to ensure that the result of consultation is known only to the papal legate and his masters in Rome.

Clearly the most important bishop in the process is the papal legate, who is sometimes a full nuncio. The nuncio by tradition is dean of the diplomatic corps, but in fact his diplomatic activity is of minor importance. His *raison d' être* is to act as the Vatican eyes and ears in church matters, and above all to filter out undesirable candidates for appointment to bishoprics. It is almost impossible to overestimate the importance of this role for the church in the country concerned. A good nuncio generally means good bishops – and vice versa. Jean Jadot, a Belgian, who was nuncio to the United States in the seventies, is often mentioned as one who made a number of very good appointments throughout the US hierarchy. Pio Laghi, his successor now a cardinal, made a similar number of poor appointments. Gaetano Alibrandi was nuncio in Ireland for an unprecedented twenty years. He once said to a friend of mine in an unguarded moment that his recommendations were always accepted by Rome. But such indiscretions are rare – normally the nuncio gives the credit for appointments to the Holy Father, if not the Holy Spirit.

Bishops from around the world may be appointed to the Congregation of Bishops in Rome who supervise appointments world-wide. This of course is a post of considerable influence. Cardinal Conway, Archbishop of Armagh, was a member of this commission, and made a point of never missing its meetings. Thirty-four cardinals and six bishops form the commission today. Looking at the list of cardinals involved, one can understand better some of the appointments that have been made in recent years.

When the Congregation of Bishops makes its nomination, the pope is of course free to reject the recommendation. Some examples from the past illustrate the human way the system works. How the system works in Asia, Africa or other continents I don't know but I would guess that it operates more or less as it does in areas with which I am more familiar. Here are a few examples. I cannot, of course, offer documentation for it is not available, but the details, I believe, are substantially correct.

The Diocese of Ossory

In 1962, when Bishop Collier of Ossory, in Ireland, was getting on in life, it was agreed with Rome that he should have an auxiliary bishop to help him – bishops didn't retire in those days. He asked for one of the priests from the college, a Fr Loughry, and apparently understood that he would be given the man of his choice. So when the rescript arrived from the nuncio to inform him of the appointment of his coadjutor, the bishop told his man to go away for a day or two so he could be out of the way until after the public announcement was made. What the elderly bishop failed to do was to look at the name on the rescript. So the bishop's candidate went away fishing and came back to the seminary lunch table on the day of the announcement, where everybody but himself now knew that he expected to be appointed and that he had not been appointed. Peter Birch, a Maynooth professor, had been appointed instead.

Dr Birch was an unusual choice, and from my experience of him as professor in Maynooth, he would not have appeared to be a particularly good one. He was Professor of Education and lectured us about the necessity of preparing our classes and talks and sermons. But he never seemed to prepare his own, and sometimes even admitted it. He spoke about love for the Mass and flew through it every morning in about ten minutes (a habit some professors got into when it was normal for the sixty or so priests in Maynooth to say Mass every morning at separate side altars and without a congregation).

In my opinion, Dr Birch wanted to be a bishop and, with that in mind, he cultivated the Archbishop of Dublin, John Charles McQuaid, to whom he displayed uncharacteristic servility. Birch did a lot of work for John Charles in the educational field and was in and out of Archbishop's House in the period before the appointment. The Archbishop of Dublin being what's called 'a Metropolitan' has some say in appointments to his suffragan dioceses, Ossory, Kildare and Ferns. My guess is that John Charles intervened without telling the old bishop, and Peter Birch got his reward. Bishop Collier was furious of course, but could do nothing – except keep Bishop Birch from any say in running the diocese for as long as he was able.

After all that, it must be said that Bishop Birch turned out to be a very good bishop – the darling of the Irish Vatican II Catholics. The priests in Ossory itself were never that enthusiastic about him, but he galvanised the laity in Kilkenny and organised one of the most efficient social service organisations in the country. He was more honest in answering questions than most bishops were expected to be, so the media loved him too. He was a loner in the hierarchy, however, most of whom considered him a maverick. But by and large they recognised his qualities and rejoiced in them in so far as they helped to give the hierarchy a better public image.

The Archdiocese of Westminster

When Cardinal Heenan died in London, everybody knew or thought they knew that Mgr Derek Worlock would be his successor. The normal screening had taken place, and Derek had been chosen by the Congregation for Bishops. The appointment was so certain that Derek was told about it (bishops do often get advance warning).

At the same time, three influential English Catholics, the Duke of Norfolk, the premier English Duke, Mr Rees Mogg, editor of *The Times,* and Norman St John Stevas, MP, went to the Vatican Delegate, Bruno Heim, and suggested the name of Basil Hume, Abbot of Ampleforth, as a suitable candidate for Westminster. They must have made a good case; and they knew their man. Archbishop Bruno Heim's hobbies were heraldry, cordon bleu cookery, and cultivating the British upper classes.

Rome too has always been deferential to the British nobility – as Irish bishops and politicians often learned to their cost, especially in the last century. Anyway Heim went directly to the pope, where it probably did no harm to mention as well that Hume's brother-in-law was secretary to the British Cabinet. And so the decision was altered, and Hume was appointed to Westminster. Mgr Worlock received the lesser but important see of Liverpool. Worlock was naturally upset, and never tried to hide it. But who can say that good wasn't done?

Both of them have done well in their respective dioceses. The late Bishop Agnellus Andrew told me that story.

The Archdiocese of Dublin

When I made educated guesses as to who would or would not become bishops, it was rarely on the basis of advance information, because there usually wasn't any. Rather it came from a growing understanding of the selection process. Take Dublin for instance. One day Dermot Ryan, Professor of Semitic Languages in University College Dublin, came into my office in the Communications Centre. He was at the time considered relatively radical in outlook. I don't think that was true, but he had had some semi-public run-ins with his archbishop, John Charles McQuaid and that was enough at the time to make one a radical. Dermot was a member of the UCD council of IFUT, the Irish Federation of University Teachers, and on the Committee of the Irish Theological Association. They were promoting the idea of theological degrees in the Irish universities, and had drawn up a document (which I still have) to present to the bishops. Dermot had already sent me a copy for comment, and I had read it carefully. Passages like the following caught my eye:

> A truly Christian and truly academic faculty or department of theology of whatever Christian denomination should, by definition, be ecumenical ...

> If bishops and theologians are to work together most effectively for the good of the whole church, their relationship should be marked with an atmosphere of mutual trust, confidence and freedom – freedom even to make mistakes, since theologians, like bishops, can sometimes be wrong. The best way to have theologians' errors corrected is by free discussion at a scholarly level. A theologian is therefore not irresponsible in publishing hypotheses for critical evaluation by scholars ...

I said to Dermot, 'Did you ever consider that, barring accidents, you are likely to be next Archbishop of Dublin?' As might be expected he denied such an immodest thought. 'Well,' I said, 'John Charles's resignation is likely to be accepted when he reaches seventy-five' (this was a correct guess). 'Look around the age level in the diocese from which the next appointment is likely to be made. Who else is there? You studied in Rome, you have a reasonable academic record, you have shown some pastoral interest, you have languages, including the most important one, Italian. Probably the only thing you can do to avoid being appointed is to worry the nuncio or annoy the bishops. And some things in this report may do just that.'

I don't know what happened to the IFUT report, because we never discussed it further. But even as archbishop, Dermot never did much to implement it, and there is still no theological faculty in UCD.

I once thought, in my simplistic way, that the problems of the church would soon be solved when younger men, steeped in the documents of Vatican II, were promoted as bishops. That handy and happy thesis proved to be false for two reasons. The priests steeped in Vatican II were not promoted as bishops; while the office changes the man rather than the man the office.

I once read a book about social psychology. It gave an example of how when a Colonel in the army is promoted to General he brings his army cronies together to celebrate. 'Now Tom, Bill, I don't want our relationship to be changed in any way by this appointment. We have always said what we think to one another without fear or favour and that is the way I want it to continue. So let's have a drink on that.' But six months later, if Tom and Bill don't click their heels, salute and say 'yessir' like everyone else, he thinks something has gotten into them.

Dr Ryan was on the Executive Committee of the Catholic Communications Institute for several years, chaired for a time by Dr Ivor Kenny, Director of the IMI. In fact, shortly before his appointment as archbishop, he and I were dining with Ivor and his wife Maureen in their home. There was never any question of anything but first names. A few weeks after the appointment I was in Ivor's house when the phone rang. Maureen answered and came back laughing. 'It's for you, Ivor. He says, "It's the archbishop speaking".'

On another occasion, Cardinal Conway was staying overnight in Pranstown House where Fr Jim Lennon – later auxiliary bishop in Armagh – and I were living. The Cardinal was always open with us about church affairs. And Jim after all was, or had been Chairman of the Armagh Priests' Council. The three of us were sitting in the drawing room when Archbishop Dermot arrived. Jim and I remained, though knowing Dermot I guessed it wouldn't be for long. True enough, after a few preliminaries, the archbishop asked Jim and me to leave while he and the cardinal talked church business. We went out like two schoolboys to the kitchen. I laughed, because it was so typical. But Jim, who was normally the mildest of men was annoyed – in fact I never saw him so annoyed – choleric might be a better word for it.

Archbishop Dermot Ryan

My relationship with Dermot Ryan was complicated, and I won't go into all the details. To begin with, my uncle and his father were friendly. His brother Andy was around my time in school. When he was professing in UCD he used to visit my eldest sister for the occasional meal. The late Fr Peter Lemass, the resident Radharc interviewer for twenty-five years, was his closest friend and golfing companion for thirty years. I invited Dermot, when he was in the university, to chair the committee which took an overview of publications in the Communications Institute, of which I was Director. Enough?

What this meant in practice was that, although we were never what you call friends, when he became archbishop I was never overawed by him. In point of fact I met him rarely, and when I did, I generally said what I thought, and maybe he didn't always want to hear it, which could partly explain our infrequent meetings.

I remember on one occasion meeting him in St Rita's, 143 Stillorgan Road – he had bought the house as a university professor, and continued to live there after he became archbishop. Visitors to St Rita's were normally entertained in the front room – dominated by a large framed caricature of Dermot in his student days riding on a Vespa through the streets of Rome. The caricature was unflattering, but it did at least manifest the correct Roman pedigree. As usual the archbishop did most of the talking. But at one stage I broke in and said mischievously, 'You know, Dermot, you're getting more and more like John Charles every day.' To which he replied, 'Maybe I understand John Charles better!'

Archbishop John Charles McQuaid

The appointment of John Charles McQuaid, Dermot's immediate predecessor as Archbishop of Dublin was quite out of the ordinary, and if I had been of age and interested at the time, I probably would have been as surprised as everyone else seems to have been when it was announced. Dr McQuaid was not the choice of the bishops, but the nominee of Taoiseach Eamon de Valera. The Irish Ambassador to the Vatican was instructed to inform the Vatican Secretary of State that de Valera wanted the President of Blackrock College as Archbishop of Dublin. Peter Lemass heard that many years later from the ambassador who was involved in the incident.

Perhaps if de Valera had asked for somebody unknown out of the blue, the request mightn't have been granted; but John Charles had been president of Blackrock during the 1932 Eucharistic Congress and, as such, had hosted garden parties for dignitaries from the Vatican, and was noted favourably by them. Mr de Valera and Dr McQuaid were of course friends, though more so in early than in later life. De Valera had once taught mathematics at Blackrock College, and when later he was Taoiseach and lived in Cross Avenue – about a hundred yards from the back gate of the college – Dr McQuaid used to come most Sundays to lunch. As is well known, de Valera also consulted John Charles during the preparation of the text of the 1937 Constitution, and had him draft material for him. But de Valera was by no means overawed by John Charles. He used him and then made up his own mind. Within the relationship, Dr McQuaid was in very much a subordinate role. His letters to de Valera at the time convey a sense of deference which is in marked contrast to the kind of imperial missive he could so well write as archbishop to his clergy. The late Bishop Patrick Dunne was my source for this information.

The Bishop of Clonfert

Another traditional source of bishops are nationals who serve the Roman curia, and for one reason or another become redundant, or want a change.

Mgr Tom Ryan was a big likeable Tipperary man – a farmer's boy if ever there was one. He worked in the Roman diplomatic service and his great glory was to come into the entourage of Cardinal Roncalli, later Pope John XXIII. He is supposed to have taught the pope English. A Roman monsignor once said to me, by the way, 'Fr Dunn, when you speak English I understand nothing, but when Pope John speaks English I understand everything!'

The witticism going the rounds at the time was that Tom Ryan used teach Pope John by getting him to repeat phrases in English after him, phrases like, 'the Archdiocese of Cashel is vacant, the Archdiocese of Cashel is vacant'. Anyway, one of John's last acts was to appoint Tom to Clonfert – admittedly the smallest diocese in Ireland but still a diocese. There Bishop Tom lived out his days, lonely in a way he could probably never have imagined, being a naturally gregarious man. I called on him once in my capacity as director of the Communications Institute; it was about six o 'clock of a winter's evening. The bishop's house was a mansion standing alone at the edge of the lake. The gate seemed a complicated affair but eventually it opened by remote control. It was a new invention, the bishop later explained, and helped to keep the cattle out (or was it in? I forget). As I parked the car I could see his big shape silhouetted in a small window to the side of the hall door. The bishop welcomed me in shirt and braces and said he was finishing his tea, and pointed to a cosy alcove by the side of the hall where there was a chair surrounded by evidence of bachelorhood: milk cartons in use and out of use, unwashed cups, tea bags and half a loaf of bread. Somebody gave him lunch he explained, but he got his own supper. He might have been happier, I felt, if he'd stayed with his friends in Rome.

How to become a bishop if you really want to

There were several French Sisters of Charity working in the Senior Infirmary in Maynooth. The infirmarian, Sr Louise, had been there since before anybody remembered. She had been married before becoming a nun, which may help to explain her no nonsense approach to life. She, a nun, and I, a student, were friendly, which was unusual in those days. I remember well her commenting to me on one of the applicants for an academic post in Maynooth. 'That man – I've seen his application. Ever since the first day he came into this college he has had his eye on only one thing – a bishopric.'

Well, he eventually made it.

Looking back over the history of Irish appointments during my time as a priest, one can see a pattern. And if I expand a little on this pattern, it is not to be in any way cynical about bishops. I have noticed that when people get annoyed with them, they sometimes say, 'Oh bishops are irrelevant anyway.' I don't think bishops are irrelevant. I think in the organisation of the Roman church to which I belong they are supremely important. Which is why I am interested in how a person becomes a bishop. If we want better bishops, then it is within this process that any change must come.

So how do you begin?

1. *Get educated in Rome*. It is not necessary but it is a great help. Four years in Rome at an impressionable age brings home to one the majesty and continuity of the church: those twenty centuries of history with the bones of Peter interred below the greatest of all basilicas. It can weld a man to the Roman thing for life. Papal audiences, trattorie, Frascati, the Colosseum, theological teachers who later become cardinals and curialists. And who may well someday put in a good word for you.

2. *Get to know bishops and be of service to them*. People don't appoint strangers, they appoint people they know to leadership positions – to do otherwise is to be reckless and stupid. If you are a member of any select group, you will be anxious to have people you know and trust around you. Bishops are the only ones who can put your name on the candidates' list. Knowing this, of course, can lead to awful sycophancy, which I have at times witnessed. I remember well a priest fawning on an archbishop in my presence where the archbishop seemed as embarrassed as I was. But it didn't hinder his appointment some years later to a diocese.

The most important bishop to know is of course the nuncio. Nuncios are usually, though not always, Italian, and rarely have a good command of English. Being able to speak Italian is an excellent start. Gaetano Alibrandi, who was nuncio in Ireland for twenty years until he retired relatively recently, was never happy in English. His boast that his recommendations were always accepted in Rome was probably a slight exaggeration, but only a slight one.

3. *Give public sermons and retreats.* A bishop is rightly expected to be a spiritual person, and if not, at least to be able to express spiritual thoughts in an acceptable way. So to be in demand for public sermons on special occasions, or to become a fashionable director of clergy retreats, would be considered good indicators of this ability. It is said that Dr Edward Daly, who recently retired as Bishop of Derry because of ill-health, first came to the nuncio's attention when he was working as religious adviser to RTÉ (the Irish radio/television network) and had occasion to give a public sermon where the nuncio was in attendance. And Dr Daly, of course, had studied theology in Rome.

4. *Be ambitious.* A layman once asked me to make it known in the right quarters that he would like to become a knight of St Gregory. I expressed some doubts as to whether this direct approach might be the best way to go about it. 'Listen,' he said, 'I am long enough in this world to know that nobody gets much of anything that he doesn't look for.'

I am not suggesting that it is always politic to ask to become a bishop, although some saints have done so. There is a letter from St Oliver Plunkett in the archives of Propaganda in Rome addressed to the Cardinal Prefect begging him 'to honour me with the Archbishopric of Armagh'.

Given that power is sought for the right reason, I think it is right for a priest to desire to be a bishop, and to take such steps as may further that objective. Power, in my opinion, rarely comes to those who don't seek it (or at the very least make themselves available to receive it). I think it right for the right kind of person to be ambitious. In fact I wish that a lot more of the right kind of persons would be more ambitious. We might get better bishops.

5. *Don't criticise the wrong people.* Unfortunately it is easier to be ambitious for worldly rather than spiritual reasons. And even if one is not worldly, and feels one might have something to contribute, a certain amount of diplomatic dissimulation will probably be necessary. Because if one ever is known to have seriously criticised central church policies, or shown less than an unquestioning loyalty to the current Holy Father, one will be automatically excluded. Many years

ago, I said to a brilliant colleague who would have made an excellent bishop, 'Please, please, lie low. Keep your thoughts to yourself. At forty-four you will be a bishop and then you will be free to speak.' His answer was that if he were once to do that, the bad habits would surely remain. He is still a priest.

An influence beyond death

One of the reasons why episcopal appointments are so important is that their influence for good or ill may be felt long after the bishop is dead. For instance, one of the reasons why there were few obvious candidates to succeed John Charles McQuaid as Archbishop of Dublin is that John Charles rarely sent independent minded people for postgraduate study. Once when I was going through a list of students with the dean of studies of Holy Cross College, hoping to find some young priest who might work part-time with Radharc, the dean said to me, 'You're wasting your time, you're looking for people like Des Forristal and Peter Lemass – we don't have people of that quality any more.' Yet Des and Peter were never sent to do postgraduate work in theology, which would naturally be the case where a young priest was considered to be possible future episcopal material. They were independent-minded, and that was the reason.

To give an example of what I mean in vulgar terms: where one has a safe, tame, dull bishop, he chooses safe, tame, dull students for further studies, who become safe, tame, dull theologians, who become safe, tame, dull bishops. There are exceptions, of course, as there always are, to prove the rule.

Conclusion

Many committed Catholics in the church seem unhappy about appointments to the episcopacy – the end result, I mean, because they can know little or nothing about the process which is buried in secrecy.

I have tried in this chapter to remove some of the mystery and secrecy – not simply to pass on clerical gossip, but because I feel one should understand the human process as it is, before considering how it might be.

There are no perfect ways of appointing leaders. At the same time, there are differing amounts of imperfection in the imperfect ones. In the case of bishops, some of these are the following:

1. Laity and priests have little or no say in who is to rule over them. Everything is decided for them between Rome and (sometimes) the local hierarchy, in total secrecy.

2. The local hierarchies do not have enough say, and too often have unsuitable candidates forced upon them.

3. Rome places too much emphasis on loyalty to the Holy See, to the detriment of other important leadership qualities.

4. The system is consequently too open to manipulation.

6
PUTTING THE HOUSE IN ORDER
Growing opposition to the appointment of unpopular bishops

Imagine a very large government agency, with ninety-eight principal officers. And imagine a situation where seventy-two of those ninety-eight officers signed three petitions, one addressed to the President, one to the Senate and one to the House of Representatives asking for the removal of the head of their agency. And imagine the President, the Senate and the House never even acknowledging the petition or replying to the letter. And imagine that several years later the tensions in the department remain the same.

It sounds incredible, but that is a fairly exact parallel of the situation we found in 1992 in the diocese of Recife, in Northern Brazil, and in a number of other important dioceses in other parts of the world as well. Seventy-two out of the ninety-eight priests in Recife wrote to the pope, the Congregation for Bishops and the nuncio to remove their bishop. Their letters were never acknowledged.

The situation in Recife – more perhaps than other dioceses – attracted world attention because the former bishop, Dom Helder Camara, was a much loved figure with an international following. He was a modest, humble man who championed the poor. He lived in simple quarters at the back of a church in preference to the episcopal palace. He was forbidden by the military government to speak on Brazilian radio or TV, or even to be quoted in the newspapers. But if the local press couldn't quote him, the world press could and did, because he was always eminently quotable. 'Wealth,' he said, 'is like the rain. There's plenty of it but it is very unevenly spread.' Or again, 'When I give food to poor people, they call me a saint. When I ask why the poor people have no food, they call me a communist.'

We made a programme about Dom Helder in 1977. It was directed by a colleague, Fr Dermod McCarthy, so I can say, without taking any credit, that it moved me. Speaking in the film to students Dom Helder said:

> I don't like people who agree with me 100%. I don't always agree with myself 100%. At times I find myself arguing with myself. It is very important that we learn to dialogue, that we learn to hear others.

When Dom Helder reached the retiring age, Rome appointed Dom José Cardoso Sobrinho, a Roman canon lawyer, who it seems, in the view of the majority of Recife priests, never learnt to dialogue, and *does* agree with himself 100%. Don José makes no bones about the fact that his instructions on his appointment were 'to put the house in order.' Which gives some inkling of how the Vatican must have felt about Dom Helder Camara. So far this clean-up has led to the closing of two seminaries, dismissing the Justice and Peace Commission and suspending one of the best known priests in Brazil (who was also the elected representative of the Recife diocesan clergy *vis-à-vis* the Brazilian Conference of Bishops). It also involved calling on the military police to re-occupy churches taken over by parishioners, driving the poor from the grounds of the archbishop's palace, forcing seventeen priests to leave the diocese, and, of course, the frequent humiliation of Dom Helder Camara.

To comprehend the anger all this caused, one has to recall that the police were one of the strong arms of the military dictatorship that ruled Brazil from 1964 to 1982, and were responsible for much torture and killing. And to help understand why Rome appointed Dom José Cardoso, and maintain their support for him when he has lost the support of his priests, one might pick this piece of our interview with him:

> If someone comes to me and says he doesn't agree with the pope, and so on, I would answer, 'I prefer to eventually be mistaken with the pope than to be certain with you.' So for me it's a question of faith. And I promised this on the day of my ordination. And I hope with God's grace to fulfil this until death.

Having made films around the world for thirty years, one can't help noticing a remarkable deterioration in the quality of the world's bishops, a representative number of whom I would have, at some time or another, met and interviewed, and others I would know about. This is particularly true of the last twelve years. But lest I sound alarmist, I mainly confine myself, in the following tour of different countries, to quoting, not my own opinions, but other sources.

The United States

Writing in his archdiocesan newspaper, Archbishop Weakland of Milwaukee said that when the church was afraid of new cultural and intellectual challenges, too often it reacted by picking leaders for 'the rigidity of their orthodoxy, so that second rate and repressive minds, riding on the waves of that fear' took over. The archbishop warned in particular against a return to the authoritarianism which was the church's response to Modernism at the beginning of this century. Then, under Pius X, 'seminaries were closed, theological periodicals were suppressed, a network of informers in each diocese was organised, oaths were repeatedly taken, intellectually rigid bishops appointed and fear and distrust were everywhere in the US.'

With the sole exception of the appointment of Archbishop Joseph Bernardin to Chicago, every major episcopal appointee since John Paul II's election 'has been more hard-line than his immediate predecessor,' Fr Richard McBrien wrote in the *New York Times*. These appointees 'tend to be loyal to the pope and his curial associates, rigidly authoritarian and solitary in the exercise of pastoral leadership and reliably safe in their theological views,' the article said. 'The result has been a lowering of the morale of the church's most engaged and effective priests, nuns and lay members. Many of them are edging to the conclusion that the church's present leadership is irrelevant, if not even inimical to their deepest religious and human concerns.'

Latin America

In February 1989, *The Tablet* reported on a meeting of ninety liberation theologians, historians, pastoral workers and publishers in

Latin America, where reports from country after country highlighted the systematic appointment of right-wing bishops – forty-nine in Mexico over the past few years, a similar number in Brazil and proportionate numbers in smaller countries – except Guatemala where the local hierarchy held firm.

In June 1992, Fr Sean McDonagh of the Irish Columban fathers reported on a visit to four Latin American countries:

> In conversation with lay people, religious, and priests I have heard bitter complaints about recent episcopal appointments ... there are few courageous bishops left to speak for the poor. The prophets who used to call attention to these issues and challenge Catholics to address them in a systematic way, have been replaced by bishops who preach an alienating other-worldly Marian piety, reduce morality to sexual ethics, and have allied themselves with middle and upper class movements. The assertion, often made during papal visits, that the church is the 'voice of the voiceless' has a hollow and hypocritical ring for many pastoral workers at the coal face of justice issues today. They echo the biblical indictment against the shepherds of Israel that the people have been scattered and for want of a shepherd have become the prey of wild animals. (Ezek 34:8)

Tensions in the Philippines

In June 1990, the *National Catholic Reporter* ran a story on the church in the Philippines:

> Fr Florante Sapalaran, the resigned Chancellor-secretary and Fr Desmond Quinn, Columban superior in Bacolod, say the priests think their new Bishop Gregorio is betraying the church as the priests know it, and has an agenda completely different from the former Bishop Fortich. The priests accuse Gregorio of repeated lying and of putting money donated for refugees from government/rebel fighting into his personal bank account, then saying he had only personal funds to give the refugees, which had to be repaid. The priests have written to the pope to explain the situation as they see it ... Plantation owners and military men have let it be known that they like Gregorio. 'We now have our man as bishop,' one planter said.

Austria

The following quotations relating to Austria and Switzerland are from *The Tablet*:

May 87: Kurt Krenn was appointed auxiliary bishop of Vienna with special responsibility for 'the artistic, literary and scientific world'. On TV on April 2 he was unable to name a single contemporary Austrian artist, painter, poet, sculptor, novelist, musician or scientist. Even his theological credentials were deeply suspect.

June 88: Dr Paul Zulehner, Professor of Pastoral Theology at the University of Vienna, said that the manner of appointment of Hans Groër to succeed Cardinal König in Vienna, and of Kurt Krenn as auxiliary bishop, suggested that Rome considered ... that those who were at the time responsible for the church in Austria could no longer be trusted.

The appointment of Bishop Krenn as auxiliary to Vienna was enthusiastically greeted in right wing conservative circles, including neo-nazis such as those associated with the nationalist newspaper *Deutsche National-Zeitung*. Some of these right-wingers talk of the bishop as their 'fellow party member.'

Jan 89: Archbishop Eder, recently appointed to Salzburg, is sixty and is known to be militantly anti-Communist. His New Year sermon underlines the importance of Our Lady's message at Fatima in its condemnation of atheistic bolshevism. He continues to say Mass in Latin, and has called AIDS 'a punishment inflicted by God.' The Austrian Chancellor has recently deplored the deterioration of church-state relations. He said he could not remain silent when a man of the church such as Archbishop Eder questioned democracy in provocative terms.

July 91: Current tensions between Archbishop George Eder of Salzburg and his council of priests have led to the archbishop's decision to suspend the council. The archbishop said he had taken this step because some members were seeking confrontation rather than dialogue.

August 91: Bishop Helmut Kräzl, the senior of three auxiliaries in Vienna, analyses Roman selection criteria for bishops. 'The appointments suggest that bishops are being nominated on the basis of how they stand on three specific points: contraception, the pastoral care of remarried divorced couples, and discussion of women's ordination.'

I met Bishop Krenn and Cardinal Groër at the launching of the German edition of the Universal Catechism in Vienna in May 1993. Groër is a kind good man, whom the Viennese respect, but consider an inadequate successor to Cardinal König – one of the great churchmen of the second half of this century. Krenn is a Friar Tuck character with a ready smile, who obviously doesn't care one jot what the media think of him. His friends say he breakfasts with the pope when he is in Rome. I later attended another function, the opening of an exhibition of Russian icons, where both cardinals were present. Groër was introduced and got a quiet clap from the audience. König was then introduced and received an enthusiastic ovation lasting several minutes.

Switzerland

May 88: A letter addressed to the apostolic nuncio in Berne and the Swiss Bishops' Conference has been signed by 267 priests in the diocese of Chur calling on the new bishop Wolfgang Haas to renounce his right of succession to the diocese of Chur as a 'sign of respect and reconciliation', and the cathedral chapter has made a similar request and is examining the legality of the procedure adopted for nomination. Half the members of the chapter did not attend the service of consecration last Sunday. Outside the cathedral some 200 protesters lay on the ground, their legs across the pathway so that the dignitaries entering the cathedral were obliged to step over them. Their banner read, 'Whoever steps over us ignores us.'

June 89: The Canton of Schwyz has asked the Swiss Government to intervene and take the matter of the Haas appointment up with the Holy See. If the new diplomatic moves fail, the Canton warns, it may be forced to take action such as suspending payments to the diocese.

July 90: The Catholic synod of the Canton of Zurich voted to cut off all payments to the diocese, and the deaneries of the canton passed a motion of no confidence in the bishop, who continued to avoid meetings and remained isolated.

September 91: The bishops of Switzerland have postponed the election of a President and Vice President of the Conference of Bishops. The current president, Bishop Josef Candolfi has explained that it is difficult to find two candidates acceptable to the majority.

And so the division enters into the Bishops' Conference.

Divided dioceses

It is very upsetting to visit dioceses like Recife where unpopular authoritarian bishops have been imposed, and to find so many good people who only want to live according to the light of the gospel, and yet cannot help becoming dispirited and disillusioned. Instance an Irish priest in Recife speaking of a local bishop:

> I feel that the man hasn't the ability to deal with priests. We don't know what exactly is behind his appointment, but we feel that he is a forerunner of a line that the Vatican is trying to impose on the Latin American church. He is one of 38 bishops who have been appointed recently who are following a line laid down in the Vatican of a church without any preferential option for the poor .

The President of the Recife Justice and Peace Commission, whose Commission was fired *in toto* by the new bishop:

> We had in the person of Dom Helder Camara permanent support and incentive. He took part in our meetings and sought us out to help him resolve problems. But when the new archbishop came, he made it clear that he had no interest in supporting this work. And he began to demand that every time we made any statements, we must clear the text with him beforehand.

I have a great respect for the office of bishop. I believe they exercise a vital leadership role in the Christian community. And I have met many of them who make me proud to belong to the same church. But leaving Ireland aside, I cannot remember meeting many bishops appointed by Pope John Paul II whom I would not prefer to see replaced.

The mind of John Paul II

Perhaps John Paul's appointments can be best understood in line with his background and beliefs.

1. His views on contraception

Karol Wojtyla has always taken a hard line on contraception. In a book he wrote as early as 1960, called *Love and Responsibility*, he anticipated the teachings of *Humanae Vitae* which banned all artificial means.

He urged Pope Paul VI to hold a synod on the subject of *Humanae Vitae* to bring vacillating bishops into line. When he himself became pope, his first synod was on this theme. Dissent was crushed. It is quite clear now that no person of whom it can be shown that he ever wavered, even slightly, in accepting *Humanae Vitae, will be appointed bishop. But since in countries where statistics are available (e.g. the US) the vast majority of priests have doubts about Humanae Vitae, this drastically reduces the talent available for appointment.*

2. His hatred of Communism

The pope has had a bitter experience of nearly forty years of brutish Nazism and Communism, so one must be understanding of his feelings in their regard. Any priest who is thought to have been tinged with Marxism is crossed off John Paul's list of candidates for bishop. This includes all the liberation theologians and their sympathisers in South America – which doesn't leave that many good theologians left. There is a lot of evidence that powerful minority elements in the Latin American church (and outside the church as well) have consistently played on the pope's dislike of Marxism to put down liberation theology and its preferential option for the poor. Most of the Latin American bishops of note (appointed in previous reigns) have at one time or another been labelled communists. Archbishop Romero was one of them who spent time in Rome trying, without much success, to persuade important people that he wasn't soft on Communism. It is said that, at the time of his death, the pope had already decided to foist a conservative auxiliary on him.

A good illustration of this aspect of Pope John Paul's character comes from a film we made in Mexico in 1986.

Arturo Lona, Bishop of Tehuantepec, had spent all his life with impoverished Indian people. He tried to take seriously the option for the poor, which meant that he was denounced as a dangerous Marxist to the Vatican. The apostolic delegate put pressure on him to go to Rome. He tried to opt out saying he hadn't the fare. But the fare was supplied by the delegate and he had to go. Eventually he came to present his report to the pope, and here I let him tell the story as he told it in our film.

He (the pope) was thumbing through the report, reading and listening to me telling how the diocese is divided, distribution of priests, sisters, mission houses, the pastoral work beginning with diocesan objectives, pastoral priorities, the hope of the kingdom realised, when he said.

'Your work is not Marxist?'

(I thought to myself, it was worthwhile coming to Rome.)

And I asked him, 'What did you say, Your Holiness?'

'... That your work is not communist, it's not Marxist. Continue right on.'

Well I was so happy and grateful ...

The latest victim of this 'Reds under the bed' syndrome is Bishop Samuel Ruiz García, from San Cristóbal de las Casas, in Mexico, with whom we made a film in 1986, and whom I came to admire. According to reports, Cardinal Gantin, Prefect of the Congregation for Bishops in Rome, wrote to the papal nuncio demanding Ruiz's resignation. Gantin's letter accused him of using Marxist analysis in his interpretation of the gospel. It has been well known for years that certain elements in the Mexican government wanted Ruiz removed because of his support for Indian rights in Chiapas, Southern Mexico. Reportedly close to one thousand international groups came out in support of Ruiz, which apparently helped the Vatican to change its mind. There also seems to have been a change of mind on the part of the government, who after the recent Indian insurrection in

Chiapas, were happy to be able to call on Ruiz to help negotiate with the rebels

3. *The roles of laity and clergy*

Another of John Paul's favourite themes is the essential distinction between the roles of clergy and laity. When Cardinal Roger Mahony of Los Angeles once said that 'lay ministry' was a contradiction in terms, he was echoing the pope's thinking. Ministry is for clerics. The role of the laity is in the world, raising a family, bringing Christianity into business and politics.

About two weeks before the papal visit to Ireland, the priest in charge of arrangements for the papal visit, Mgr Tom Fehily, now parish priest of Dún Laoghaire, returned to his office about 10:30 pm to find Archbishop Dermot Ryan waiting for him. Dermot wanted to know the position of lay ministers of the eucharist during the papal Mass. Tom showed where they would be.

'I told you they would have to be put out of sight of the altar.'

'You didn't,' said Tom.

'Well, I told Des Forristal to tell you.'

The archbishop suggested that perhaps students from the religious orders in Dublin might be used instead of lay people. Tom said it was impossible at this stage. A compromise was agreed that the lay ministers would move down from the altar flanking a priest so that it might seem to the pope that they were just attendants.

This view of ministry colours John Paul's episcopal appointments in a positive and negative fashion. Negatively, in so far as it excludes clerics who are felt to have dabbled in politics (except of course where they oppose Communism). Positively, in so far as the men he chooses seem to share his own views about training for ministry. For instance:

The Theological College in Recife, which Dom José Cardoso closed down, was open to lay people, men and women, and was situated in the middle of a poor district. The seminary on a hill in the more upmarket district of Olinda, which Dom José refurbished will be open only to males studying for the priesthood – that is a pattern being repeated throughout the world. John Paul is unsympathetic to the practice of making up for the absence of celibate priests by appointing trained lay ministers, and especially if these are women. He is against it in principle. But I also suspect that he feels it leaves a chink open to eventually bring pressure to admit married laymen to Holy Orders, or even worse, women to the ministry. And in that he is probably correct.

4. A celibate clergy

Bishops who say 'we need married clergy' don't become cardinals (and priests who say it don't become bishops). Celibacy for John Paul is an absolute. Speaking to a Canadian bishop, he once said that while the church might look foolish in the eyes of the world for refusing to change its policy on the celibate priesthood, 'if we are being brought to our knees by the need for more priests, it may be that the church will have a better understanding of the priest's role.'

5. The need to keep theologians in their place

As long ago as 1971, Karol Wojtyla, then Archbishop of Cracow, wrote an article in which he said that ever since the Vatican Council, theologians were usurping the role of bishops, and needed to be put in their place. Their task was to defend the pope's teaching, and not to disturb the faithful with new ideas.

So John Paul likes to appoint men who are tough, who will rein in the dissident theologians, speak disapprovingly about Marxism, see the faithful are not disturbed with new ideas, and keep the layperson and cleric in their respective places. Dom Helder Camara would never fit that identikit. Dom José Cardosa Sobrinho and Bishops Wolfgang Haas and Kurt Krenn are a better fit.

7
STOP THE CLOCK
Contraception — the great debate

There is a digital clock outside the railway station in Inchon, Korea, which shows the population of the country in figures visible at half a mile. The clock is one of many linked to a central computer which monitors the increase in births over deaths throughout the whole country. It was erected as part of a government programme to bring home to people the need to curb the growth in population, which had doubled in the previous twenty-five years. When we watched it, the figure seemed to increase by an average of one person per minute, which would mean, if it were a real average, a growth of over half a million a year.

In the course of our filming we interviewed an Irish sister working in Korea.

As a Catholic nurse here and as a sister, I accept *Humanae Vitae* now but after much struggle. When it was first promulgated in 1968, I really wept tears, because at the time I was working in the maternity department, and they have many, many very poor mothers who had very many children, and another baby would endanger the lives of some of them, obstetrically speaking. And they would say to me, 'Sister, please help me. Can't you do something for me?' And I couldn't do anything.

Some years ago, I said half in jest to people I work with, that if and when I decided to make a television programme about Humanae Vitae, they would know that I must be contemplating retirement. I leave you to work out the reasoning! But I have no doubt in my mind that it was and is by far the most significant story in the Catholic Church in my lifetime – and the most dangerous for a priest to tackle in such a public medium. (I have no plans to do so!)

Inevitably the subject did come in by the back door, because we took up the problem of overpopulation in Indonesia and Korea, and looked at natural family planning in Korea and Australia. The Indonesian story, called 'The Overcrowded Island' contained a significant witness to dissent which I hoped my bishop would not notice at the time. The Archbishop of Jakarta, Leo Soekoto, told us in an interview:

So the Catholics of Indonesia are supposed to do the family planning through abstinence, but in reality now and then we get some problems. Take this for instance: if there are a husband and wife who are really not able to afford to have another child, but on the other hand they are really not able to use the abstinence to prevent the birth of a new child, so I think we cannot ask the impossible. And therefore the bishops of Indonesia have said that in this predicament, people are allowed to use other means (i.e. contraception) provided it is not abortion and not sterilisation.

Q. What was the feeling in Rome about the Indonesian bishops' stand?

Of course there was a reaction. The first reaction was from Rome...

The archbishop told us later off camera that the Indonesian bishops were put under severe pressure to come to Rome to get brainwashed (his expression).

So even if we have never made a programme about the church's ban on artificial contraceptives, the subject has come up often enough to require that I read and think about it.

The significance of Humanae Vitae

There is a case to be made that the issuing of the encyclical, *Humanae Vitae* was the most significant happening in the church since the declaration of papal infallibility in 1870. More significant therefore than the Second Vatican Council. Why?

Because it touched more people in the most intimate part of their lives

The procreation, nurture, and education of children – moral, physical, emotional and intellectual, is the most serious of all purely human concerns. *Humanae Vitae* forbade the use of modern means of control over this activity under pain of mortal sin. This was of much more serious concern to the laity than whether, for instance, the Sunday Mass should be said in the vernacular or in Latin, or whether one was free to attend a Protestant service.

Because it called into question the competence of the magisterium, or teaching office of the church

Weltbild is a German Catholic journal that is very loyal and devoted to the pope. A survey among 6,000 readers in 1988 showed that only 12% of the faithful under fifty years of age, and only 25% of those over fifty were prepared to listen to the present papal teaching on questions of sexual morality. Any teaching!

A study of the Catholic priesthood in the United States in 1970, (two years after *Humanae Vitae*), revealed that 87% of the Catholic clergy no longer insisted on acceptance of the official birth control teaching in the confessional, whereas twenty years before, few Catholic priests would have been willing to give absolution to penitents who declined to accept the teaching.

Similar findings have resulted from surveys in other parts of the world.

Because it has led to sharp divisions over the appointment of bishops

In 1983, John Paul described to a group of American bishops the kind of priests he wanted to make bishops. In his own words, he wanted 'priests who have already proven themselves as teachers of the faith as it is proclaimed by the magisterium of the church.'

The evidence of faith that impresses John Paul is public opposition to birth control, to married priests and to the ordination of women.

Since only about 13% of the priests in North America support the Vatican's teaching on birth control, the pool of talent from which to appoint bishops is correspondingly small, and naturally reflects the more authoritarian elements in the priesthood. Furthermore, when the pool is small and the criteria clearly known, there is more incentive for priests motivated by worldly ambition to trim their beliefs to the theological wind and thereby earn promotion.

Because anger at the teaching appears to have undermined support for the church

In 1960, Americans in general gave an average of 2.2% of their income to the church regardless of whether they were Protestant or Catholic. Today Protestants still give 2.2%, while shortly after *Humanae Vitae* appeared, Catholics reduced their contributions to around 1%! This is quite an extraordinary statistic that requires some telling explanation. In purely financial terms, this drop in revenue amounts to some six or seven billion dollars a year every year for twenty-five years. In the view of Fr Andrew Greeley, the sociologist, cutting down on their generosity was not a kind of sudden meanness. 'It's anger,' he says, 'anger at the church over *Humanae Vitae*.'

The historical background to church teaching

I can't remember any serious theologian ever suggesting that Christ was married. He appeared to favour celibacy for his close disciples, and his remarks about becoming 'eunuchs for the kingdom of heaven' certainly gave sexual morality an ascetic twist. He was strong and uncompromising in his support for the marriage bond and condemnation of adultery, but apart from that he hadn't much to say about sexual matters, much less birth control.

Tribal society in Western Europe condemned contraception (and abortion) long before Christianity arrived. So the prohibitions were not of particularly Christian origin. Christian attitudes towards sexuality were very much influenced from the beginning by great teachers like St Jerome and St Augustine, who in turn were influenced by pre-Christian as well as Christian values.

Without wishing to enter a scholarly discusssion about the views of the Fathers of the church on sexual morality, and whether these views may be of pagan rather than Christian parentage, I will give two examples which may help to indicate how far on occasion two of the influential fathers were prepared to go.

Jerome, for instance, wrote that he valued marriage only because it caused virgins to be born! St Augustine, who was even more influential in these matters, taught that married couples commit a venial sin every time they indulge in sexual intercourse beyond the need to make babies or prevent adulterous acts. Married people were seen by him as being in constant battle against 'their animal natures'. He wished Christian couples could find a way to practice complete continence in order to be united 'not by the bonds of the flesh, but by those of the heart.'

Such views persisted in church circles up to about 250 years ago. And while nobody supports them nowadays, recalling them should help to make the theological heirs of Augustine and Jerome more careful and more humble when they lay down the law today.

Our forebears were, of course, influenced in their attitudes by the scientific beliefs of their day. As late as 1845, the sperm was thought to contain the whole human embryo – the word 'semen,' remember, is the Latin word for seed. The act of intercourse was like planting a seed in fertile, or as the case may be, barren ground. Contraception was therefore viewed as a form of abortion and considered a sin of homicide under the fifth commandment, 'thou shalt not kill'. I think it is very important to remember that if one is to understand the origin of church teaching.

When the Lambeth Conference of the Church of England approved the use of artificial means of contraception for the first time in 1930, Pope Pius XI felt it necessary to condemn that view in an encyclical, *Casti Connubii*. And so the matter rested until Vatican II.

The Vatican Council

In a famous TV interview during the debate on marriage at the third session of the Vatican Council, 1964, Cardinal Ottaviani said that the church's teaching on marriage would never change since it was based on 'the natural law and a few texts of scripture'. Ottaviani spoke with authority, being the cardinal in charge of the Holy Office, official guardian of the Catholic faith.

Against powerful opposition from the Roman curia, the bishops at the Vatican Council did bring about one very important change in the church's teaching on marriage – though it might not seem significant at first sight. Instead of defining procreation as the primary end of marriage, as the curial theologians proposed, the council was content to describe marriage as 'the intimate partnership of life and love'.

Once the stress came off procreation as the primary purpose of marriage, then other values could come to the surface – the bonding power of sexual intercourse, for instance, more important than ever as life expectancy increases.

When at the last session of the council, Cardinals Alfrink, Léger and Suenens, and Patriarch Maximos IV spoke out in favour of admitting some means of contraception, their interventions were applauded by the whole assembly. Pope Paul, however, removed the issue from the council agenda. In retrospect, some say that the Fathers of the council should have fought out this issue then and there, and tried to win back the confidence of the Holy Father. Because Paul's action was the beginning of the process that led him to his lone, non-collegial decision.

The Birth Control Commission

Having withdrawn the topic from the council agenda, Pope Paul enlarged the small commission previously set up by his predecessor to review the problem. This commission, whose full title was 'The Pontifical Commission for the Study of Population, the Family and Birth', was reformed at different stages, and ended up with sixty-eight members. With some exceptions, the theologians appointed were conservative in outlook, and expected to confirm traditional teaching. However, between the years 1963 and 1966, the Commission moved from being in favour of upholding the ban on artificial contraception to opposing it. The final alignment was said to be 64-4 in favour of change. Even the four who remained opposed to change admitted that they had no arguments left (and many had been brought forward and critically examined) – except that to reverse the position would severely damage the authority of the church.

What happened afterwards was described by John Marshall, a member of the Commission, twenty years later:

After submission of the final report there followed months of silence. These were not months of inactivity however. A new body was established in great secrecy containing three officers and seven consultors of the congregation. There is reason to believe that an encyclical might have been published at this stage but for the intervention of some cardinals ... Yet another body of twelve

119

experts, all clerical, was then set up which produced yet another report which was again not accepted.

Cardinal Suenens was one of those who worried about what was going on, and in particular the control the curia was exercising over Pope Paul. Cardinal Villot, Secretary of State, had warned him that the Holy Office had effectively isolated Paul, and asked him to come to Rome to try and exercise some counter-influence. Suenens sought an interview with the pope and afterwards sent him a strong letter which Suenens published in his recent autobiography.

The feeling of general unease, in my opinion, does not stem from any specific issue *per se,* but rather from the fact that Your Holiness has reserved for yourself the right to choose the appropriate solution, whatever it may be – thus foregoing the possibility of any collegial input or analysis by the bishops. As a result, discussion of certain issues was forbidden at the council and again at the recent synod.

The good of the church would be dramatically endangered, in my opinion, if the Holy Father were seen to take upon himself the role of sole defender and guardian of the faith and of moral standards – if he were to stand before the world alone, cut off from the college of bishops, from the clergy, and from the faithful.

We know full well that Your Holiness has engaged, and continues to engage, in private and secret consultations. Far from dispelling the unease, this type of consultation feeds it. It is felt that these controversial issues need to be studied openly and thoroughly by qualified theologians and experts who are recognised as such, and that the results of their work should then be submitted to the bishops for discussion. As long as there is no such open debate, it will be impossible to create the receptive climate essential to any authority.

Suenens' letter was brave, to the point, and prophetic. But it didn't have any effect. On the 25 July 1968 the encyclical, *Humanae Vitae* appeared, drafted, it is said, largely by Bishop Carlo Columbo and Fr Gustave Martelet.

Why did Pope Paul reject the commission report?

There is no evidence that Pope Paul rejected change because he was convinced by any new arguments about the intrinsic evil of contraception. All the arguments had been examined *ad nauseam* by the Commission and found to lack coherence and be unsustainable. Indeed Paul seemed to recognise this in his encyclical when he told priests that though the arguments might not convince them they should accept them in obedience. The paragraph is worth quoting:

> Beloved Sons, you who are priests ... in the performance of your ministry you must be the first to give an example of sincere obedience, inward as well as outward, which is due to the magisterium of the church. For, as you know, the pastors of the church enjoy a special light of the Holy Spirit in teaching the truth. And this, rather than the arguments put forward, is why you are bound to such obedience. [par 28]

What did weigh with Paul were the curial arguments which had little to do with birth control and much to do with the credibility of the teaching authority of the church.

Most ordinary Catholics at the time would have understood the pope's point of view – better perhaps than their children twenty-five years later. They were brought up in a church where the claim to infallibility, which they would understand in non-theological terms as preventing the church from making serious mistakes in its teachings, was very much emphasised. A majority of Catholics today, more than 70% overall in Catholic Spain and 69% in the 15 to 34 age group in Ireland, seem now to reject infallibility. (And perhaps *Humanae Vitae* itself was a significant factor in bringing about that change.)

From the early days of Christianity, the church taught that to use artificial means to prevent conception was a serious sin. Which meant that if couples did so, with full knowledge and full consent, they would forego their right as children of God to the happiness of heaven. If that were so, how could the pope now turn around and say, 'From this moment on, use of contraceptives is morally neutral, and maybe even praiseworthy'?

This aspect of the question was of course much debated in the Commission itself. Fr Zalba, one of the more conservative theologians said once during a meeting, 'If we change the teaching, what of the millions of people we have in former times sent to hell?' To which Mrs Patty Crowley, from the Christian Family Movement, replied, 'Fr Zalba, are you sure God took all your instructions?'

In sum, the conservative argument amounted to this: one can find no period of history, no document of the church, no theological school, scarcely one Catholic theologian, who ever denied that contraception was always seriously evil. The teaching of the church is absolutely constant. So it must be true. Because to say otherwise would be to admit inadmissible consequences, e.g:

1. Even if infallibility isn't strictly involved, it would seriously weaken the idea of an infallible teaching church, a church which in crucial areas of faith or morals, was protected by God from making mistakes.

2. Admitting that the heretical Anglican Church was correct in accepting contraception at the Lambeth Conference, whereas Pius XI was wrong in condemning its decision in his encyclical, *Casti Connubii,* (1930) – tantamount to admitting that the Holy Spirit had been with the heretics and not with the one true church!

3. Opening the floodgates. If contraception was a mortal sin, and now it isn't, what about homosexual acts? What about divorce? What about abortion? Perhaps they will be next to be legitimated?

4. Asking forgiveness for imposing an intolerable burden on the laity down the centuries under pain of damnation. ('Alas for you lawyers, because you load on men burdens that are unendurable ...' Luke 11:46.)

5. Depriving the Roman curia of much of its reason for existence.

The laity reject Humanae Vitae

Opinion polls in western countries clearly show that the majority of Catholics – and it increases with the younger generation – rejected the teaching of *Humanae Vitae* on birth control. They do not, however, appear to consider themselves any less part of the church, and most would not even consider the use of contraceptives as a matter for the confessional.

So an extraordinary situation has arisen where no encyclical in recent history has been so massively rejected by the laity, and yet no encyclical has been so forcibly reiterated by the central authority.

How has that rejection been justified?

The laity were aware that Pope Paul never claimed to be making an infallible statement

The late and much respected Bishop Butler, Auxiliary of Westminster, whose orthodoxy was as impeccable as his theological positions were moderate, used always quietly to insist on the status of *Humanae Vitae* as a non-infallible document – a distinction which, however, Rome has always sought to blur.

Note that the blurring occurs because some curial theologians claim that even though the pope didn't intend to call upon his full powers to define *Humanae Vitae* teaching as infallible, the fact that the ban on contraception is the constant teaching of the church means that it shares in the infallibility of the church quite apart from the pope's intention.

The encyclical didn't fit with the laity's understanding of marriage

People's understanding of marriage has changed noticeably, even radically, in the space of the last hundred years. In the older understanding, the man was provider and leader, the woman bore children and looked after the home. So long as there was no unfaithfulness, the marriage was considered good. Love was not essential, which is why marriages could be arranged by parents and accepted by their children. If love was present, or developed, that was an added bonus, but what was essential was commitment to each other, and the acceptance of whatever children God might send them.

Gradually in this century, a new understanding of marriage has emerged where love has moved centre stage. People fall in love, which is partly governed by biological mechanisms. But within marriage that mutual attraction is expected to deepen into a more permanent love. This loving seeks intimacy, communication, sexual fulfilment and the acceptance of equality between the sexes.

The strength of the newer understanding is the intimacy which encourages ever closer union between husband and wife. This in turn mirrors more closely St Paul's model for marriage, which was Christ's love for his church, and Christ's own model of two in one flesh. When all the basic needs are met, as they are for most in Western society, people naturally seek self-fulfilment. And because the human being is animal and rational, that includes emotional and sexual fulfilment as well as intellectual fulfilment.

In addition to this, it now seems universally accepted that sexual intercourse plays a critical role in the healing process in marriage. Two people cannot live together without sometimes falling out of love. Nature provides a remedy. And given the fact that people live longer and longer, that remedy is of increasing relevance.

So sexual intercourse, in current thinking, has to do with a lot more than making babies.

Medical technology had changed the human situation

At the height of the Roman Empire, when Christian thinkers first began to write about sexual morality, average life expectancy was less than twenty-five years. Only four out of every hundred men, and fewer women, lived beyond the age of fifty. So the Empire expected its citizenry to spend considerable time and energy begetting and rearing legitimate children – just to keep the society going. And up to the nineteenth century, the statistics wouldn't have been very much different. So if we take sixteen years of age as being adult, and present life expectancy at seventy years, then on average adult life has been extended in comparatively recent times by a factor of about six – from nine years to fifty-four years, with a corresponding dramatic effect on the average length of a stable marriage. Add to that the fact that (in developed countries) almost every child born today, and every woman bearing a child today will live, and one has a very significant change in the data for moral decisions about marriage.

Because of the complexity of modern society, children need higher levels of education than in the past, which require greater investment of time and money by the parents. So there is greater need to control and space the growth of a family. Science and technology provides the means for control.

Leaving aside for the present, the natural methods of birth control, a Catholic couple either practise quite heroic levels of sexual self abnegation, which may in ways damage their marriage (although this can be argued), or they end up having sixteen children whom they can't afford to educate.

The benefit of the human sciences, including medicine, is to give men and women more control over their lives. If a couple wish to visit an area in Africa where malaria is endemic, they can take a pill which will help keep them free from disease – or anyway used to. If they wish to avoid smallpox, they take a smallpox vaccine – although this last interference with nature was also once condemned in former times by the church! Human beings want to have that sort of control over their bodies when it is available to them. And one of the most elemental human needs is to control the number and spacing of children within the family.

The laity sensed that the clergy were with them in nuancing the papal teaching

Most people who were aware of the encyclical and its contents were also aware of the stance of a number of Conferences of Bishops who obviously had to show respect for the papal teaching, but at the same time pointed out that the ultimate decision must rest with conscience, and if a couple sincerely believed that the use of contraceptives was lawful, etc, etc.

They were also aware of significant dissent among professional theologians – aware that in the United States for instance over six hundred theologians signed a statement dissenting from the pope's decision. And it soon became known in parishes which priests took a broad-minded view of the question in confession.

They noticed too that whereas priests preached sermons affirming the church's teaching in other areas of sexual ethics, like divorce or abortion, very few sermons were preached about birth control.

Traditional theology gave a basis for dissent

If contraception were a matter of church law, then the pope clearly has authority to make laws, and there is not much further argument about it. But in the case of birth control, we are repeatedly told that it is a question of God's law, which by definition the pope doesn't make, but only helps to explain.

Where the pope teaches without calling on his infallible authority, this teaching must still be treated with great respect. At the same time, where he calls on arguments to explain God's teaching, his arguments must be open to the normal human process of examination.

In traditional Catholic teaching, 'enlightened conscience, even when honestly mistaken, is the immediate and ultimate arbiter of moral decisions'. In the case of authoritative but non-infallible teaching, like *Humanae Vitae*, there is a long-standing theological tradition that Catholics are free to dissent where they have sufficient objective and tested grounds for doing so.

A note on natural family planning

Our programme 'Stop the Clock' was in part about natural family planning. But we also produced a full programme on the subject in 1978 in Australia, home of Dr Billings, who of course was the first to work out the practical details of the method. We called it 'Doing what comes naturally'. I remember filming interviews with comfortable middle-class Australians around a swimming pool near Sydney. If it hadn't been Australia, there might have been more embarrassment about the fact that the chairperson of the natural family planning association whom we interviewed was visibly pregnant. And it wasn't planned!

Natural family planning is attractive to Western society because it is natural, in the sense of avoiding barriers, lotions and pills. But the method requires education, commitment and care on the part of both partners to the marriage, and periodic abstinence.

So far as one can judge, from what I have read and heard, when the rules are kept strictly it is an effective method. If problems arise, it is because one or other partner lapses in their commitment. Increased knowledge of the process of human reproduction has helped to refine the method much beyond what used to be pejoratively called 'Vatican Roulette'.

But in Korea, for various reasons, including the fact that many of their flock are married to non-Christians, the bishops seemed resigned to the fact that it was not a credible option for more than a small minority. So little effort was put into its promotion.

Lay people, and many theologians also, seem to see little difference in principle between wearing a condom and confining intercourse to infertile periods, or indeed prolonging the infertile period, which is what the basic contraceptive pill is designed to do.

It is perhaps worth noting that women have, to some extent at least, a built-in family planning system. The discovery of the hormone 'prolactin', which suppresses ovulation and menstruation while a mother is breast-feeding, points to nature providing its own contraceptive for spacing children. In the past, women breast-fed for two years or more, as is still the case in some developing countries.

Vatican reactions to the reception of Humanae Vitae

1. Find a scapegoat

Fr Lambert Greenan OP, until recently editor of the English language edition of *Osservatore Romano*, helped to explain the Roman viewpoint on *Humanae Vitae*, talking to Radharc in 1989. He put it down to a general rebellion against authority, theologians forgetting about the magisterium or teaching authority, and a false Protestant emphasis on private judgement.

I came here in 1968 and there was a whole crisis of authority in the world at large; there was the rebellion in the schools, the universities – you remember in America – and it was inevitable that this attitude of rebellion should enter into the church and it did. It entered into the church on a very emotive issue, which was *Humanae Vitae*, and it was, if you like, unfortunate that it was on that particular emotive issue that the clash with authority came ... These theologians forgot about the magisterium, in other words, it too was tossed overboard. It reminds me of something Ronald Knox wrote – he wrote a famous parody on the poem by Dryden,

'Absalom and Achitophel,' which he called 'Absolute and a Bit of Hell' and I often think that two lines in that poem can describe very well the situation that developed after the Vatican Council in the theological field. So I quote them for you:

'So freedom reigned, and priests dismayed by nought,

Sought what they liked, and mentioned what they thought'.

There it is, we're back now to the question of private judgement. Knox also spoke at the same time about Jonah being thrown overboard. I'm afraid that in the aftermath of the Second Vatican Council there was a great deal more than Jonah thrown overboard. And the question now is, how to bring back the theologians and others to the fundamental principles of their science. *Humanae Vitae*, to my view, has become the touchstone of orthodoxy with regard to moral theology nowadays – just as *Homoousios* was regarded in the fourth century ... It could never be changed.

2. *Choose a pope to reaffirm the teaching*

It is perhaps going further than the evidence to suggest that the curia chooses the pope. However on purely *a priori* grounds one must presume that it has a very important input.

There is no question that the curia considered Pope John XXIII a disaster: many important members said so – privately of course. And there are other indications: some bishops at the Vatican Council wanted to make John a saint by acclamation shortly after his death but they weren't allowed to do so. Thirty years after his death, there is no obvious movement on his cause, while the controversial founder of Opus Dei, who died long after John, was recently beatified!

In curial terms, John was a disaster because he returned power from the centre to the periphery. When he called a council, the curia prepared their documents and tried to get the bishops to rubber stamp them and return home. John empowered the bishops to reject the curial documents and write their own.

So it would be perfectly reasonable for the curia to try to avert a similar disastrous (from their point of view) papal appointment. And how would they do that? Well they have all the files. Information, rumour and innuendo are the things which help or hinder people when it comes to getting appointed to any position.

The curia have all the time to study the field and test different candidates. And drop the right name in the right place. They invited Cardinal Wojtyla to give a retreat to the papal household when they knew Pope Paul was terminally ill. That is a good way of sizing up a man. They would know from the files that he had asked Pope Paul to make the affirmation of *Humanae Vitae* and the outlawing of dissent against it the subject for the next synod. And many other things.

Most of the cardinals live outside Rome, and they are busy in their dioceses. They may hardly know each other, and certainly don't have the information available to the curial cardinals when trying to make a decision at a consistory. So they are open to be guided – I won't say manipulated.

Most people seem to think that the election of a pope is a surprise, and pious cardinals will say afterwards that the choice was made not by them but by the Holy Spirit. But John XXIII told his friend Giulio Andreotti before the consistory that he expected to be elected pope. When Andrew Greeley, was in Rome during the last papal election he put all the rumour and information he could collect into a computer with a programme to predict the result. When the printout arrived he dismissed the conclusion because it seemed a bit stupid. Who would elect a Pole like Karol Wojtyla? Who indeed!

3. Affirm the teaching at a synod

Pope John Paul II chose marriage and the family as a topic for his first synod. According to what I heard in Rome at the time, and subsequent press reports, there was a determined effort by English-speaking bishops to open up a discussion on *Humanae Vitae*, but the whole weight of pope and curia moved in immediately to prevent it. The emphasis was switched to the need to defend the papal teaching. At the end, Pope John Paul himself drew attention to the role of theologians who, he said, were to help explain why the conclusions already arrived at in papal teaching were true.

4. *Appoint bishops who will support Humanae Vitae*

Fr Lambert Greenan OP again put the Roman case to us:

> Now they (160 German theologians who criticised *Humanae Vitae*) also objected to his appointments of bishops. I can understand why they'd object to that. Naturally the pope will want to appoint bishops who are going to support his magisterium – he'd be very ill-advised, wouldn't he, if he were to appoint bishops who are not going to support him – those who are going to remain silent on these vital issues, or even perhaps go against him. That wouldn't be a very wise thing to do. So the pope, naturally and rightly so, will appoint bishops who are going to support the magisterium of the church and his own magisterium and in particular will support this doctrine of *Humanae Vitae*.

5. *Establish institutes to promote the teaching of the encyclical*

One of John Paul's initiatives was to set up Institutes of Marriage and Family, with the parent one in Rome under the direction of Mgr Carlo Caffarra.

Mgr Caffarra continues to raise theological eyebrows with some of his public statements. He is reported to have said, for instance, that if one spouse has AIDS, the married couple must practice total abstinence. But if such abstinence might lead to adultery or grave harm to conjugal peace, the couple may licitly have unprotected sex and risk infection. (Liberal translation: let both parents die and leave orphaned children, but no birth control).

Addressing a meeting of Mgr Caffarra's Institute to mark twenty years of *Humanae Vitae*, Pope John Paul said that in spite of 'unjustified criticisms and unacceptable silences, ' the years since the publication of *Humanae Vitae* had shown its 'prophetic meaning and living relevance.' The church now had to explain its teaching more fully.

6. *Invest the fallible with infallibility*

The first draft of the Constitution on the Church, prepared by a pre-conciliar commission under the direction of the Roman curia, laid down that after the ordinary magisterium had taught on a controverted subject, the matter was no longer open to discussion by theologians. This first draft of the conciliar document was rejected by the council. But this is the curial mind. They want as much infallibility as possible, and try to ensure that important non-infallible teachings like *Humanae Vitae* be treated as if infallible.

At the twentieth anniversary celebrations of *Humanae Vitae*, the pope, according to reports, declared that the teaching of Paul VI was not man made, but was 'written by the creative hand of God in the nature of the human person.' To dispute it was 'the equivalent of refusing to God himself the obedience of our intelligence, and could threaten the very cornerstone of Christian doctrine.'

The pope stated that the church's teaching authority, or magisterium, was instituted by Christ to 'illuminate the conscience.' To consult one's conscience specifically to contest the truth of the teaching of that authority was a refusal both of that authority and of moral conscience. No 'personal or social circumstances' could justify exceptions to the moral norm taught by *Humanae Vitae*. At this stage, the shadow boxing between pope and theologians ends and the straight fighting begins.

Liberal theologians maintain that such a denial leads inevitably to contradictions. To deny the right to dissent either means (a) that a non-infallible teaching can never be wrong, which is a contradiction, or (b) that while a non-infallible position may be wrong, ecclesiastical obedience demands that we say it is always right, which is preposterous.

Bernard Häring, the great moral theologian of Vatican II, wrote a long and strong public letter to the pope on these questions, and concluded:

> If only one particular theological tendency is accepted in the Vatican, and indeed with such severity as in the case of the congress of moral theologians organised by Carlo Caffarra, then for all of us innumerable and very painful questions are raised.

7. Deny that probabilism applies

When we were in the seminary studying moral theology, we had to learn about probabilism. Probabilism is a system one can call on to help decide difficult problems about right and wrong. Where one is doubtful as to which course of conduct to follow, and there are different opinions among experts (e.g. moral theologians), then a person may lawfully follow the opinion in favour of liberty, provided it is truly probable, even though the opinion for the law in question is definitely more probable. The general adoption of probabilism was largely due to the influence of St Alfonsus Liguori, founder of the Redemptorist Fathers, who formulated his own carefully balanced version of it.

Some members of the Roman curia have tried to maintain that there can be no probable opinion opposed to the clear teaching of the Roman magisterium. According to that opinion, once the pope or Roman congregation take an official position, there is no longer room for the legitimate doubt upon which probabilism is based. Many, if not most theologians would reject this view.

They, the theologians, would say that such a position can only be reasonably maintained if the Roman magisterium can be shown never to have erred in its authentic moral teaching. Which isn't possible because it demonstrably erred often. Furthermore, they would maintain, the system of probabilism is not a favour granted to the church by a benevolent ruler, but a hard won victory of the forces of compassion over a rigoristic authority in the eighteenth century.

Why has the curia been so vigorous in its efforts to preserve the traditional teaching?

There are two broad views of the papacy, which one can express in extreme form (although nobody normally would), as a help towards understanding.

In the first view, the pope is purely a symbol of unity in the church and enjoys a 'Primacy of Honour' – i.e. everyone is prepared to look up to him provided he doesn't try to tell them what to think or what to do. In this view, the pope would hardly require much more staff than he needs to exercise his primary function as Bishop of Rome.

In the second view, the pope is emphatically the Vicar (i.e. takes the place) of Christ. In practice, the bishop becomes the pope's local representative, for all policy is made centrally, and most of the other decisions as well. I say in practice, because in theory this idea of bishops as local representatives was explicitly abandoned at the Second Vatican Council.

But if power in the church is to be centralised, and the role of Peter's successor is central to that centralisation, then the pope needs a curia – a sort of international church government. And the more decision-making power the pope exercises, the bigger and more important the curia becomes.

What vastly strengthens the pope's universal role is the association of infallibility with his office – the Holy Spirit guarantees his teaching in a way that doesn't apply to other bishops.

The Vicar of Christ – which means the person taking Christ's place – is obviously the best person to appoint bishops. And to provide the information for his decisions, he needs to have a nuncio in every country in the world. That is quite a bureaucracy for a start. A modern pope like John Paul II has to make a lot more decisions simply because of the improvements in communications. Matters which in the past might have had to be decided in other parts of the world, now can be decided in Rome – by fax if necessary. So the pope needs more people to help him make all these decisions. The Brazilian bishops need to be told what aberrations are to be corrected in liberation theology. The religious priests and sisters in Latin America have to have a Secretary General appointed for them in place of the sister they had elected, since a woman would not have the doctrinal and theological qualifications required for the post. The North American bishops wish to substitute the phrase 'The word of the Lord' during the Mass, in place of 'This is the word of the Lord'. Should they be given permission or should they not? Decisions, decisions!

If pope and curia were to have to admit to being wrong on such an important matter as contraception, it would undermine the whole basis for central decision making, and – pardon the pun – pontifica-tion. And threaten jobs at the curia. Anyone who knows anything about humanity knows that the primary function of any organisation is to safeguard its reason for existence.

What will the future hold?

John Paul II declares that those who practice contraception are failing to recognise God. Yet the majority of Catholic couples do use contraception and share the eucharist. They act, not in a moment of passion or weakness, but as a consequence of a deliberate moral decision.

Contradictions of this magnitude between professed teaching and daily practice undermine integrity and destroy credibility, not only in this area but in all other teachings of the church.

Some say the subject is best left to rest. People are making their own moral decisions, and history shows that Rome never publicly retracts. But this point of view does not take into account the problems of conscience of some individuals who are deeply disturbed to find themselves in opposition to their pope, and to be told by him that they are acting against God. Nor does it take into account the difficulty of bringing information on family planning to many parts of the Catholic world where overpopulation is a problem, but where the Vatican actively opposes the introduction of birth control technology or information.

If the ban on birth control is ultimately laid to rest by a future pope, what arguments might he use?

1. The confirmation of the Holy Spirit was lacking

Paul VI was confident that the Holy Spirit not only acts in the church's teaching authority but also 'illumines from within the hearts of the faithful and invites their assent'. He expected this assent to *Humanae Vitae* to be forthcoming and to confirm his teaching. If the assent in fact be lacking, as it manifestly is, then the confirmation is lacking too.

2. Pope Paul was unwise to act alone

Pope Paul's teaching authority was very much weakened when he separated himself from the college of bishops, and allowed them no part in the process of coming to his decision. Particularly when it seemed clear that the majority would almost certainly disagree with him.

While reaffirming papal primacy in the church, Vatican II taught that the pope cannot teach or make rules for the universal church in such a way as to exclude the bishops from collegial co-responsibility.

3. *Reverses in non-infallible teaching are not really new*

Pope Nicholas V, in 1454, granted to King Alphonso V of Portugal and his son Prince Henry the Navigator 'full and free permission ... to capture, conquer and subjugate all Saracens and pagans whatsoever and other enemies of Christ ... and to bring their persons into perpetual slavery'. This permission the pope granted by apostolic authority from sure knowledge and from the plenitude of apostolic power. A century later, Pope Paul III totally condemned the practice of slavery.

Pius IX, in *Quanta Cura,* condemned 'that erroneous opinion which is especially injurious to the Catholic Church and the salvation of souls, called by our predecessor, Gregory XVI, a derangement, namely that freedom of conscience and of worship is the proper right of each man ...' The Second Vatican Council completely overturned this teaching.

Pope Pius XI's encyclical, *Mortalium Animos,* (1928) condemned the movement for Christian unity as leading to indifferentism and confusion. Again Vatican II reversed the teaching.

Popes and their moral theologians have justified, with great confidence and certainty, torture, burning of heretics, suppression and forced conversions of colonial people, and over a period of centuries, the castration of choirboys. At various times the church has forbidden usury, limb amputation, kidney transplants and even smallpox vaccination. The history of theology provides ample reasons for modesty on the part of all who teach on moral issues.

Will there be change?

There are some straws in the wind:

At the European Synod in Rome in 1993, Bishop Norbert Werbs from Germany said he doubted whether the distinction between natural and artificial means of birth control is demanded by the gospel. Since then, the head of the German Bishops' Conference,

Karl Lehmann, asked whether it might be time for the church to rethink its position.

The retired Cardinal Archbishop of Vienna, Franz König, recently insisted that 'the question of world population cannot be ignored'. He referred to the irritating distinction between birth control as natural (approved) and artificial (condemned) – 'as if from the moral point of view what is important is the trick of cheating nature'.

Helmut Krätzl, auxiliary bishop in Vienna, spoke not long ago of the church's need 'to win back its credibility on questions of sexual morality'.

Every human indicator leads to the conclusion that immense pressure will be put on Pope John Paul II's successor to alter the church's position.

Positive effects of the Humanae Vitae saga

There is a saying about God writing straight with crooked lines. I am an optimist in the sense that I believe all things work towards good (and enough of a realist to expect trouble on the way.)

Humanae Vitae was a curial victory over collegiality. If it proves to be a pyrrhic victory, the curia must take the blame.

Pope John XXIII did much during his reign to share power with the world's bishops, power which the curia had to surrender. However, John did not live long enough to be able to consolidate this achievement. He died, the bishops went home, and the curia won back lost ground.

A lot of theological effort in the past has been devoted to explaining away changes in church teaching. Because nobody wants to say baldly 'the church was wrong', one tries to say that the church was right but ... This involves much digging around decrees and encyclicals, giving benign interpretations here, stretching a meaning there. Whereas the honest approach would be to say simply that the church did its best, but it made a mistake.

Humanae Vitae, however, is not a case where fudging could get over the problem. Too much has been said, and put into the record, and remains in living memory for that to be an option. There is no way of covering a retreat. If it goes now, very, very serious error must be admitted.

Creeping infallibility has become one of the greatest obstacles to church unity. It may well be that a humbling of the curia is a very necessary part of the Holy Spirit's providential plan for the united Christian church of the third millennium.

A note on what might have been

While the Birth Control Commission was sitting, it became fairly clear, through the inevitable leaks, which way the thinking was going. The Irish representative on the Commission, Thomas Morris, Archbishop of Cashel, expected a change. He hinted as much to me at the time. We both expressed our shared fears of the consequences. It is clear to me now that the Irish hierarchy felt it opportune to prepare the clergy and faithful for a change. Fr Kevin McNamara, professor of dogmatic theology in Maynooth, and later Bishop of Kerry and Archbishop of Dublin, served the hierarchy as a trusted theological workhorse. He prepared and read an obviously inspired paper to a conference in May 1967, which was later published in *The Furrow*. The following extracts give a flavour:

> Taking a general view of the church's history, one could speak of a law that was justified in the existing circumstances ... in an epoch when medical science was undeveloped and the excess of births over deaths, or even the equality between the two, could by no means be taken for granted, the ban against contraception was wise and necessary.

> It would still have to be conceded, however, that the church in the past shared in the defective understanding of marriage of mankind in general. No doubt implicit in the church's general doctrine about marriage, lay the value of the mutual love of the spouses and the goodness of its expression and development through intercourse ... These aspects, however, were not brought into focus, their hour had not yet struck.

> In changed circumstances, the ban against contraception might be withdrawn. Today it could be argued such a change exists. The problem today is over-population, not under-population. Today too the status of women is completely different ... the danger of

exploitation is greatly reduced. Education of children too, has become universal and expensive to the point where it requires a limit on further children ... Man is seen today as called by God to harmonise nature and by his own ingenuity make it a more perfect instrument of his rational purpose.

The existence of error in one aspect of the tradition would still have to be granted, viz. a failure to distinguish between the substance of the natural law and a contingent and changeable expression of it, culminating in the formulation of Pius XI that contraception was intrinsically evil ...

To conclude. It is not now clear that the ban on contraception cannot be revoked. (Kevin liked double negatives.)

The article makes ironic reading nowadays. Kevin was a good if rather dull theologian whose instinct pointed him to absolute obedience to authority. So when *Humanae Vitae* appeared, he fully supported the ban on contraception, despite the groundwork he had done in anticipation of change.

Personal impressions of the commission

Pat and Patty Crowley were one of three couples invited to join the Pontifical Commission for the Study of Population, the Family and Birth. In 1992, before dinner in her apartment on the 88th floor of the John Hancock building which looks out over Lake Michigan, Patty spoke to us about the human side of the deliberations.

We arrived in Rome and took a cab to the Spanish monastery, and when we got there they said that Pat would stay at the monastery with the priests while the women would go about a mile away to stay with the nuns. Well, needless to say, we were a little dismayed, but we thought, well we won't rock the boat, we won't say anything.

When we got back to Chicago after the meeting, we were asked by the *Ladies Home Journal* for an interview. We didn't say too much: the only thing we did say was that we thought it was sort of strange that they separated the husbands and wives, and Pat said, 'Well it's a good way to solve the problem, you know, split them apart and there won't be any problem of birth control!' But the next time we went to Rome we did have an apartment, so Pat said the pope must read the *Ladies Home Journal.*

When we were first married everything was forbidden – there was a period when even the rhythm method was forbidden. Then they had rhythm and many couples found it very difficult. My husband also thought it was so stupid a thing; it was so unnatural really.

After the first session of the Commission, everybody got some homework to do. We were asked to find out what couples thought of the rhythm method, those that were practising it. So we prepared a questionnaire with the help of the University of Notre Dame Sociology Department and sent it out to many couples in the Christian Family Movement around the world. And when we started getting them back, it was really heartbreaking to read the letters we received. I often felt that those letters had a lot to do with the majority opinion on the Commission. The stories they told ... how one couple had had six kids one after the other, and they just felt they couldn't have more children. And you just could feel that all the couples that answered were loyal to the church, and were not practising birth control.

Between the first and second sessions of the Commission, the theologians met. Most of the theologians, I know, were conservative, because I think most of the people on the Commission felt that the doctrine should never be changed. But when they came back after the second session and reported their findings, that 95% of them felt that birth control was not intrinsically evil, and that the doctrine could be changed, to me that was the most important part of the Commission: as a married couple that really affected us because if it wasn't intrinsically evil that made such a difference for us.

But I must say, the sad thing about it for us was that after the last meeting we left and we never heard one word from Rome. We never received the final paper, we never had a letter from anybody thanking us for coming. It was an honour to be there, but it was difficult because it was over a year or two and we had children, and we didn't like leaving them for so long. And so we never heard a word from anybody, nor did any priest in the United States talk to us about what happened to us.

It was very strange because, you know, we never knew anything about what the pope was going to say. In the middle of the night, we had a call from some pressmen, and we were freaked out naturally, and they said 'What do you think of the pope's encyclical?' Well of course we didn't know a thing about it, and all Pat said was, 'Well no, we didn't know.' And so they told us what it said, and all Pat said was, 'I don't believe it.' And, you know, it took a long time for it to sink in – that all the time that was spent trying to seek the truth, what the truth was – you know we sort of wasted our time.

Well, after twenty-five years, it still disturbs me that every time I see the pope going to a Third World country or going any place, he always come out and says that birth control is intrinsically evil and that couples shouldn't follow it. Really you know, you just sort of wonder why is this happening? And so I think I've been more disturbed about it recently when I realised that no priest talks about birth control from the pulpit – they talk about abortion often but never birth control. Yet it is sort of hypocritical that it is classified as evil and yet they don't talk about it, just ignore it. So it really bothered me recently. I think if Pat were here we could talk about it and we could sort of get over it ... (Pat died in 1974.)

8

SIMON PETER, THE LORD, AND HIS SPEEDBOAT

Marriage and celibacy in the South Pacific

Picture a little bay surrounded by coconut palms in the South Sea Islands, with the outline of a venerable cathedral just visible through the trees.

The five day annual diocesan retreat is over and the sisters are going home, a journey of some twenty miles across the lagoon. The Bishop of Tarawa, Nauru and Funafuti, Paul Mea Kaiuea, with many other friends from the Catholic community, is down at the wharf to see them off. There is some delay because the sisters' aluminium boat has sprung a leak. The water is bailed out and the rate of inflow assessed, and after some discussion the decision is made to leave nonetheless. The boatman turns on the petrol and pulls the rope to start the outboard engine. Nothing happens. Again and again, and again. Nothing happens. So the mechanic is summoned, and removes the cover of the engine. Through the telephoto lens of the camera I see him waving a bit of wire in the air, and giving off loud peals of laughter which echo round the gathering. Gradually the word spreads and with it the wild merriment. The engine, it appears, had been stored in a shed for safety, and while the sisters prayed the rats ate up the electrical connections!

When the merriment dies down, the bishop's new speedboat is trundled out and the sisters' luggage transferred. Nobody minds that much about the delay. The bishop's boat is faster and more comfortable, and one won't have to keep bailing it out to keep abreast of the leaks.

I am sometimes asked what part of the world I would like most to revisit, and usually have skated around without answering the question, because, truth to tell, I never formed an opinion. But I have been thinking recently about Kiribati and the islands East of Australia, and I do now have an opinion. I'd like to revisit the South Pacific!

Surf sand and coconut trees: doesn't one get tired of them? Maybe yes. But there are sometimes other features to make a varied landscape. And the people are very different, and interesting. And they laugh a lot.

In Kiribati, land comes in little strips – necklaces of narrow islands surrounding large lagoons. Getting around atolls can be quite difficult; for the most part travel and transport has to be by boat – or sometimes, if one is lucky and the islands are close, there may be a pedestrian bridge.

On the largest and most developed atoll in Kiribati, Tarawa, one can drive for about fifteen miles on a good road. On one side the surf pounds the beach. On the other, the calm waters of the lagoon: one or other seems always in sight. For Tarawa is just a series of sand banks joined by causeways and bridges – no part of it more than fifteen feet above sea level.

The most important mode of transport is still the outrigger canoe with lateen sail. Astonishing distances are covered in these frail looking craft: in fact the islanders believe that their ancestors came from far away Samoa in outriggers some thirty generations ago. Even today the position of families within the social structure, their title to land and fishing rights is dependent on their being able to trace back their descent from these Samoan invaders.

For a Gilbertese man, the outrigger canoe is part workhorse, part family transport, part sports car – and great love and patience goes into its making. A good canoe can reach twenty knots or more, and remain stable in heavy seas.

I saw people making dugout canoes with modern tools and terylene string, a unique blend of ancient and modern technology, where the one unchanging factor was a design proved by aeons of usage. The hull is carved out of one piece of timber – perhaps the earliest and most primitive form of boat construction. At the same time, the keel of that hull is very precisely curved to compensate for the drag of the outrigger, which would otherwise keep pulling the boat around in a circle.

Houses without walls

Despite the fact that the soil is poor, and nothing grows with ease except the coconut, Tarawa is thickly populated.

The typical Gilbertese house is a small raised platform with coconut leaf roof, and no walls. When it rains the occupants hang up a few mats to keep out the damp: perhaps also when a family needs a little privacy – though privacy does not appear to be highly regarded in Tarawa. I found it very strange to stand at the edge of a village and literally stare through house after house! Nobody seemed to mind.

Home is for sleep and for sex and for storm shelter: the rest of life is spent out and about – preparing meals, which is often done in common, or fishing, or socialising in a large communal building called the Maneapa.

Every village has at least one Maneapa, whose grandeur will depend on the size and importance of the village. They have been built up to 120 feet in length, and as high as a four or five story building.

The Maneapa is at once the council chamber, the dance hall, the feasting place and the recreation room for the whole village. Because of its importance it is treated as sacrosanct. No brawling or dispute may take place under its roof. Its supporting pillars may not be struck. The building may not be spoken of in jest.

At any one time, there may be a dozen things going on in the Maneapa. In one corner a family celebrates a homecoming with exotic foods. In another a wedding is being arranged. Where I sat the people were playing cards – several teenagers, two young married couples, grandmamas with skin wrinkled like old prunes. There they chatted and laughed the day away, gambling a few cents on the fall of the cards, seemingly unconscious of the generation gaps.

The carefree attitude to sexual matters which Europeans presume is part of the tradition of noble savages is not very manifest in Kiribati. The traditional punishment for a straying wife was to have her nose bitten off by her husband! Within living memory, male adulterers were punished by being put into a canoe without food or water or paddle, in a strong offshore wind, which was normally a sentence to a slow and certain death.

Full unemployment

In the sense that we usually use the word, almost everyone in Kiribati is unemployed. Apart from the few who work for the government, there are no jobs worth speaking of, and there never were. And yet everybody seems housed and healthy. Coconut trees supply an amazing range of needs, both in food and building materials. A family may also have use of a bit of land which with added humus will grow taro and yams. For the rest there is the sea where fish can be found when you want them.

One of my abiding images of Kiribati is of powerful supple bodies gleaming with health and vigour – seeming proof that all human dietary needs can be met by fish protein and coconut.

One product of the coconut, whose manufacture used to be a secret shared only with the Caroline and the Marshall islands, may also contribute to the aforementioned merriment. If you cut through the spathe or stem of the coconut blossom and gather the sap which exudes, you get a refreshing drink which may be given to children. Left for more than fifteen hours, it turns into a potent beer, highly nutritious and full of vitamins.

For those satisfied with traditional ways, life in Kiribati is good. But for those who want to share in Western-style consumer goods like cookers, refrigerators, hi-fi, videotape or television, there is no alternative but to go abroad and earn money.

The Gilbertese are a Christian people. Christianity came to them first, not through missionaries but through some local people who went to work in Tahiti and brought the faith back to their own people.

Pacific Christianity

The Missionaries of the Sacred Heart arrived from Europe in 1888, and brought the Mass and the sacraments. Britain made the islands a protectorate four years later, and under European influence some aspects, good and bad, of the unique culture died. The British had different ways of doing things, and they did not approve of petty warfare. Gilbertese men always had plenty of time to indulge in the male propensity for war games: a genuine Gilbertese sword, if you can find one today, is edged with razor-sharp sharks' teeth.

Nowadays the British have gone, and the last of the old missionaries await their eternal reward; but the tradition of lay ministry has been kept. In Kiribati where local priests are few, preaching and administration of the sacraments is carried out largely by lay catechists.

Bishop Paul Mea has, in area at least, the largest diocese in the world – four million square kilometres. Only one four-thousandth part of the whole area is dry land. To serve that immense and scattered diocese he had, in 1982, nine local priests and ten ageing foreign missionaries. Even that sounds better than the reality, because at any one time the number in pastoral work was about half the total, between priests on special work, priests studying abroad, or on holidays, or sick.

'Before, when we had more priests,' the bishop told us, 'they used to reside on one island, but now because of the shortage, one priest is taking say two or three islands. Where the priest does not reside permanently, the catechists are doing the work which normally the priest should do – like officiating at marriages, performing baptisms, conducting Sunday service during which they distribute Holy Communion.'

Bishop Mea has over 300 lay catechists working for him who carry out most of the duties that elsewhere might be carried out by a priest. The bishop's method is to go to the island or village where a catechist is needed and explain the need, and the qualities the candidate should have to be selected. The community meet then to discuss the matter and make their own selection. From then on the community has to support the catechist, his wife and family. In the outer islands, where people have little or no cash income, they support their catechists by giving food; or they may open their coconut groves to him to collect a specified number of coconuts which provide copra for him to sell.

A married couple in the presbytery

We had afternoon tea with Catechist Simon Tonganibeia, and his wife and family, on the veranda of what was once a mission presbytery. Simon is only a nickname, but it stuck because just as

Simon Peter followed the Lord Jesus everywhere, Simon Tonganibeia seemed to go everywhere with the Lord Bishop!

Simon has access to a truck owned by the diocese which is not needed for diocesan work all of the time. Motor transport is rare in Tarawa, so the parishioners who support him expect a little help now and again with their transport problems – moving some second-hand palm leaf roofing tiles, or selling off a better than usual haul of fish.

There can be a lot of demands on the catechist's time; however, he does have natural motives to be of service to his community. The community provide his upkeep, and this may be more or less generous depending on the goodwill he creates. With so much to do in the parish, we asked Simon whether this interfered sometimes with his responsibilities to his family.

It is our main and basic duty to look after the welfare of our families. Fortunately the people are very understanding and considerate about that. They usually have their own arrangements whereby they give money or food, and whatever else we may need to meet the unexpected events or occasions, for example births, funerals, and so on. In other words, the well being of the catechist's family is the special concern of those people we work for.

We asked him whether he thought the married catechists should be ordained priests.

Our former bishop, Pierre Guichet, was the first to put forward the idea and pose the question of ordaining married catechists to the priesthood. On our part, we as catechists were willing to accept ordination for the sake of the people. However there was a block and great opposition from the people themselves, and more strongly from the older people. They were just not willing to accept the idea of a priest with a wife.

Celibacy or the eucharist?

Kiribati is one of the many places in the world that forces one to think seriously about the tie between priesthood and celibacy. Less than a dozen priests flitting from island to island over four million square kilometres, leaving large amounts of consecrated hosts which

146

the catechist may distribute over the months when no priest can be present. How does one reconcile that with the famous formula of Vatican II which says that the eucharist is 'the true centre of the whole Christian life'? + Family

Pope John Paul II has said some stirring things about the importance of the eucharist. He tells us that the spiritual drawing together of the people of God in the eucharist 'expresses the church and brings her into being.' That 'eucharistic worship constitutes the soul of all Christian life.' And that we should do 'all we can to ensure that the eucharist may become an ever greater source of life and light for the consciousness of all our brothers and sisters of all the communities in the universal unity of Christ's church on earth.' The reality that I have experienced, and Kiribati is by no means the worst case, is that in many parts of the Catholic world less than one per cent of the people attend Sunday Mass because 99% have no Sunday Mass to attend. Some places have Mass only once or twice a year. If 'eucharistic worship constitutes the soul of all of Christian life', then many millions of Catholic Christians are being sorely deprived of what is their due.

In Kiribati the people have accepted a Sunday service which is a blend of scripture reading and hymn singing. But the reaction has been different elsewhere in the Pacific. Elsewhere the laity have pointed out that to have services without a priest is to do what the Methodists or Presbyterians do, and often not as well as they do. If Catholics haven't the Mass, they haven't much to make it worthwhile being a Catholic.

Protestant fundamentalist groups have been very active in recent years throughout the Pacific islands. They teach a very personal spirituality, with simple readings and prayers based on the scriptures, and group services with enthusiastic singing and fervent preaching. It's a mode of Christian spirituality which has many positive values especially for people of simple culture. It's certainly not a eucharistic spirituality, but it is often better than what the Catholic Church can in practice offer without priests. So why should Catholicism be preferred?

147

Celibacy makes sense for religious and for missionaries. As a celibate a missionary is not tied to family or place, he belongs to the whole church. But within the village community, where a married person is known and respected for virtue and prudence, and who like Simon Tonganibeia is accepted as the natural religious leader, many bishops feel that person should be officially designated as the one to preside at the community eucharist.

It is ironic in a way that the church is willing to accept indigenous people as catechists and teachers, qualified to expound the scriptures, but not to provide the eucharist. After all it requires a lot more education, natural intelligence and judgement to preach effectively than it does to remember and repeat what Jesus asked us to do 'in remembrance of me'. That requires faith and reverence more than education and intellect.

It also seems ironic that while the church lays down that only males who accept celibacy as a lifelong commitment may be ordained to the priesthood in the Roman rite, there are frequent allegations and some evidence that in many parts of the world where a married priesthood would seem most necessary, a high proportion of the small number of supposedly celibate priests are not in practice celibate. There are no statistics, possibly because nobody in authority wants to know the statistics. But I heard from a reliable and authoritative source that in Bolivia up to 70% of priests live in concubinage. Students live celibate lives in the seminary; after ordination they are sent to remote regions where they live alone, far from other clerical company, and where the local community insists that they follow the conventional pattern and take to themselves a woman. In the Philippines I was told – less reliably – that about 50% of the local clergy were celibate. We filmed a fiesta many years ago on the island of Luzon in honour of the patron saint of the local fishermen. During the celebrations, the saint's image was carried on a barge round the bay. All the participants were expected to get wet, and those who didn't jump into the water voluntarily were pushed in, which gave me many anxious moments operating the film camera. After the celebrations we were invited back to the presbytery to dry out and get something to eat. We left our equipment in the bedroom. I couldn't help noticing that the 'housekeeper' seemed a bit more than a housekeeper, that the clothes line had its share of children's washing, and that the priest had a large double bed. However, as I say, there are no statistics. But if the picture is as I have painted it, then there seems to be an acceptance of a situation where men who are unfaithful to their ordination vows continue to be licensed to perform the eucharistic liturgy – so long as they stay quiet about their infidelity – while leaders of living Christian communities faithful to their marriage vows are denied the privilege of providing the Bread of Life for their people.

The contradictions between the words and spirit of countless papal and Vatican pronouncements about the eucharist, and the realities in many countries, are so glaring that one wonders at times if we all live in the same world.

I am not one who thinks that celibacy has no value – far from it. I argue the case for it, I hope cogently, elsewhere. The value of celibacy is not in question: the question here is of priorities in particular situations. Which has priority in Kiribati – a disciplinary church law or the right of Christ's followers to share in the celebration of the eucharist?

In 1980 three White Fathers wrote to *The Tablet*:

> Many of us missionaries here feel that it is almost useless to go on baptising Christians into a non-sacramental church. Without a eucharistic or liturgical renewal throughout the developing world, one can only envisage masses of weak Christians ... Here in Tanzania, and indeed in most Central African countries, the eucharist is largely unavailable and consequently not central to most Christian lives.

And didn't the Lord himself say to us, 'If you do not eat the flesh of the Son of Man, and drink his Blood, you will not have life in you'?

9.

RELUCTANT REVOLUTIONARIES

A trip into the mountains with the guerrillas
With some thoughts about war and revolution

There was a problem initially on how to reconcile my priesthood with the revolutionary movement. But when the theology of liberation reached the church in Negros, little by little we perceived the justness of launching the revolutionary armed struggle in order to really effect radical changes in our backward and corrupt social system in the Philippines. We believe that even Pope Paul VI in his papal documents has emphasised the right of any people of any country to rebel against their government if that government has become oppressive and no longer works for the welfare of the people.

— *Vicente Pelobello, NPA Revolutionary, and former Parish Priest.*

A call to arms

Two open trucks drew up smartly in the yard of the Columban House in Batang, Negros, in the Philippine Islands. The white truck contained the spokesman for the New People's Army, Vicente Pelobello, and four companions. They weren't obviously armed, but they looked vigilant. The second red truck contained a CBS camera crew from San Francisco. It was 8 o'clock in the morning. John Madden, sound recordist, and I were having a leisurely breakfast prior to getting ready to film some local fiesta later that day.

We never in fact got to the fiesta, but ended up instead in the main training camp of the New People's Army, deep in the mountains of Central Negros. It happened this way.

I had met Pelobello secretly some days before. After recording an interview, I asked him if it might be possible to film the NPA in action. He said he would see, but I hadn't expected much to come of it. I now got my answer. 'There is a party going to our training camp in the hills. I have arranged permission for you to film. Do you wish to go? And if so can you be ready within fifteen minutes?'

Now fifteen minutes isn't a lot of time to prepare for a safari which might last up to three days. In addition to equipment and film, I threw in a hat for the sun, a windcheater, and some mosquito repellent. I never thought of what in the end we most needed – water, and warm clothes.

Within fifteen minutes, we were in the back of the truck holding on grimly to the more delicate parts of the equipment, and on our way into the unknown.

Stated in the simplest terms, the NPA is a highly motivated peasant army hoping to bring about a less unjust society by military force. If any real social progress were to be made by other than violent means, then their membership and support would almost certainly melt away. The movement is often called 'communist' by the military, and Marxist terminology and ideology may sometimes be invoked by the leadership, but by and large the words don't ring true in Filipino mouths or Filipino situations. Nor is there much evidence of support from communist powers, or any knowledge or interest in communism among the peasants who form the backbone of the organisation.

In 1989, the NPA claimed 30,000 full time cadres with 10,000 modern weapons – mostly M-16s, the American rifle used in Vietnam. More than 100,000 have been killed in the civil war, mostly innocent peasant farmers.

According to their stated aims, the NPA would like to see a more equitable distribution of wealth and resources, especially land. They would like political power to be shared outside the tiny minority who have exercised it to date. And they would like to end foreign domination in political and economic affairs. It is only in the Philippines that such a programme could be considered revolutionary.

The NPA is likely to continue to be around for a long time to come because none of these worthy aims seems likely to achieved by normal political means. While there have been several attempts down the years to bring about land reform, all have failed through massive opposition by the rich and powerful.

People join the NPA either because they see no hope of change in an intolerable situation without the use of force; or they join for emotional reasons – because they or their relatives have been the victims of institutional violence at the hands of rich landowners, or their servants, the military.

If the military knew what this Radharc camera crew were up to, and caught up with us, we might learn a little about institutional violence as well.

The base camp

It wasn't far to what one might call base camp: ten minutes of asphalt, perhaps fifteen to twenty minutes of dirt road, around a few fields and up to a small house hidden among trees.

The CBS crew were in their own truck, so we didn't have any opportunity to find out what they proposed to do; and when we arrived they hadn't time to tell us because they began to record material immediately with an electronic camera. (We were using film.) I had presumed they would be coming up the hills with us, and it was only in the course of the next hour or so that it became clear that they proposed to complete their story at base camp.

While they were working I took a look around. The trucks were parked outside a typical Filipino peasant house – wooden frame, bamboo infill and coconut matting. There was one interior room, about 15 ft x 10 ft, with access through a large veranda.

In front and below the house, there was a valley with trees and shrubs and pathways – an ideal jungle film-set. On cue, the men with guns acted their parts for the camera – moving in single file through the undergrowth searching for imaginary hostile forces. After recording various shots of intrepid freedom fighters/dangerous communist guerrillas (take your pick), the filming concluded with an interview with Vicente Pelobello against the background of a fallen tree trunk draped with gun-toting volunteers. (We realised later that most of the 'gunmen' were locals engaged to carry our equipment up the hills, and not really NPA soldiers at all! But that's television for you.)

There were four in the CBS team, and when they finished their work they became more communicative. They told us that they proposed to fly out that afternoon to Manila, edit the story there, and send it by satellite to California where it would be shown on the main evening news. They left at 10.30 am, and we looked forward to making a move.

Instead, the men returned and hung around the veranda, playing with their guns, or going off quietly to sleep. The women moved in and out of the house, busy with children and household chores. I could see Pelobello having a meeting with a small group of men inside.

Nobody seemed in a hurry, so we took out the camera and started to photograph men cleaning guns, men fondling guns, men sleeping with guns. One of the guns looked new and short and fat and vicious, and lessons were being given in how to dismantle it. An older man tapped the handle and said with obvious disgust, 'Plastico'!

In the corner someone else chattered on a portable radio. It was explained to us that he was trying to make contact with our destination up the hills, but hadn't so far succeeded. Nothing much left to film so we put the gear away again. And sit and wait.

John Madden gets impatient and says so. I tell him we're like patients in a hospital. Things will be done for us and to us, but we won't be told when or why, and we're not expected to ask.

Another hour passes – by this time we've been hanging around for three hours, and our patience has reached its limit. I decide to go inside the house and make my presence felt. Fr Pelobello is still having his meeting – the men sit on the floor, the women are lying on shelf beds at each end of the room. I apologise for interrupting, and say that we feel it's important to leave as soon as possible.

'We will have lunch first,' said Pelobello.

'When we're filming we are accustomed to skip lunch.' I said hopefully, 'We would much prefer to reach the camp in good time to get pictures.'

'You will be in good time,' he said.

The long walk

Our party eventually left at 1.25 pm. We had been nearly four and a half hours hanging around without anything to drink since breakfast, although water was offered us at the meal. I asked had it been boiled, and when one of the women said it hadn't, I declined to drink, and suggested to John that he do the same.

Water is the main danger when going native in third world countries. Food will normally be cooked, and cooking destroys bacteria. Fruit is fine if one does one's own peeling: but water can carry strains of typhoid, dysentery, hepatitis and many other diseases to which the locals may have built up an immunity, but which pose a much greater danger for the unprotected foreigner. Water has to be boiled, or treated with tablets to render it safe for Europeans. We didn't have any tablets and it didn't seem worth the fuss of having it boiled, so we left without taking a drink. One forgets real thirst after a while, and anyway a little temporary suffering is better than recurring bouts of dysentery. (One member of a former Radharc team in the Philippines suffered from dysentery for years after his return).

We never did find out why we were kept waiting. There may have been military activity in the area; or the bearers may have been unwilling to walk in the midday heat, or leave without a meal, knowing that food was scarce in the hills. Or maybe there was something in what we were told about the need to establish radio contact with the training camp – though I doubt it.

There were eleven in our party, one NPA soldier with an armalite at each end, seven men to carry our equipment, and the two of us.

The unhappy image of Victorian explorers following their native bearers came to mind, so John and I made half-hearted gestures in the direction of carrying some equipment. Fortunately we were told it might be dangerous to do so – being unused to the difficult terrain we could easily lose our balance. In light of this not unwelcome advice we agreed to let others do the carrying, which was fortunate, because I surmise we wouldn't have got more than a few hundred yards before having to give up ignominiously.

For the next four hours and ten minutes, we walked through the foothills and table land of the Negros central mountains. What started as a rough road rapidly became a track. Occasionally there were a few banana trees to provide welcome shade, but most of the time we walked in the tropical sun.

After the foothills, there was table land where the walking became easier. Twenty years ago this land had been rainforest – one was reminded of the fact by the occasional tree stump blackened by fire. Where hundreds of thousands of species of plants and insects and animals and birds flourished for millions of years, one useless plant, the condo grass, and a few orange-flowered bushes were all that seemed to survive. Bird-life was almost non-existent – all I remember seeing was some species of swallow.

From the crest of a hill one could see steep valleys where some of the original vegetation remained. But what the international logging companies left as uneconomic to remove, the local population are now cutting down for themselves. We passed two men with water buffalo dragging blocks of timber to be sold below. And so the destruction will shortly be complete.

About the halfway point, the party stopped at a little oasis where there was a house by a stream and a group of coconut trees. The youngest of the bearers was despatched to seek out the owner in a nearby field and ask permission to sample his crop. A single coconut was thrown down for evaluation, and when approved by the group leader, a large bunch followed. The water of a coconut is cool and sweet at all times. On this occasion it tasted like nectar.

When four o'clock came and went, and there was still no indication that we would soon reach our goal, I began to get desperate. The sun was sinking fast; it seemed more and more likely that after all the effort we would arrive too late to get much useful material on film. I moved up and down the line trying to speed up the party, thinking to myself, 'Here am I, heart pounding, muscles crying out in protest from unaccustomed exertion, exhorting these locals to greater efforts – young mountainy men half my age who if they wanted to, could run up a steep slope as if it were flat ground.' They smiled and nodded, but it didn't seem to make any difference to our pace.

The worst part of the climb came at the end – one had to pull oneself up by the bushes, and try and make footholds in the loose earth. But after that the pathway descended gently into a saucer shaped valley surrounded by hills.

A passing-out parade for guerrillas

Below us to one side there was a large parade ground lined with several hundred people. A detachment of the New People's Army were lined up in formation. Somebody was making a speech over a crude public address system. Clearly the passing out ceremony was well under way, if not nearly over. I grabbed the camera case from the bearer and ran towards the crowds. The equipment had all been broken down for transporting, and had to be put together again. John Madden and I sat on a rock and worked like madmen. I was in fact mad, mad that something relatively unique in film terms had been in our grasp and was rapidly escaping. In the end we did get just enough to put together a film sequence which included the singing of the *Internationale,* and a half serious half comic ballet performed by heavily armed men. But if we had been ten minutes later we would have got nothing.

As the ceremony ended, ranks broke, and the proud new graduates in the techniques of guerrilla warfare met their even prouder relatives. There were hugs and kisses, smiles and tears from mothers and fathers, children and girlfriends, wives and husbands (some of the soldiers were women). We left the camera and sound recorder rolling, possibly for too long. But we had missed so much that I was trying to make up. It was a very emotional scene, and I was glad to have plenty of it later.

As we put away the gear I began to reflect on the fact that we had met nobody on arrival, that we had photographed without asking guidance or permission, and most surprising of all, nobody seemed to mind. In my previous experience, guerrillas usually like to hide behind dark glasses, and red handkerchiefs. Here people didn't seem to care – it might as well have been a conferring of university degrees instead of a passing out parade for left-wing guerrillas, soon to take their place in a deadly serious war against an army five or ten times larger, and backed by US know-how and technology. I remember reading somewhere that the average life span of a Filipino guerrilla is four years

Statistical information about the New People's Army in the Philippines is not easy to come by. They are understandably not forthcoming on such matters themselves. One of the few sources of information is the Philippine Army, who may however have reason to inflate figures. Be that as it may, it is reported in Manila that the military believe the NPA have established a presence in nearly 20% of the whole country's 41,600 villages.

According to some military experts, a troops to guerrilla ratio of at least ten to one would be required to eliminate the NPA by military action. The ratio in 1987 was nearer five to one. So the NPA, it seemed, might be around for some time.

We surveyed the camp while there was still a little light to see by. There were two large open spaces set in the hollow of some hills – the parade ground where the ceremony had just taken place, and adjoining it an exercise ground with the kinds of apparatus that military use to train for difficult physical tasks – crawling under barbed wire, crossing rivers with ropes, jumping from heights in full equipment. All the apparatus was home made in rough timber. One couldn't help feeling that its purpose would have been pretty obvious to any passing helicopter, or indeed to one of those US satellites that can photograph Yeltsin jogging around the Kremlin. Most of the houses, on the other hand, were hidden among wild banana trees so it would have been difficult to estimate how many people lived there. We were told about 500, but whether that was for the occasion, or whether it was the normal complement, I couldn't make out. Accommodation that night was clearly at a premium, since the relatives who came for the passing out ceremony had to stay overnight. A young woman who spoke English reasonably well told us that she had travelled for two days to be here with her boyfriend.

We had packed all the equipment away before we were approached for the first time by somebody who appeared to have official status. He didn't give his rank or name, but remarked that we had been expected earlier. I explained with ill-concealed testiness that we had intended to come earlier and were quite upset about being detained at the base camp for over four hours. But that was water under the bridge: what could he arrange for tomorrow? He promised there would be a meeting that night to arrange activities for us to film. In the meantime, we would be brought to our sleeping quarters.

'Would it be possible to buy a beer or a soft drink?' I asked.

The request caused much amusement among some bystanders who clearly understood some English.

'You don't find beer in the mountains,' he said quietly.

A night in the jungle

As for sleeping quarters, we wondered what to expect. I had hoped that they might make some concessions to European habits of soft living, but that was not to be. Quarters were allotted to us in a small traditional house, one of two close together under banana trees. Our house had an outer room, approximately 6 ft x 6 ft. One side had a shelf where a woman lay resting. The floor of this room consisted of bamboo slats on a wooden frame, about a foot and a half off the ground. One side was completely open – there were no windows or doors. Further in there was another room, one step below the outer room level. Two girls and a man appeared to fill this space. Ben, the leader of the bearers, John Madden and I had the outer space to sleep in. I asked for the outside position since I knew I would get cramps during the night after such unaccustomed exercise and dehydration, and would need to be able to get out quickly to bend and stretch the muscles in spasm.

There was no moon. The darkness was lightened somewhat by stuffing a wick in a bottle of paraffin. When more light was needed the bottle was tilted to increase the flow. In such cramped quarters there was no place to put the camera and recorder except on the ground underneath where we slept. I tried not to think of £30,000 worth of precision equipment lying on the damp earth, awaiting an invasion of ants.

The lady on the shelf watched us all the time, but didn't say anything. She had a tiny transistor radio which was barely audible, but I recognised 'Born in the USA'. Ironic that she should be listening to American pop – the culture and the music of the one clear enemy.

John moans for a drink – we have had nothing since some coconut juice on the journey up. Neither of us drink from the large square can of water in front of us, although it looks so tempting. We ask to be permitted to boil some of it, but there is only one fire, and the rice is cooking. It will be possible later.

Perhaps we could get a coconut? (I had seen coconut trees around earlier.) Unfortunately there were no coconuts. What about the banana trees, didn't they bear fruit? No. They were either wild or didn't have any fruit just at the moment. I didn't quite believe all this, so I made it known that anyone who brought us any kind of fruit could have a hundred pesos (more than many people in the Philippines would earn in a week). But nobody took up the offer.

The evening meal consisted of lumps of poor quality rice, with some chopped-up chicken – bones and all. After the meal they put a can of water for us on the fire. We asked for boiled water – what we got might at best be termed pasteurised. We shared a filthy glass to drink it. It was now 8.30 in the evening of a day in which we had climbed for over four hours in the tropical sun on a morning coffee and half a coconut.

And so to bed. The woman on the shelf had been replaced by a man. Bed was a coconut mat which someone kindly rolled out over the slats of bamboo. The slats had gaps between them and the mat was very necessary to reduce the strong under drafts. People slept in their clothes. While others tried to settle down to sleep, I sat on the edge and watched two men make a bed in the open from dry banana leaves. As they lay down, and indeed every time they moved thereafter, there were rustles, snaps and cracks, which provided a light background of timpani for the frogs and animals and insects that sang to each other in the tropical night.

I put on the windcheater and the second shirt, made a flat pillow out of the film-changing bag, and lay down on the matting hoping to sleep. We must have been several thousand feet above sea level, but even so it felt a lot colder than I expected. (I read in the paper later that it was the coldest period in the Philippines for over fifty years.) Around twelve midnight, the wind began to blow up. I dozed off, but woke up not long afterwards, shivering uncontrollably, and had to get up and do some vigorous exercise to restore warmth. After that I sat on the edge of the house, which was also the edge of my bed, and tried to think how to keep body heat in. I had no extra clothes: the film-changing bag would have been useful but I needed it as a pillow. I remembered reading about tramps in London who kept warm at night by surrounding themselves with cardboard. So I took one of the film boxes from underneath the house and pulled it apart, trying to make as little noise as possible. Opened out, it was large enough to cover my sides and chest. I crumpled the cardboard so that it would fit more closely to the body, and put it between shirt and windcheater. It made enough difference to permit fitful sleep.

The noise of the wind wakes me up again. Something warm and firm is pressing into my back – the buttocks of a younger warmer body. I think of Abishag of Shunem, and remember the last time I felt the sensation when as a small child I climbed into my parents' bed when I couldn't sleep.

A woman moans in the inner room. The hard floor seems to get harder. Cocks crow in the distance even though there is no sign of dawn. In fits and starts, the night passes.

Morning

One of the women from the inner room steps over us, takes a little water in a coconut shell from the big can, dabs it on her face, combs her hair, and disappears into the undergrowth. That appears to be the way one performs the morning ablutions.

For breakfast there was more rice, and a hunk of bacon fat.

By 9 am, when nobody had come to announce the programme for us as promised, we began to get worried and impatient. Communication with those immediately around us was a problem, because the NPA is truly a peasant army, and peasants in the Philippines don't speak much English. After much determined effort however, we were brought to meet a man introduced to us as 'Ando' – whether Ando was his real name or not I couldn't say – most NPA guerrillas address each other under pseudonyms. Ando wore a kind of skirt and turban, and looked like a pantomime pirate, but he was clearly very much in charge. We expressed our great anxiety to get filming quickly and he said he would see. (The plural 'we' is apposite; John would normally have left such arrangements to me, but this time he took an active role, fearing even more than I did that we might have to stay another night!)

In fact, after a late start, everything worked out to our satisfaction. One of the companies performed the kind of complex movements troops are expected to do on a parade ground. We were then treated to something a little more spectacular – crossing canyons on rope pulleys, overcoming obstacles carrying full equipment, and lastly, at our request, some more realistic manoeuvres through jungle territory, of which there was plenty close to the training grounds.

Returning to the sleeping quarters, we interviewed two soldiers – one of them a woman – as to why they joined the NPA. In each case the reason amounted to a reaction to harassment on the part of the Philippine army. I was impressed with their reasonableness and determination.

NPA discipline and morale are high partly because they are very careful as to who they admit to their ranks. Candidates must have resided in the same place for at least three years, and be well known locally. They must have shown leadership qualities, at least at village level; they must have a stainless moral record, and must prove their determination and capacity to bear the rigours and dangers of guerrilla life.

We left the camp at two o'clock in the afternoon without saying goodbye to any of the bosses; we couldn't find them – perhaps they were having their siesta. But as we went over the side of the hill, somebody ran after us to say that there were reports of military activity below, and that we should keep a special look out because we might meet government patrols. John and I were told that if we were overtaken by military we were to say that we were taking pictures of the mountain scenery, that we had brought three people to carry our bags, and that they in turn had met friends of theirs whom we knew nothing about. The story wasn't so far from the truth as to cause a crisis of conscience because we were also working on a film on missionary attitudes to the destruction of the rain forest. However, I was glad in the end not to have to explain all that to a military patrol.

The way down was naturally easier, but to our surprise took nearly as long as the journey up. In light of the suspected military presence, I would have felt more comfortable if the fellows at the front and rear of our party could have hidden their guns.

Everybody we met on the way was questioned about the military. It appears that they had passed through earlier, and were probably just as anxious as we were to be home before dark. As it was, our party would have been stuck for the night at base camp if we hadn't, by good fortune, met a lorry loading sugar cane, and with the owner's permission, climbed aboard. Between the cab of the lorry, the running boards, the front bumper and the bonnet, space was found somehow for our equipment and fifteen people! We made it back after nightfall to cold drinks, good food and a soft bed. Bliss.

The nine bearers asked for forty US dollars to share between them. We gave them sixty.

Clerical revolutionaries

Looking back on the trip to the hills, we had done better from the point of view of pictures of the New People's Army than I had originally anticipated. However there were disappointments. My original idea had been to build a film around Vicente Pelobello, spokesman for the National Democratic Front in Negros, of which the NPA is the military wing. My understanding was that Pelobello would be following us up to the training camp in the hills. In fact he never turned up, and the only film we had of him in the end was an interview. So the programme had to be cast differently, although the theme remained the same – why and how do sincere Christians rationalise their involvement in guerrilla warfare?

Vicente Pelobello is a sincere Christian, he is in fact a former parish priest of the diocese of Bacolod in the island of Negros.

From what we were told, it would appear that a significant number of Filipino Catholic priests are sympathetic to the NPA. Over the past twenty-four years, at least fifty priests have actually joined the organisation. At least fifty others have worked with NPA-led united front groups. In Bacolod, six diocesan priests have left their presbyteries and gone to the hills to join the guerrillas. Antonio Fortich, their bishop up to 1989, said he did not condone or approve of their action. But he admitted that he could understand what had driven them to do so.

Pelobello is one of these six priests. For many years pastor of a suburban parish, he still considers himself very much a priest. Born in 1939, he had a quiet, middle class and protected childhood. In addition to the normal studies for the priesthood, he was chosen to do further studies in canon law, and in later years headed up the Marriage Tribunal in the diocese. In due course he became parish priest of one of the better parishes, and might, if he had played his cards carefully, have become a bishop. Instead he resigned his comfortable living some eight years before we met him – much to the grief of Bishop Fortich – and chose to embrace a life of great austerity, moving from place to place in the hills, living on poor and inadequate food, in constant danger of being caught and tortured, or simply shot.

When I asked him why he gave up his parish, he recalled instances where as a young priest he became involved with the Young Christian Worker movement and was shot at by the military on a picket line in the city of Davao. And how he earned the anger of local ruling families who tried to oust him from his parish when he supported the cause of starving sugar workers .

Negros is a place where the poor have been ground down in a manner that cries out to heaven for redress. Europeans who have been many years in Negros say that the people are worse off than they were twenty years ago. For much of the year people starve in a land where all could have and should have food in abundance.

In recent times, and particularly since the Second Vatican Council, the Catholic Church has laid special emphasis on training lay leaders. Apart from the intrinsic correctness of this policy, it has also become part of a survival policy, with falling vocations to the priesthood. Training begins with study of the bible, and application of its teachings to real life. Lay leaders in primarily rural areas like Negros come from the peasantry, and because of the miserable situation in which they live, can't avoid becoming involved in issues of justice. And so they say to their priests, 'We are doing justice work because of what you taught us, and we are being hit and we are being killed. We have to fight back.'

Ed de la Torre, a priest who was jailed under President Marcos for nine years, spoke to us about priests who join the NPA:

Priests don't start out trying to overthrow a government, they are trying to defend themselves and their lay leaders ... They join the revolutionary struggle on that basis – part of it is because the military is about to kill them anyway. But I think knowing them personally and having had conversations with them, priests are reluctant revolutionaries. We prefer not to be in armed struggle; but those of us who have decided to take it up, do so resolutely. But we would prefer if there was a more peaceful way. So I think we should not think of priests going to the hills in a romantic way, and kind of glorify them as warrior clergy. It is imposed by the situation, and by the need to continue and be part of the same process, and with the same companions who before travelled the non-violent, the peaceful way of reforms.

His comments reminded me of a film we made in Ireland twenty years before about Fr John Murphy of Boulavogue, one of several priest leaders of the 1798 rebellion. In 1798 it was church policy in Ireland to dampen down any signs of unrest. Faithful to his bishop's ruling, John Murphy encouraged and cajoled his parishioners to hand in to the authorities any arms they might have hidden away. It was only when they had done this under his instructions, and were raped, pitchcapped and persecuted mercilessly by the military as soon as they were defenceless, that John Murphy became involved with rebellion. For him it was a question of self defence, and the moral justification for self defence is very solid in Christian theology.

Violence and force

The justification or otherwise of Christians getting involved in armed struggle is something that has always fascinated me. I have met so many of them in different parts of the third world – El Salvador, Nicaragua, Guatemala, Sri Lanka, Burma – committed Christians, lay and clerical, who give religious reasons for engaging in armed struggle. I always remember my own sense of shock when a sincere little priest said to me in Nicaragua that the most beautiful thing in his life after Jesus Christ was the revolution.

I have often tried to clarify my own mind on issues of peace and war, but have only ever got a certain distance. But one thing I am sure of – to say that the use of violent means is evil is not only pointless but tautologous; for violence by definition is 'the unjustified use of physical force'

The use of force may be good or bad, justified or unjustified, depending on factors like circumstance, motivation etc. So when a policeman arrests a robber after a bitter struggle, that is force on the part of the policeman and violence on the part of the robber. On the other hand, if a policeman on duty arrests a car thief during the day and then kidnaps a parish priest in the evening as part of an Ulster Freedom Fighters mission, the two acts may be materially the same, but in the first case he used justifiable force, in the second, violence.

There is of course a complicating factor, and that is the level of force used. If a policeman uses karate to knock out a car thief, that is justifiable use of force. If he shoots him dead, it may well be violence.

Force can be exercised by physical means, or by psychological means such as brainwashing, or by structural means – for example, by preventing free association, preventing the formation of trade unions, preventing the wider ownership of land, by denying education to sectors of the population, and so on.

Structural violence shows itself where resources and control of resources are the property of one group who use them, not for the good of all but for their own profit. Examples may come to mind from the old apartheid system in South Africa.

Forms of structural violence, many believe, make up the most serious overall infringements of human rights, and the most difficult to deal with. Wars, even dreadful wars, affect a proportion of a population. Structural violence may oppress everybody – apart from a small wealthy oligarchy who are responsible for it.

Christians and war

In the abstract, the use of force is justifiable to support legitimate just government, or to overthrow illegitimate unjust government.

A legitimate government, to be viable, has to have certain powers of compulsion. For the state or its citizens to renounce physical force of any kind would be immoral because it would involve renouncing liberty. In principle that is fair enough. In practice Christians split when it comes to the question of taking human life, either by sentencing wrongdoers to death, or engaging in warfare.

Some claim that Christ was totally opposed to war as, it seems, were all the early Christians. No serving soldier would be accepted into the first Christian communities; nor any one involved in executions either. Few nowadays seem aware of this early Christian witness, which seems to me most significant.

Some, on the other hand, claim that there is no direct reference to war in any of the teachings of Christ. Nor any indication of how a community should act when threatened by aggression. Nor how the oppressed should conduct themselves when subject to structural violence.

But whatever stance concerned Christians take up, they all seek to justify their views by appealing to, or explaining away, seemingly relevant texts in Holy Writ. Some of the texts often quoted as condemning violence and warfare are appended here, with some of the comments/arguments used to explain them away.

Matt 5:21ff: 'You have learnt how it was said to our ancestors, "You must not kill, and if anyone does kill he must answer for it before the court." But I say this to you, anyone who is angry with his brother will answer for it before the court ...'

Comment: Christ was thinking of interpersonal relationships and not of war. The Old Testament explicitly sanctions both war and capital punishment.

Matt 26:52: 'Put your sword back, for all who draw the sword will die by the sword.'

Comment: 1. These words were not used by Jesus in a political situation where they might be held to relate to the problem of war. They were said in relation to the question of whether or not Jesus should be prevented from accepting the role of the Lamb who would take on himself the sin of the world.

166

Comment: 2. The fact that Jesus did not put himself at the head of a nationalist freedom movement says nothing against the use of force. His role was to save, not one nation, but the whole world.

1 Peter 2:21-23: 'Christ suffered for you and left an example for you to follow the way he took. He had not done anything wrong, and there had been no perjury in his mouth. He was insulted and did not retaliate with insults; when he was tortured he made no threats but he put his trust in the righteous judge.'

Comment: Not to retaliate may have been good advice in the circumstances of the time – when the only feasible course of action was non-resistance to the might of the Roman Empire. But it is not necessarily valid when there is some hope of achieving change by resistance.

Matt 5:38,39: 'You have learnt how it was said: eye for eye and tooth for tooth. But I say this to you: offer the wicked man no resistance. On the contrary, if anyone hits you on the right cheek, offer him the other as well.'

Comment: This is to be understood simply as forbidding one to cause vindictive harm: the New Law as opposed to the Old, expressed in a colourful, poetic way.

The early Christian tradition

After seeing what the bible has to say, it is reasonable to look for guidance to the earliest Christian tradition, formed at a time when people could read the New Testament in the language in which it was written, and identify closely with the world in which Christ lived and spoke about.

The witness of the early Christian writers seems consistently opposed to warfare. Origen (185 to 254 AD) commented in a tract against Celsus:

And to those who enquire of us whence we come, or who is our founder, we reply that we are come, agreeably to the counsels of Jesus, to 'cut down our hostile and insolent worldly swords into ploughshares, and to convert into pruning hooks the spears formerly employed in war'. Nor do we 'learn war any more', having become children of peace, for the sake of Jesus, who is our leader.

Athenagoras, writing about 180 AD, and referring to the circus games, forbade Christians to attend; for 'we (Christians) cannot endure even to see a man put to death, however justly.'

Tertullian (160 to 235 AD) advised soldiers who became Christians to leave the army immediately:

> Shall it be lawful to make an occupation of the sword, when the Lord proclaims that he who uses the sword shall perish by the sword? And shall the son of peace take part in the battle when it does not become him even to sue at law?

The Apostolic Tradition, a document which many think was written by Hippolytus, represents the teaching of the church at Rome around the year 200. The document lists occupations or professions which were forbidden to candidates for church membership. Three articles address the question of warfare:

> A soldier who is of inferior rank shall not kill anyone. If he is ordered to, he shall not carry out the order, nor shall he take the oath. If he does not accept this let him be dismissed (i.e. as a candidate for church membership).

> Anyone who has the power of the sword or the magistrate of a city who wears purple, let him give it up or be dismissed.

> The catechumens or believers who wish to become soldiers shall be dismissed because they have despised God.

Christian attitudes to war and militarism were fairly constant up to the time of the Emperor Constantine, who in 313 AD gave religious liberty to Christians, and significant privileges to the church. Even though Christianity did not become the official religion of the Empire until 380, churchmen began to think more kindly of the civil power, and the force it used to maintain its existence. This change in attitude was complete by 416 when the Empire required all its soldiers to be Christian! The *volte face* was also influenced by the Barbarian threat: Rome was sacked by the Visigoths in 410, and as every schoolboy knows, St Augustine died as the Vandals stormed the gates of Hippo.

Athanasius, writing in the fourth century gives a good example of this new thinking on warfare:

> It is not right to kill, yet in war it is lawful and praiseworthy to destroy the enemy. Accordingly, not only are they who have distinguished themselves in the field held worthy of great honours, but monuments are put up proclaiming their achievements. So the same act is at one time and under some circumstances unlawful, while under others at the right time it is lawful and permissible.

St Augustine sought to justify theologically the participation of Christians in warfare. Christians, he said, may justly wage war only when the lawfully established authority orders it. However, once the Christian has been officially ordered to kill, he must do so with untroubled conscience:

> What indeed is wrong with war? That people die who will eventually die anyway so that those who survive may be subdued in peace? A coward complains of this ... No one must ever question the rightness of a war which is waged on God's command. God commands war to drive out, to crush or to subjugate the pride of mortals.

This is the kind of theology that justified the Crusades, and the war against the Albigenses and the religious wars of the seventeenth century.

The weakness of this theology is that it grew, like all theology, out of a context, and that context was a bad context – the gradual adoption of Christianity as the official religion of the Empire. The state supported the church so the church rationalised its support for the state. I never liked Augustine much, and his views on warfare only increase my dislike.

One interesting and significant aspect of the early belief that being a Christian and indulging in warfare were incompatible occupations remains to this day: clergy in Christian countries are exempted from military service. I think this is very significant, because it seems to be a recognition of the early view that killing people – even in so-called just wars – is not a Christian way of acting, and that permission to kill is a concession to human weakness.

My own views in this tortuous field are tentative. Quite apart from my clerical status, I would never have been prepared to kill in warfare, no matter what the penalty to be endured.

I think, in addition to considering what Christ said – or did not say – about the use of force, we should ask ourselves what, in our circumstances, might Christ himself do. And if we were to do that, I think the fundamental Christian instinct would be to return violence with love.

I suppose all Christians would agree that the path of non-violence is always preferable. But what often isn't recognised is that certain conditions are required if non-violence is to be a worthwhile option, conditions which are not always present. Gandhi is held up to all as a successful proponent of non-violence, and so he was. But the British Raj were prepared to tolerate Gandhi. In Nazi Germany and Stalinist Russia, not to speak of some Latin American countries, Ghandi mightn't have survived long enough to accomplish anything.

Critics of non-violence should take account too of the huge dispro-portion between the resources given to military development and the resources used to develop techniques of solving problems by non-violence – probably no more in a year than would buy two tanks. Surely one of the most important initiatives Christians can take is to encourage funding for studies of non-violent approaches to problem solving.

In my opinion, the major moral scandal in the contemporary world is the amount of resources spent on armaments, the ingenious devices which have only one purpose – to kill or maim other human beings. I came across a table recently which spelt out the annual costs of global programmes which would be required to solve the majority of contemporary human problems. They are as follows:

Eliminate starvation and malnourishment.	$19 billion.
Provide safe clean water supply.	$50 billion.
Provide health care.	$15 billion.
Provide shelter.	$21 billion.

Retire developing nations' debt.	$30 billion.
Eliminate illiteracy.	$ 5 billion.
Prevent acid rain.	$ 8 billion.
Prevent global warming.	$ 8 billion.
Provide clean safe energy.	$50 billion.
Stop deforestation.	$ 7 billion.
Stop ozone depletion.	$ 5 billion.
Prevent soil erosion.	$24 billion.
Stabilise population.	$10 billion.

The combined total cost of all these worthy programmes is approximately one quarter of the world's total annual military expenditure.

The ultimate dilemma

The dilemma which sincere Christians like Vicente Pelobello have such difficulty in resolving is how to oppose and overcome manifest structural injustice and physical violence against the people they feel called upon to serve.

A maniac on a roof is shooting innocent people in the street below. You can see him clearly from your window, you have a gun, and you are a crack shot. It would seem that the law of love might require you to shoot that man.

In practice most Christians are not pacifist. They believe in the right of an oppressed or attacked people to take up arms in their own defence.

At the same time they accept the special role of the clergy to keep alive the virtue of compassion in the nation at war, to remind the fighters that his enemy is also his brother, and that the public peril cannot justify private hate.

Some modern Christian thinkers seem able to make revolution appear very respectable. Paolo Freire says that the oppressed, fighting to be human, take away the oppressor's power to dominate and suppress, 'and restore to the oppressors the humanity they have lost in the exercise of oppression.' But what if you have to kill him or her in the process? The case of the maniac on the rooftop is relatively clear. Few other cases are that clear.

The people of Negros are held in a kind of serfdom by a tiny rich land-owning class. While the poor get poorer and the rich richer, the rich oppose any protest with military might, and at government level stymie any attempt at land reform. It is institutional violence to a high degree, and often physical violence as well. Does the law of love not require one to use force on behalf of one's suffering neighbour in this case as well? People like Vicente Pelobello have decided that it does.

But waging war affects people in negative ways, and often gives new expression to some of the evils it seeks to destroy. Few people come to power by military means without being scarred in the process. And where in the past there have been successful revolutions against tyrannical regimes, the revolutionary leaders often turn out to be more oppressive than the tyrants they replace. The Imperial Czar, it should be remembered, was succeeded by Joseph Stalin.

It is far easier to start a war than to control its outcome. The armed struggle may generate military counter-struggle with immense suffering and devastation for the poor, whom the struggle is supposedly going to benefit. This is what appeared to happen in Guatemala in the 1970s and 80s, where one million people were displaced within the country, 350,000 left as refugees and perhaps 120,000 mostly innocent people killed.

The unfortunate fact was that Guatemala, like El Salvador and Nicaragua and the Philippines, and a number of other countries where many good and sincere people argued that social revolution was needed, in fact came within areas where the United States feared political change.

The United States, which itself was born out of a revolution against colonial oppression, has consistently opposed by covert and overt, moral and immoral means what it chose to see as communist inspired revolutionary movements around the world.

And so the revolutionary wars in Central America over the last twenty-five years have led to 300,000 deaths, with countless more wounded and displaced, and economic misery and destruction. And all to little avail. The landless poor and the persecuted around the world may have justice on their side when they take up arms against their oppressors. But as long as the United States remains a world power, they are unlikely to be allowed to win. After twenty-five years of the NPA activity in Negros, and much suffering, the people are poorer than they have ever been, and there has been no land reform.

Ned Gill is a senior Columban priest who has worked most of his life in Negros. We interviewed him for this film about the NPA:

To me one of the great tragedies of the present situation in the Philippines is that you have in this country, where 80 per cent of the people are very poor, you have an army of 300,000, and they have no external enemy, so they're supposed to be engaged in hunting down the NPA which is the military arm of the communist party. During the past number of years they have had very little success there. As a matter of fact, the NPA have grown enormously within that time, and one of the reasons has been that the military do not go after the NPA in the same sense that you expect an army to go after an enemy. They go into the mountains, they have an operation, they're very indiscriminate in whom they kill, like down in the South here a few months ago, they went in and did quite a lot of shelling and bombing, and at the end of it, I think they had got very, very few NPA, but they had displaced an enormous amount of people. As a result it's very easy for the NPA to come along and to gain recruits. So they keep growing all the time. And the army do not want to stop. They're interested in creating incidents because the more incidents there are, the more there seems to be a need for the army. They're the ones who sent in the report on the number of NPA killed, and in actual fact it would be very interesting if you followed the papers and totalled the number of NPA that have been killed according to the military, and how do you tally that against the fact that they have been increasing all the time?

Fr Niall O'Brien, who was imprisoned for fourteen months in the Philippines for championing the rights of the poor, took time off

173

afterwards to study and write about non-violence. We interviewed him after his return to the Philippines:

When you think about it, there is a massive consensus throughout the world in favour of violence. I mean look at it, the capitalists, the communists, the Muslims, the Christians, all believe that there's such a thing as a just war and a just revolution. And looking around at the world at the moment, the world is torn apart by wars, resulting basically from the belief that there is such a thing as a just war and a just revolution. I think it's time for a more radical solution and that radical solution lies in the direction that if people withdraw their consent from despots and from those who want to make war, then they will not be able to make war. How to make people withdraw their consent is the science of revolutionary non-violence, and that's the science which I feel is the science of the future.

He has since published two books on the subject.

In the meantime wars continue, and the morality of most of them seems to be very questionable. If I have to sum up my own position, I think of Christianity in the simplest terms as the imitation of Christ. And I cannot in any circumstance imagine Christ with a gun. At the same time, I accept that people in intolerable circumstances cannot be condemned if they judge in the abstract that the exercise of physical force may help to bring about a more just society. In the concrete, however, they must take into account the reality that the great powers, and in particular the United States, have opposed with arms, money and know-how pretty well every popular armed revolutionary movement since World War II – usually successfully, and with horrific human consequences.

10

MALACHY:
A PROPHET WITHOUT HONOUR

Making film documentaries often depends on good luck!

Fr Liam Swords and I were working on a film about St Malachy of
Armagh who was a close friend of St Bernard, and spent some time
at his friend's monastery in Clairvaux in France, where, indeed, he
died on the feast of All Saints, 1148, at the age of fifty-four.

So we had to go to Clairvaux to get material for the film. We arrived
shortly after lunch, drew up at the front door of the ancient monastery, explained our mission and said we proposed to take a few
pictures of the exterior. A uniformed gentleman politely explained
to us that Clairvaux was now a high security prison, the monks having
been driven out some time ago – by the Emperor Napoleon in fact.
Because it was a high security prison we couldn't take any photographs without permission, and if we wanted permission we could
write to the Minister of Justice in Paris.

Well you win some and lose some, and we were not prepared to lose
just yet. The idea of leaving Clairvaux without some pictures of the
monastery just because of a stupid bit of officialdom pleased neither
of us, so we decided to go for the high ground, and get some pictures
of Clairvaux at a safe distance with a tele-photo lens. There was a
hill nearby – it was wooded, but woods always have clearings, and
if there isn't a clearing there's always the other side of the wood; so
there seemed little to lose. We got into our car and started climbing.
Now there had been a fair bit of rain the same day, and the road
through the wood was slippery. The slippery road then became
mucky, and the mucky road became very mucky – and still there was
no clearing, and no sight of the end of the wood. So we decided we
had better turn back and try another way. Our hired car was heavy

175

and low slung, and in the attempt to turn it, the wheels got stuck in the mud. We tried to put brushwood under the wheels, but they went in deeper and deeper. Another shower of rain made things worse. By four o'clock, the car had sunk down to its chassis, and there was no way we would ever get it out without help. Having lived in France for years, Liam Swords was the obvious person to strike out for the village and see if help could be organised. He arrived back in about an hour in a Renault 4 with four amused French policemen. Having pulled us out of the mud they ordered us down to the police station.

Sometimes the truth doesn't sound very plausible. Two Irishmen trying to take surreptitious photographs of a French high security prison! When we arrived at the gendarmerie, what looked like the local sergeant was waiting for us. He sat at a high desk with a quizzical expression, pen in hand, ready to write a full report for the Ministry in Paris. Liam waxed eloquently on the friendship between Saints Malachy and Bernard and informed the astonished policemen that because of Bernard, the name of Clairvaux was as familiar to every Irish schoolboy as Paris or London! Furthermore he foretold enormous interest in our film documentary – which would help cement cordial relations between Ireland and France. Some or all of our explanations and peculiar behaviour were written down in longhand, for which we duly signed.

Early on in the proceedings, one of the gendarmes had asked me would we like to meet somebody who was knowledgeable about St Bernard, and I said we would, though I was too preoccupied with our present predicament to think much more about it. But when the signing was complete, we were introduced to a youngish man whom I had noticed entering earlier and who had been waiting around for the official proceedings to finish. He was a French lawyer with a doctorate – the subject of his doctorate being the writings of St Bernard. He hoped some day to be a judge, and as part of the career pattern of French judges he was spending a period working with the prison system. His current post was Deputy Governor of the Clairvaux High Security Prison!

So about an hour later, we were having aperitifs in his quarters in the prison, before proceeding to the stone vaulted dining room. Once the laundry of the monastery, it had been recently restored with great taste to provide a magnificent staff dining room, with tables grouped around a large pool in the centre. We sat at table and enjoyed a leisurely meal with both the Deputy Governor and the Governor. Now there are reasons for everything. The Deputy Governor was very interested in restoring parts of the prison which dated from the time of St Bernard, and had made certain progress. But he felt the project would move faster if he had more support from the Governor. The fact of an Irish television crew coming to film about St Bernard was an indicator of international interest which he hoped might impress the Governor. So Liam did his best to play a supporting role.

Next morning we had permission to film what we liked – all doors were open to us, even where sometimes this literally required three keys. We also had an interview with the deputy governor, who drew an interesting parallel.

The prisoners live in cells. They don't go outside. They have no wives, no private life. This is about the same way of living as the monks long ago. Of course, the very big difference is that the prisoners have not chosen to be here, while the monks did!

I have indulged myself telling this little story, not because there are big issues arising from it, but because in making films for Radharc we have often been very lucky, and I just want to celebrate that fact.

11

THE 16TH CENTURY IS ALIVE AND WELL AND LIVING IN NORTHERN IRELAND

The rationale of inquisition

Belfast, late October 1987. Methodists and Roman Catholics were meeting for the first time ever to discuss their theological differences in St. Clement's, the Redemptorist retreat house on the slopes of Cave Hill. The excuse was the 250th anniversary of John Wesley's conversion and Alphonsus Liguori's death. (St Alphonsus was founder of the Redemptorists and John Wesley of the Methodists.) The occasion was meant to be an opportunity for peaceful dialogue and reflection, but the Reverend Ian Paisley M.P., unionist politician and minister of religion had other ideas. Paisley spoke vehemently against the meeting on the radio, organised a protest meeting, arranged for a large picket to parade up and down with offensive banners outside St. Clement's, and invited his supporters to a service at his Martyrs Memorial Church.

A service in Dr Paisley's church

I sat through Paisley's full service which lasted nearly two hours. It was only for the experience, because filming in his church isn't permitted. There were two other preliminary speakers, readings and hymns. It bored me after the first twenty minutes – right up to the time when Paisley himself rose to speak, some forty minutes from the end. But his was a devastating, wicked, winning, theatrical performance which had the whole auditorium hanging on his every word. The Catholic practice of Confession was one of his first targets:

> How great would be our wonder if we saw a person invested with the power of changing a Negro into a white man. (Voice dripping with irony.)

178

But the priest does what is far more wonderful, for by saying "Ego te absolvo" he changes a sinner into a friend of God, from a slave of hell into an heir of paradise (pause). They mustn't be working too hard at it. If they are changing men into the heirs of paradise and the friends of God, that is not the way they turn out of the confession box. For they turn out tenfold more children of hell than when they went in!

And my friends, it's *priests* that these Methodist men are with, it's these men that are claiming this power every day, and I want to tell you that at 8 o'clock on Wednesday, they gather together and they will hand up this pancake of bread and water. And they will all kneel down, and I will not be there, but the Methodists will be kneeling with them. Such is the great delusion – God shall send them a strong delusion that they might believe a lie: that they all might be damned who had pleasure in unrighteousness.

This is the thing that made the martyrs fight the battle. It was because they set their face against the Mass that they were burned.

And I have said from this pulpit and I will say it again – that the day will come when we will be burned for preaching the true gospel of Christ.

Let us face up to it, the martyrs band are not all finished, you know. There are still more martyrs to come ...

And when the battle rages, (gradual crescendo) and when men would replace my Saviour with a human priest; would dethrone my Saviour with Mary; or would take me down into the cesspool of the sewers of Liguori's confessional instrument, I will raise my voice (pause) ... and stand up (pause) ... for Jesus!

When religion flourishes at that kind of high emotional level, there is generally a good political reason. One saw it in Poland under the Communist regime, when Catholicism was the rallying point for political opposition. One finds it in the North of Ireland where Catholic Nationalists have political reasons to be friendly with Protestants, and Protestant Unionists have political reasons not to be friendly with Catholics. Because if they really became friendly with Catholics, the reason for having a border to divide Protestant and Catholic would disappear. Which explains why, as a Church of

Ireland rector once told me in Armagh, when he holds an ecumenical service in his church, the congregation is 90% Roman Catholic.

Reformation/Counter Reformation, a human tragedy

The North of Ireland is one of the few places left in the world where one can still see strong tensions in the community resulting from the tragedy of the Reformation/Counter Reformation, which was a human and spiritual disaster of the megaton variety. It was a human disaster because of the wars it provoked, the ruin of many countries including our own, and the suffering of countless millions of people down the centuries. Let me explain.

Every plantation of Ireland by foreigners was absorbed by the local population up to the Reformation. The planters intermarried and became 'more Irish than the Irish themselves'. But after the Reformation, intermarriage became virtually impossible between Roman and Reformed, and the two tribes thereafter developed separately – the planters in a state of siege, the dispossessed nursing their grievances. And so we have the division, the hatred, the killings. The death of every person through political violence in the North is an indirect result of the Reformation.

The sixteenth century church was desperately in need of reformation, but reformation within the concept of one church, rather than a division into many. The fight for reform would have been better pursued inside the organisation – quitting is often the easy option. If the leaders of reform had been clear in their own minds about the value of unity, they might have tried harder to find ways of staying within. The reform might have taken longer, but presumably goodness and truth would have eventually triumphed – our Christian belief demands that confidence.

I know I am again being naïve, and unmindful of the passions once aroused by different theologies, but I am making a point for today. The progress of the church is best served when men like Hans Küng and Charles Curran and Bernard Häring are determined, despite persecution by the Holy Office, to remain and work within the fold. It is less well served by theologians like Charles Davis and Leonardo Boff who, by giving up their priesthood, are more easily marginalised. I believe that is true as a general rule, with admitted exceptions.

Reformation/Counter Reformation – a spiritual disaster

The Reformation/Counter Reformation was also a spiritual disaster for the reason that for centuries the energy of good and holy people was directed to attacking their opponent's beliefs, real or fictional, and the shoring up of their own characteristic institutions and traditions, even those of negative worth. Clashes concerning discipline became clashes of personality, clashes of personality became clashes about doctrine, because human beings always proceed to rationalise their conflicts – so that they appear to be about issues rather than egos.

At the Second Vatican Council, the Roman church eventually embraced most of the great ideas of the Reformation – the emphasis on the dignity of man, the importance of personal freedom, the need for a vernacular liturgy, the centrality of the bible, the need for decentralising authority. (Or perhaps I should say more or less accepted, because there has been some clawing back since.) But for centuries all these ideas were Protestant ideas, enemy ideas, and brain power and energy and ink were spilled in sternly refuting them on that ground alone.

A Protestant observer at the Vatican Council said to me that if the changes brought about at the council had only come 400 years earlier there would have been no need for the Reformation. My reply was that if more of the reformers had stayed within the Roman church, the Vatican Council reforms might have come 300 years earlier.

The Protestant fear of Rome

The Reverend John Dunlop, a recent Moderator of the Presbyterian Church, said to us in interview:

> Many Northern Ireland Protestants see themselves as being threatened on two scores, by the imperialism of Irish nationalism which wishes to take over the whole of Ireland, and by an ecclesiastical imperialism from Rome which understands itself to be the one true church, and perhaps wishes to absorb within itself, everybody who is at present outside that communion. So it's a twin imperialism of nationalism and Roman Catholicism.

Some years ago I might have been dismissive of those fears of ecclesiastical imperialism, but nowadays rather less so. The recent record of the Vatican in trying to muzzle theologians and stifle theological debate is of very sincere concern to many Catholics as well as to Protestants. The treatment of Leonardo Boff is one of the worst of many examples.

Leonardo Boff and the Holy Office

Leonardo Boff was a Franciscan theologian in Brazil. He was summoned to Rome to appear before the Congregation for the Doctrine of the Faith – which most people still call 'The Holy Office'. One of the criticisms made of his lectures and writings was that he was promoting a grassroots church, parallel to and opposed to the hierarchy. So Cardinal Arns and Cardinal Lorscheider, two Brazilian cardinals, took the unprecedented step of coming specially to Rome with Boff to support him in his inquisition. So much for fears of him representing a parallel church!

At the end of the inquisition, the Holy Office issued a document which said that some of Boff's opinions 'endanger the sound doctrine of the faith.' Nothing specific was found to condemn in the way of heresy, or even error. Boff accepted the admonition humbly. Yet two months later he was silenced, forbidden for an unspecified period to give lectures, or publish.

Cardinal Arns of São Paulo wrote about the episode afterwards. 'For me it was a really surprising measure to punish a man who accepted everything from the Vatican in such a humble and friendly way.' Ten other Brazilian bishops called the action against Boff 'an attack on the rights of man and on the freedom of research in the field of theology, as well as an insult to the Bishops' Conference.' The apostolic nuncio in turn rebuked the ten bishops. That was in 1985. The silencing of Boff lasted ten months.

In 1989 Boff was required to resign as editor of *Revista Ecclesiástica Brazileira,* a theological magazine.

In May 1991 the Holy Office swung into action again, removing Boff from the editorship of the cultural magazine, *Vozes,* published by the leading Catholic publisher in Brazil. Boff was told to stop writing about controversial subjects like the exercise of power within the church, and to stop teaching at the Theological Institute for an unspecified period. The Vatican also appointed a group of censors to control the total output of the *Vozes* publishing house, as well as Boff's own writings. This censorship was vigorously applied.

In April 1992, Boff's superiors in the Franciscan Order told him that in view of the continuing pressure from Rome they would prefer him not to return to his teaching post in the Theological Institute as had been planned after another enforced sabbatical.

In July, Boff wrote a moving letter of resignation from the Franciscans.

> Everything has a limit. I arrived at mine ... My personal experience of dealings over the last twenty years with doctrinal power is this: it is cruel and without pity. It forgets nothing, forgives nothing, it exacts a price for everything. To achieve that end – the imprisonment of theological intelligence – the doctrinal powers take all the time necessary and use all the means necessary. They act directly or use intermediaries or force one's brethren within the Franciscan Order to exercise a function which by canon law belongs only to those who have doctrinal authority.

If that is what happens to someone who 'endangers sound doctrine' what might happen to a real live heretic!

Boff wrote about his experience of being summoned to the Holy Office:

> The church today lacks the political means for punishing those accused of heresy, but the fundamental mentality and proceedings of the past have changed little. Physical torture has been abolished but psychological torture continues: the juridical insecurity of the doctrinal processes; the anonymity of the denunciation; the lack of knowledge as to the reasons behind the charges; the judgements apart from the process; no acknowledgement of offered explanations; repeated accusations to known questions; long intervals between correspondence; the insecurity and uncertainly as to whether the process is being continued or discontinued, or whether the procedures have been further refined. All of this, accented even more by the marginalisation one suffers in the local church due to the scrutiny of the Sacred Congregation for the Doctrine of the Faith, leads some theologians to the dark night of lonely suffering, psychological worry, and even physical death.

How quickly the words of Pope John XXIII at the opening of Vatican II have been forgotten. The church, John said, 'considers that she meets the needs of the present day by demonstrating the validity of her teaching rather than by condemnations.'

When Cardinal Angelo Sodano, Pope John Paul's choice for the post of Vatican Secretary of State, heard of Boff's resignation he commented that 'even at the time of the apostolic college, there was a betrayal; and it is not that the Lord had not chosen Judas carefully!'

The inquisitorial attitude

The inquisitorial attitude has of course a hallowed place in the Christian tradition – one which in earlier days the Reformers shared equally with the Roman church. But it is part of a past which nobody is proud of, and most Christians today, I believe, would prefer to consign it to history.

There is a permanent exhibition of torture instruments in Amsterdam – I once made a special point of going to see it. I think that every new recruit to Cardinal Ratzinger's Congregation of the Doctrine of the Faith (or Holy Office) should be required to visit the exhibition and write a study paper on it.

Here are the tools of the Inquisitions of which the Holy Office is the heir. There are headcrushers, thumbscrews, ladder racks, breast rippers, knee splitters, oral, rectal, and vaginal pears, shrew's fiddles, iron maidens, heretic forks, and Spanish spiders – with woodcuts, engravings and documents to show how they were used.

Pope Gregory IX reserved the apprehension, trial and punishment of heretics for the church and its agents, the Inquisitors, in 1231. The use of torture was authorised by Pope Innocent IV twenty years later. In fact six different popes justified and authorised the use of torture during the thirteenth century. However, these directives were largely ignored. Pope Clement V (1305-1314), however, was anxious to find the Templar Order guilty of heresy, idolatry and sodomy, so that he could confiscate their wealth and possessions for his fellow Frenchman, King Philip the Fair. In Aragon, Castille, Ravenna, England, Scotland and Ireland where torture was banned, the Templars got a fair trial and were found not guilty. Pope Clement refused to accept the acquittals, and ordered a retrial everywhere with the use of torture until confessions of guilt were obtained. When King Edward complained that torture was against the Common Law in England, the pope threatened him with interdict. In May 1310, sixty-three knights who had withdrawn their confessions made under torture were burnt at the stake as relapsed heretics. Four years later, the Grand Master and his chief supporters also withdrew their confessions and were burnt at the stake.

Had the next pope denounced the principle, or at least withdrawn the order, one could dismiss the matter of torture as an aberration. But subsequent popes endorsed the position, and enforced it ruthlessly through the Inquisition. And while the maximum penalty within the Inquisition's power to impose was life imprisonment, there was of course the catch – the condemned could be handed over to the secular powers to be dealt with as they saw fit.

An elaborate manual produced to support an exhibition of torture instruments presented in various European cities in the middle 1980s states that between 1450 and 1800 somewhere between two and four million women condemned of witchcraft were burnt alive at the stake in Catholic and Protestant Europe. Others quote 100,000 as a more realistic figure. Either way the reality is horrific.

I find it hard to come to any satisfactory conclusions about the Inquisition in its different manifestations. When Catholics and Protestants were at each other's throats, and that wasn't too long ago, the Inquisitions of the Church of Rome were the subject of propaganda on one side, and cover-up on the other. So it is very difficult to be objective in one's judgement. Furthermore, one has to try and judge according to the mind of the times. Little went on in the dungeons of the Inquisition that would have seemed excessive, let alone unusual, to any commoner, prince or burgher of the day. And the Reformers were just as capable of torture as any Grand Inquisitor. In Lutheran Germany the leaders of rebellious peasants were hung up by the ankles and sawn in two parts from crotch to head.

However, even with the most beneficent reading of the evidence, the record provides the gravest warning of the dangers involved in inquisition, and in the capacity of otherwise good men to get involved in the most terrible and totally unchristian deeds in the name of

Christ. Nowadays the church doesn't condone the use of physical torture; but there are other methods, as Fr Boff pointed out in his moving letter to his brethren explaining his resignation.

The rationale of the inquisition

The idea of a pluralist society is a recent invention. In the past civil rulers saw religious differences as breeding political instability. And who could say they were wrong. *Cujus regio ejus religio* (the religion of the King is the religion of the State) was the norm most often applied. Which is why there were martyrs throughout Europe on both sides of the Reformation divide.

God lives in inaccessible light, the scriptures tell us. But he also seeks our love, and to that purpose gives himself to us in a form we can perhaps understand, his Son in human flesh. Because of who he is, the Son's message is of supreme importance and must not be corrupted. The church is there to guard his teaching, and to be single minded about opposing those who try to twist it to their own vainglorious end. Where truth is in danger, some kind of enquiry is required to find the facts, to be able to determine whether this is Christ's teaching, or a shameful distortion. The old-fashioned word for enquiry is 'inquisition'.

That is one side of the equation. Now the other. Can one imagine Christ pulling people's arms out of their sockets trying to extract admissions of heresy? Or handing them over to the civil authority to be burnt at the stake? Can one imagine Christ presiding over the tribunals like those in which Karl Rahner and Yves Congar were asked to recant of their false teachings, teachings which were later embraced by the Fathers of the Second Vatican Council, and written into the documents which now stand as part of the body of teaching of the Catholic Church? What did Christ think when men like Leonardo Boff and Gustavo Gutiérrez were called from the ends of the earth – sometimes accompanied for support by their local cardinal archbishops, successors to Christ's apostles – and subjected in Rome to intimidation and indignity, and then forbidden to write and teach, even though not found guilty of any heresy?

I leave the last word to a very charitable Lutheran, Dr George Lindbeck, who was a delegate-observer at the Second Vatican Council, and whom we interviewed in 1989:

One way of describing the limitations of the changes that have taken place in the Roman curia is to say that the Roman Catholic Church still has not learned to deal with a loyal opposition – it has not learned how to make a distinction between a loyal opposition and a disloyal one. And no church can, it seems to me, really have the kind of renewal that was projected by the Second Vatican Council unless it learns to live with those who, out of love for the church, for God, for Jesus Christ, criticise the church.

12
VIETNAM: CHURCH AND STATE
*A former colonial church adapts
to living in a communist state*

This church, when some day it finds room to express itself more freely, will amaze the rest of the world. I have travelled around the world a lot and this country is far from being alone in having to survive amid difficulties – alas there are many others. But I have rarely seen so many difficulties as here in Vietnam.

— *Cardinal Etchegaray, President of the Vatican Commission for Justice and Peace, interviewed by Radharc in Hanoi.*

Vietnam is one of the last of the hard-line Communist states with all the associated paraphernalia – secret police, re-education camps, and strict control of freedom of movement, information, and, of course, political dissent. So we felt a little more excitement than usual as we boarded the DC10 at Brussels for the first stage of the journey to Ho Chi Minh City via Bangkok.

Filming without permission

Normally we make our own travel arrangements and get whatever documentation is necessary. But the 1990 trip to Vietnam was arranged in conjunction with Mike Kelly, an Australian Jesuit with good contacts in Asia. We had worked out a way of helping each other whereby he supplied travel arrangements, research and documentation about agreed subjects in Asia or Australia, and we came together for the actual filming. In return Mike would get copies of the completed programmes for use in Australia.

This time Mike had entrusted the visa arrangements to a Jesuit office in Bangkok. When we met in Bangkok and came to collect the visas it quickly became clear we had a problem. The Bangkok office had procured tourist visas – which meant we had no permission to film. A proper journalist visa would require some weeks to process, so either we went home empty-handed, or we tried to bluff it out. We decided on the latter course.

We divided up the bags at Ho Chi Minh City airport and went through the customs as individuals. Despite some unusually shaped baggage – the tripod for instance – the customs officials neither opened anything nor asked any questions. Vietnam was trying to attract more tourists to get hard currency. Perhaps the customs official had taken note of the posters we saw later scattered around the country which proclaimed 'The Year of the Tourist' and asked all the locals to be nice to foreigners.

Without perhaps realising the value and significance of the arrangement at the time, Mike had secured accommodation at a hotel in Ho Chi Minh City through the kind assistance of an official of the US Immigration Office in Bangkok. US Immigration had personnel stationed in Ho Chi Minh engaged in screening Vietnamese who had claims to enter the US, either as a child of a US serviceman, or somebody involved with the US regime before the Viet Minh takeover. And so we stayed in the same hotel as the US officials, chatted with them over breakfast, and having been booked in through their office, came in Vietnamese eyes to be somehow connected with their operation. We learnt later that US officials thought we had permission from the Vietnamese government to film in Vietnam, which we hadn't, while the Vietnamese thought we were somehow connected with the US government operation, which we weren't. They were probably afraid to interfere with us for that reason. Anyway we were left to our own devices.

So, in the end, working in South Vietnam proved to be surprisingly easy. Most residents of Ho Chi Minh City look on the police and security services much the same way as people in Ballymurphy or Andersonstown look on the RUC or the SAS, or the blacks in Selma looked on Bull Connor and his dogs. Among themselves they still call their city Saigon, and are adept at flouting the Hanoi regime, indeed they delight in it. This is probably one of the first lessons the outsider has to learn in Vietnam: that despite the outward appearances, Vietnam is still in many ways two countries.

The North and the South

During the war, the Viet Minh talked of liberating their brothers in the South. But in the end they made the mistake of treating the South as a conquered enemy nation. Instead of proclaiming a general amnesty and making friends, they persecuted those who had been involved with the US-backed government. Inevitably most South Vietnamese had been compromised in some way or other with the old regime, and therefore felt vulnerable.

I think part of the problem was that the North Vietnamese soldiers were victims of their own propaganda. They came to liberate their brothers groaning under the yoke of foreign domination: instead they found them enjoying a much higher standard of living with luxuries available which were unheard of north of the border. The South had a share in western technology, and was well ahead of the North in manufacturing industry and the corresponding (relative) wealth that technology brings. The North had put all its energies into pursuing the war, and had gone through thirty or more years of hardship as a result. It galled the northern soldiers and officials to find that while they were making such sacrifices, people in the South had been living in relative luxury and comfort.

It was this factor I believe more than anything else that lay behind the rather savage treatment meted out by the North Vietnamese to their brothers and sisters in the South which has left a legacy of hate to this day.

Two other liaisons helped our film work in different ways. Early on we met with a Vietnamese Jesuit who took us out to his small rural parish. We went by taxi, though this seems rather a grand name for a vehicle that would in any European country have long since gone to the scrap heap. We were warned not to talk in the taxi as the driver was as likely as not to be reporting to the security police. Although a Jesuit, our friend was working as a secular priest, anxious to conceal his international contacts as a member of a religious order. In fact in every way he seemed frightened, suspicious, and secretive.

When later in the presbytery we explained our anomalous position – filming without permission — he advised us to get in contact with the Committee for the Union of Patriotic Catholics, and in particular with one of its leaders, Fr Phan Khac Tu. This committee comprised a group of concerned Catholics who advocated co-operation with the regime.

The Committee for the Union of Patriotic Catholics

We came across three different attitudes towards this committee and all those who belonged to it – some with more, some less enthusiasm. Right-wingers see the members as having sold themselves to the regime – at worst to enjoy power or privilege, at best because of a mistaken idea that their support would be to the benefit of the church. People in the middle see the members as pragmatic men making the best of the circumstances and providing a framework in which the church can survive and do its essential work. A third group genuinely support the Committee, motivated by the socialist ideal whereby, they believe, people should work for the good of the community rather than for personal gain. This group also express their repentance of the fact that the church in the past has been so closely associated with colonialist and exploitive regimes (for that read France and North America).

Although the government sponsors this Committee for the Union of Patriotic Catholics, it has never attempted to establish a national Catholic church, independent of Rome, as was done in China.

One hundred and forty-two priests belonged to the Patriotic Committee, all with the approval of their bishops. These included the rector of the seminary in Ho Chi Minh City. This Patriotic Front saw its role as helping to explain to the Catholic people the socialist way of building society, and to feed back to government the problems and aspirations of Catholics.

Among some of its projects, the Committee promoted the idea of religious orders taking responsibility for collective farms. They saw the idea as a very Christian one – committed people working together for the good of the wider community rather than purely for their own benefit. Indeed religious communities like the Cistercians, one might say, have been running collective farms for nearly a thousand years.

We visited a farm where Salesians, Cistercians and Jesuits share community work and prayer in a spirit of brotherhood.

Fr Phan Khac Tu was the leader of the group of priests within the Patriotic Union. He was also a member of the legislative assembly in Hanoi, elected from Ho Chi Minh City. This, we were told, was not quite as significant as it seemed, and simply involved attending and voting at two meetings in Hanoi each year. But he did have clout with the government, and if he showed interest in our activities, we felt he might provide us with some civil authorisation which in turn would be helpful when it came to looking for co-operation from the church authorities.

We met Fr Phan Khac Tu at his office, a substantial suburban detached house in Ho Chi Minh City provided for him by the government. The house had some ground at the rear which was now being built upon. This was to be a new ecumenical centre where visitors from overseas could come and study. We climbed around and admired the incomplete, but obviously well built structure of red brick. I can't say that we fully understood the need for this centre, but one thing seemed clear – it was not being built without government support, because the government controlled the supply of bricks and mortar.

We interviewed Fr Phan on camera, and that was important. But we also had an unrecorded interview which was just as important. We told him exactly what our position was, how it came about, and our hopes of being able to present a fair and unprejudiced picture of the church in Vietnam. He listened and said little, and at the end we didn't know whether he would do anything for us or not. I was hoping he might have been able to arrange a piece of paper with official stamps which we could show around when necessary. That never appeared, but he did arrange contacts for us which showed goodwill. And he may well have persuaded officialdom to leave us alone. But even if he hadn't, our contact with him – which we took pains to advertise – was helpful in legitimising our position with others, all of whom presumed we had official permission. For how otherwise would we be filming without it? And if Fr Phan had co-operated with us, how could they get into trouble for doing the same?

Re-educating the South Vietnamese

Our other important contact was a former South Vietnamese army colonel who had spent eleven years in a communist re-education camp – which is a euphemistic name for prison. Let's call him Cedric rather than his real name. I don't know how he came across us because we didn't look for him. In fact for some time we were very wary of him, encouraged by our local Jesuit friend who was full of warnings. However, it soon became clear that Cedric had valuable contacts with what was left of those who had prospered under the previous regime in South Vietnam. We needed to meet some of those people. Cedric seemed to be able to arrange anything, including a Mercedes car for our comfortable transport – not the newest model, but still a Mercedes. If we didn't use him more it was not because he wasn't courteous, efficient and useful, but because we were afraid to blot our copy with the regime which had held him for twelve years in jail.

The conditions he experienced in the camps included solitary confinement with a tiny portion of rice and less than a litre of drinking water a day. In the beginning there were long periods of so-called re-education in socialist principles and the new political realities. But gradually the re-education aspect faded into the background. A normal day began at five o'clock with ten minutes of exercise and ten minutes for breakfast. Then work in the rice fields or quarries. Visits were very restricted and food packets limited to less than five kilograms every two months.

Cedric showed us things that officialdom might not have shown us; the convents and monasteries and church schools that had been taken over by the government; the military graveyard of the South Vietnamese regime and the tomb of its 'unknown soldier' which had been pillaged and left to return to the wilderness. And he arranged for us to meet two priests who had only recently left prison after their long process of 're-education'.

The visit to the two priests was arranged with great circumspection. It reminded me of a visit to Moscow in 1978 when a member of the staff of the French Embassy arranged for us to meet the dissident son of the great Pasternak. The person in each case who made the arrangements gave us a map, but preferred not to come with us.

The two priest brothers were living in a room at the top of their sister's house. There were five related families living at this one address, one on each floor and the two priests in a garret on the roof. We walked up the rickety stairs through various family quarters, with figures in dark corners cooking or washing and numerous children playing on the floor.

The two brothers were in their early sixties, but looked older. Fr Peter had a long white beard like one expects to see in old photographs of French missionaries. Paul was clean shaven, dapper, and very nervous. They agreed after much hesitation to be interviewed. The room they lived in looked out on a flat roof, and had two beds, some books, and a small table for the Mass. Two windows let in plenty of light, but they wanted the shutters closed when we set up the camera because the neighbours could see in. A gathering thunderstorm with failing light compounded the problem and made compromises in picture quality necessary as Father Peter talked to us.

If we hadn't received the support we did from our family, I don't think we would have survived – the conditions in prison were so bad. But our family is poor and could only support us to the best of their limited resources. We were trying our best to stay healthy, but when eventually we became ill, this caused even more problems for the family. But if our eleven years in prison caused them pain, our two years of freedom has brought them even more trouble, because now they have to support us in the family home.

Fr Paul was very much weakened by his time in prison where he developed three different illnesses.

The first was an uneven heartbeat caused by a breakdown of the nervous system. I also have high blood pressure and part of my brain doesn't function normally – I suffer from loss of memory as a result. Every day I have to take medication, otherwise my bodily systems go out of control, and this can be dangerous. The doctor told me it would take a few years to recover, but I haven't seen any progress yet.

The two priests never found out why they were imprisoned or what the charges against them were. The only charge Peter ever heard was when a policeman told him that he was in prison because 'he was CIA.' The two brothers were forbidden to exercise their priesthood publicly after their release. Apart from leaving them nothing to do, this deprived them of some income to support themselves, and so they had no alternative but to impose on their relatives.

I felt sad for those two men and angry with the political system which can take away people's freedom in such arbitrary fashion and keep them in inhuman conditions for a decade and more without the semblance of a fair trial.

Cedric brought us past one of the re-education camps and I filmed it out the window of the car; we didn't dare to stop. We were surprised to find it in a town, and not in the open country as one might have expected. It had a strong wall, and one could see the tops of some institutional buildings inside. There were guards at the gate, of course, but if the camp hadn't been pointed out to us I would have presumed it was maybe an army depot or even an industrial site. Normal practice, according to Cedric, was to send people to camps far away from their homes, to discourage attempts to escape.

It is said that about 40,000 people were taken into re-education camps, about 200 of whom were Catholic priests. Some had been military chaplains in the army of Saigon, some incurred government wrath for something they said in a sermon, some never knew the reason.

Sermons in Vietnam must still be monitored, because shortly before our visit a prominent Redemptorist priest was sentenced to three years house arrest for suggesting in his Holy Week sermon that the government wasn't taking sufficient notice of the sufferings of the poor. Ironically this priest had been a prominent government supporter in the past when other priests might have been at best lukewarm.

An improving situation

But, truth to say, there was evidence in 1990 of an improving situation. We covered a happy occasion in the parish of Nam Dong in the very south of the country. The villagers were welcoming Fr

Chan Thau, their new parish priest and their first pastor for eight years. The church had been re-painted, and the presbytery was undergoing restoration – which it needed after being empty for so long. After the ceremony, a meal was provided for perhaps two or three hundred parishioners, served by the young people of the parish. Local communist bosses arrived in their Mercedes and joined in the celebrations.

Fr Chan Thau had been sent to a re-education camp on 30 January 1978 and released on 27 April 1984. He was quite precise about the dates. After that he was idle for six years before the government would permit him to take a parish.

There are usually delightful ironies in the situation where the church operates in a semi-covert way. We photographed a class in the seminary with Fr Giap, a scripture scholar who was lecturing on the Old Testament. Fr Giap is the image of General Giap, whom older people will remember as the scourge of the French and US armies during the Vietnamese wars of liberation. The resemblance is not an accident – the General is Fr Giap's uncle!

In 1990 only two out of nineteen seminaries were allowed to operate, and even this was a relatively recent concession.

From the beginning of the Communist takeover, the church/state struggle has centred on the training of clergy. The government wanted to control the appointment of professors, the curriculum they teach and the selection of students to attend the seminary. And because the church hasn't given much ground in any of these areas, it has been limited by the state in the number of vocations it can accept. The class of fifty-five students which we photographed were admitted in 1987. When six years of studies are completed another class will be admitted. In the meantime anyone who wants to be a priest has to wait – there are hundreds of young men on waiting lists to enter seminaries!

Madame Doctor Hoa

Within a tight-lipped carefully monitored community, it is always delightful to meet the occasional free spirit who speaks out and doesn't care. One such is Madame Doctor Hoa, who provided a medical service to the Viet Minh army through many years of jungle campaigns, and who indeed lost a son in the liberation struggle. Dr Hoa was educated in Paris, spent some time in America, and is a highly intelligent and sophisticated lady. She became Minister of Health in the first Viet Minh government, but resigned after six months. She is deeply critical of the Hanoi regime and says so openly, but she gets away with it simply because she served in the jungle with most of the present ministers, and knows them intimately; and they know too that she is too independent and too intelligent to be easily cowed.

Her main criticism of the government is that winning the peace requires different skills from winning the war. Basically the government is still in the hands of the people who won the war of liberation. In her view, they should have moved aside long ago and left the country in the hands of people with social, management and entrepreneurial skills. She is also deeply critical of the way the South was treated after the war, which turned out to be 'a conquest, not a liberation'.

She is very quotable, given a little tidying up of her English.

I was in Hanoi last year and met a very old woman in the market. I noticed the vegetable that she bought and I asked her its name. Her answer to me was, 'During the war and before the liberation it was a vegetable for pigs and now it is a vegetable for human beings.' Where then is the progress?

I said to the Politburo that it is very illogical to pay such a low salary to teachers – less than a factory worker! They gave as their reason that teachers did not produce anything and I replied, 'You'll never produce much without education and knowledge'.

When I think of the boat people, I understand their reasons which are at the same time political and economic. They don't see a future for their children – and the big majority of intellectuals who leave the country also leave for that reason.

Dr Hoa would be a force in any community, but we didn't meet many women like her in Vietnam. Whatever about priests, nuns appeared to us to be particularly cowed. We called on a group who looked after mentally handicapped children in part of the former convent left to them for the purpose. (All schools, and orphanages were taken over by the State after re-unification.) Nursing the very handicapped is a difficult, demanding job which nobody particularly wants to be told to do, which is one reason for leaving it to the nuns. Officially the nuns are regarded as nurses but, of course, the authorities know well they are nuns. The sisters showed us their very modest quarters but declined with much apology and hand wringing to allow us photograph them at prayer. They have a small oratory, and the government knows they have it, but if it were officially acknowledged to exist, it might well have to be officially closed. They told us about a priest who had got hold of a printing press and was doing some catechetical publishing. A blind eye was turned to the venture until it received some publicity – only then did the authorities feel obliged to close it down.

The church of the poor

Elsewhere we visited a Dominican Convent where the whole community welcomed us – five nuns and nine novices. The novices, who giggled a bit in appealing if predictable fashion, were paraded in front of us to perform a modest Vietnamese dance. I sat in a large chair and felt like a colonial official being entertained by samples of native culture; and smiled with patronising benevolence. The realities of convent life didn't allow for much smiling however. The sisters were abysmally poor. The novices had always to be prepared to hide in the roof when the police called because they shouldn't have been there at all – religious orders are not allowed to take novices. Furthermore, every person in Vietnam is supposed to sleep in his or her own family house, and requires official approval to sleep elsewhere – it's part of the communist way of control. The novices of course had no such permission to sleep away from home.

It is not often in life that one can feel truly munificent on a small outlay. We gave the sisters $200 – worth a fortune in Vietnam which is starved of foreign currency.

So relatively speaking, Ho Chi Minh City proved an easy place for us to work in, easier than we had expected, perhaps because there are so many still living there who regret the passing of the former regime. But Hanoi would be a different matter, and we knew we would have to be more careful.

Into the communist heartland

Our flight to the northern capital happened to be on the same afternoon as the burial of the recently deceased Cardinal Archbishop of Hanoi, Joseph Marie Trinh van Can. We would like to have been at the funeral but were told that there was no possibility of going on an earlier flight. But at least we had the opportunity to film several hundred priests attending a commemoration Mass for the cardinal in Saigon Cathedral – a most unusual sight in Vietnam. We heard from one of the priests that Cardinal Etchegaray had flown into Hanoi from Rome for the funeral – he is head of the Roman Justice and Peace Commission. An interview with Etchegaray in Vietnam might prove a useful conclusion for our programme.

So we took a taxi from Hanoi airport in or around the evening rush hour and headed straight for the cathedral. On arrival it was difficult to communicate – Hanoi had never had an American presence to force people to learn English. However, I established that the cardinal was somewhere in the office/residential complex beside the cathedral, and wrote a note to him in bad French saying I was a friend of Monsignor Diarmuid Martin, a Dublin priest in Rome who was working under him at the time and who, as a clerical student, spent one summer working with Radharc. By coincidence I had met Diarmuid at Brussels airport on our way out East. When I told him we were going to Vietnam, he mentioned that Etchegaray had visited there six months previously. He also told me that Etchegaray's lodgings – provided by the government – had to be shared with a colony of rats and that the cardinal had got food poisoning. This gave him a lot of problems during the long ceremonies which were an inevitable part of his visit! (Our experience later on was not that different. Peter Kelly got the rats in his room, and I got the diarrhoea.)

After an anxious five minute wait my liaison came back and brought me to the cardinal's simple quarters. I gave the minimum information and asked for an interview.

'I have to leave in ten minutes.'

'Ten minutes will be enough.'

Starting from scratch, three of us rearranged the furniture, erected camera and lights and completed an interview within ... well, say fifteen minutes.

I can't say it was a stunning interview, but he was lively, and including him in the programme was worthwhile. I have never been a great one for going after official representative figures. The convention of the television documentary often requires them to be interviewed because they are where the buck stops. But usually they can only say safe and predictable things.

So here we were in Hanoi. We had got our interview; now we needed some place to stay. The taximan brought us to a hotel for the night which was obviously accustomed to foreigners – most of the guests were speaking Russian. But it wasn't central, and didn't look that clean. We learnt quickly that the best and safest place for us to stay would be in the hotel where the government put visiting diplomatic staff. How could we work that one? Well Mike Kelly, our Jesuit mentor, was a friend of the Australian ambassador to Vietnam, and the ambassador was – according to reports – the Vietnamese government's favourite diplomat. He had encouraged good relations between Vietnam and Australia and had been generally positive and helpful to the government. So we made an urgent call to the embassy.

The ambassador was shocked, and groaned in dismay when he heard we were making television programmes in Vietnam without permission, and was naturally reticent about getting too much involved with us. However, he gave us a short but carefully worded letter of recommendation which Mike used to great effect at the diplomatic hotel. I think it wasn't anything the letter said so much as the Australian embassy address at the top and Mike's confident blustering that was the overriding factor in getting us by. Anyway he won the day and we got the rooms, a successful outcome which in the end proved more important than we realised at the time.

Staying in a hotel for foreign diplomats, we had to presume that the rooms were bugged, so we were very careful never to talk in our rooms about our business. I hope nobody wasted too much time recording and translating our conversations on such non-political subjects as the weather, Australian rugby and Gaelic football.

Keeping a low profile

We were naturally more careful filming in Hanoi than we had been down South, but still had some frights. The first was when we tried to get permission to visit a coastal village – without of course mentioning anything about filming. Not only did this prove impossible but the police discovered we were in Hanoi, whereas our visa only gave us permission to visit Ho Chi Minh City, and that as simple tourists. Much protestation of innocence, breast beating and a contribution of $150 straightened that one out. We were very thankful to leave the police station without too many questions being asked about what we were actually doing in Hanoi.

Another occasion was a dinner with a friend of Mike's, an Australian doctor who was in Vietnam with a film crew from an Australian programme, seen also in Europe, called *Beyond 2000*. The doctor had presented some episodes in the past, and now was doing a further series of items for the programme in Vietnam.

The Australians were having an 'end of shoot' dinner, and had invited their 'minders' from the Ministry of Information to a good restaurant – I think there were four of them altogether. 'Minders' are employees of the Ministry of Information who are deputed by the Ministry to accompany film units – supposedly to smooth their path, but in reality to keep an eye on what they are doing.

If I had known in time who they were I would have backed out of the dinner at almost any cost, but by the time I realised it was too late. One of them questioned me across the table about what we were doing in Hanoi and I prevaricated as much as I could. Fortunately then he asked where we were staying and I gave the name of the diplomatic hotel. After that he lost interest. Film crews didn't usually stay there; and we could hardly have been admitted without somebody important vouching for us.

It was only after that little run in that we realised how lucky we were. I have had experience of being saddled with 'minders' from Ministries of Information in other countries, and there is nothing I hate more. It was probably little more than a nuisance for the Australian team who were doing programmes about scientific and medical matters. But we were touching sensitive areas like religion and politics, and a 'minder' could easily have been the kiss of death.

I have pleasant memories of Hanoi. The centre city where we were staying is built around a lake and much of the original French architecture remains, and retains its beauty, even if parts are a bit tattered. There are few taxis about and almost no private cars, and that probably adds to the charm too. Everyone travels by foot or bicycle or cyclo (cycle taxi). We were of course a good mark, paying in dollars, and rapidly were cornered by three smiling cyclo drivers who kept us amused while trying to squeeze out an extra buck.

'You want us to bring you to lovely Miss Vietnam. Very good, very cheap.'

'No', I said, 'I couldn't trust the others not to tell my wife.'

Three cyclos carried three of us and the necessary equipment to all our locations. One of my favourites was the Ho Chi Minh mausoleum and museum.

Ho Chi Minh

The great Ho Chi Minh was a simple man of the people. This simple man is commemorated in Hanoi with a Lenin-style mausoleum complete with endless queues of worshippers. And that we had to photograph.

Over thirty years ago, when the army brought materials to build a museum in his childhood village, Uncle Ho stepped in and ordered the supplies to be used for building a school instead. In recent times the government has been forced to admit that in his last will and testament, Uncle Ho specifically directed that his body be cremated, and not be preserved for public adulation. But his wishes were countermanded by his devoted followers who wanted a shrine where the legend could be forever sanctified.

One wonders what he'd have said were he consulted about the marble and brass museum just completed in time for the centenary of his birth. Here almost every note he wrote, everything he wore or even touched, is lovingly preserved for posterity. The museum itself is an unusual and attractive building which may be of lasting interest; which is perhaps more than can be said of some of the contents.

Roman Catholics are the dominant Christian group in Vietnam, outnumbering others by about forty to one. Their church has been through a tough cleansing.

All mass movements have to have figures to hate as well as to love. In the struggle for independence in Vietnam, the great hate figures were the foreign colonialists – who also happen to have brought a French-style Catholicism which shared the opprobrium. In the words of Fr Phan Khac Tu:

> In the past, the relationship between the Catholic Church and the ruling French colonials was very close. Furthermore, the two last presidents of South Vietnam were Catholic. As a result, the church and the Catholic population were politically very powerful. This close relationship with the colonials brought about an emotional conflict between the Viet Minh and the Catholic Church.

This emotional conflict goes back a long way. The French defeat at Dien Bien Phu in 1954, and the installation of a communist government, caused panic in church circles in the North. Only three years before Dien Bien Phu – the final defeat of the colonial power – the bishops in a public letter had forbidden all co-operation with the Viet Minh, and called Communism evil. Catholic areas provided troops to fight the Viet Minh.

At the same time, the US was trying to bolster up the new Southern Republic of Vietnam. Catholicism's traditional opposition to Communism seemed to suggest the perfect ally. And so the Central Intelligence Agency helped to provide money and transport to assist 600,000 Catholics to migrate to the South.

More than half the Catholic population left the North, and settled along Highway One, the main road leading north out of Saigon. There they built their churches. An observer remarked that it looked as if there was one every hundred yards. A small cowed church remained behind in the North. During the rest of the long war, its members were almost totally cut off from the outside world, and as a consequence were little influenced by the Second Vatican Council. Even today the cathedral in Hanoi takes one back in time, with men on one side of the centre aisle, women on the other. Still, after thirty years of stern Communism, the Masses are well attended, and not only by the elderly.

In general, the church in the South supported the Saigon government, and prospered materially, sharing in American aid. But as time went on, the Thieu regime became more repressive and corrupt. The hierarchy remained silent. They remained silent too when 4.6 million tons of American bombs were poured down on North and Central Vietnam. And so the communist Viet Minh came to see the church as the great ally of their foreign enemies. And when victory came they took a measure of revenge.

In 1990 when we were filming, that was all in the past. Archbishop Nguyen Van Binh of Ho Chi Minh City had become the principal episcopal advocate of Catholic-Communist detente. He said that he saw no reason why a Catholic could not be a good party member. In his Tet, or New Year message shortly after unification, Archbishop Binh said :

> We have to recognise that the revolution is a great opportunity to the whole nation to get rid of injustice and oppression, evils that had degraded man and society. When the Revolution overthrew the old social structures, it also gave Catholics a chance to come closer to the gospel, because the revolutionary situation provides us conditions in which to live more simply, more selflessly, with a greater sense of service.

Fifteen years later, the Bishop of Xûan Lôc, Bishop Nguyen Minh Nhât, put it more simply in an interview for Radharc: 'If we had any faith,' he said, 'we would call what happened in April 1975 a blessing from God.'

The recent history of the church in Vietnam echoes a common thread through church history. The church grows into a powerful political position which it feels bound to defend. Suddenly all its privileges and property are removed. The trauma is great; but the church emerges cleansed and purified – and in important ways, free. And then, alas, the process starts again.

Postscript

The process started again when Cardinal Angelo Sodano, Vatican Secretary of State, sent a letter on 20 May 1992 to Bishop Nguyen Minh Nhât, as President of the Vietnamese Bishops' Conference, telling the bishops that for priests to be members of the Catholic Patriotic Association is against canon law and cannot be reconciled with the obligations of the clerical state. This view would reflect the views of some right-wing Vietnamese bishops, notably the Archbishop of Hue, who has opposed the association since its foundation, and who would have found a more sympathetic ear in Rome when Sodano succeeded Cardinal Casaroli. The Vietnamese government response noted:

At a time when relations between the Vatican and the government were becoming better, this prohibition will certainly be an obstacle ... The Vatican decision is contrary to the Constitution and legislation of Vietnam concerning citizens' rights and human rights. This decision by the government will be communicated to the church of Vietnam.

Just one month after Sodano's letter, the seminary in Ho Chi Minh was due to have its first ordination ceremony for many years. Forty-three students who had completed their studies were to be ordained in the cathedral on June 27th, with several thousand attending the celebrations. On the eve of the ordinations, the authorities withdrew permission for twenty-three candidates. Twenty were ordained two days later in the chapel of the diocesan seminary. Unquestionably this surprise move by the Vietnamese authorities was a calculated response to the letter from the Secretary of State.

13

WOMEN IN ROME

Alarums and excursions at the Synod of Bishops

It was 1980, and we were in Rome for the Synod of Bishops, a structure originally designed to keep the spirit of the Second Vatican Council alive. If the essence of that spirit was bishops working together under the pope in an atmosphere of free expression, to determine church policy and teaching, then the synods held so far have not been a success.

The topic in 1980 was the Christian family. 216 bishops came to Rome for a month, and held discussions under the watchful eye of the Vatican.

Some representatives of the religious orders were present, and fifteen married couples invited by the pope as auditors, which meant they could listen, but had no right to vote or speak. The fifteen couples were led by Dr and Mrs Billings, of natural family planning fame, and all represented the same tradition, albeit they came from different parts of the world .

A group of American women who felt, as they said themselves, that 216 unmarried men were not fully qualified to make decisions about the Christian family, also came to Rome to lobby the participants – lobbying is of course a very American tradition. They were perforce confined to cornering bishops on the streets or in their hotels or lodging houses, because admission to the synod is confined strictly to the invited participants.

The women came to Rome on their own vacation time and at their own expense. They tried earnestly to communicate to the bishops their feelings and attitudes about the matters being discussed at the synod and in particular their views about the inferior role of women in the church, and how that role might be changed. They talked to us in Radharc about their experiences and their frustrations.

DOLLY: One of the bishops said to us 'We're not talking about women's rights, were talking about the dignity of women', and somebody else said to him, 'What is dignified about being discriminated against, what is dignified about being treated as second class? Women in the church have been abused – we are doormats!' It has been said that when the pope came to the United States, he may have got things a little confused. He kissed the ground and walked on women. And I think that is very much the attitude of the church: as long as we are willing to stay in our place and to do what we're supposed to do, then we're very welcome, we're appreciated. But otherwise forget it!

ADA MARIA: I was just asking a bishop a little while ago 'How seriously do you take the laity?' And they always say yes, they take us seriously, but I think that the fact that they do not do anything to change structures which effectively keep the laity and women out of the decision making process makes me question how seriously they take us.

DOLLY: I don't think that women have had any say in the bishops' deliberations at the synod. The bishops get very defensive about any number of questions, particularly in this synod on *Humanae Vitae*. But then when we look at the lay people who are representing the rest of us in the church, they're not at all representative of any people that we know.

MARIA MASCARENHAS: This morning we were told that there are over 2,300 women religious superiors in the world, and they have only two (non-voting) representatives at the synod!

DOLLY: My question is, when mostly only male celibates are the ones that are, quote, 'the official theologians of the church,' how can you have an adequate theology of sexuality?

ADA MARIA: In our church jurisdiction is tied to Holy Orders. You have a vote and a full voice in the church only when you are a priest and eventually become a bishop and so forth. So as long as women do not have the possibility of participating through Holy

Orders in the decision making process of the church, I think we will just continue to be second class citizens.

DOLLY: I think that the time when the bishops sit together in synod, or the pope sits alone on his chair and decides for us, for anybody, is past. And the sooner the hierarchy learns that the better it's going to be; because people are not listening. This synod has meant nothing to the Catholic people of the United States. Very few people know it even exists, that it happened. So I think that if the church has to find that out, then it will find it out the hard way, I am afraid.

The women did find some sympathetic listeners among the bishops: Archbishop Hurley of Durban, South Africa, for instance – one of the important figures at the Vatican Council – was sympathetic to their views. He made a good point in the programme from his own experience:

It always makes a big difference to have people in a discussion who have an area of experience that others don't have. In South Africa, in the Catholic Church, if you go back about ten years, there wasn't much representation of black priests or black bishops – or black lay people for that matter. So it was a case of the whites trying to discuss what was best for the blacks. But since the number of black bishops and prominent black priests and lay leaders has increased, and taken a larger part in our discussions on church issues, well a whole new area of experience has been opened up. The conclusions of our discussion are very often vastly different now because they are conclusions relating to the lived experience of people who have suffered – whereas in the past we could only try to imagine their suffering.

Archbishop (later Cardinal) Godfried Daneels of Malines in Belgium was also aware of growing problems:

In the past, the relationship between the church and the workers has been characterised by a credibility gap. Also the relationship between the church and the intellectuals. But if there were to be a further credibility gap between the church and women, it would have very drastic consequences. And I think that some young women and young mothers are leaving the church silently, and this would be the most deep and dangerous haemorrhage in the history of the church.

And how does the pope see the role of women? René Laurentin, a theologian of moderate views, well known for his writings on mariology, was in Rome for the synod. He gave us his opinion:

> The pope is not at all misogynist in his speeches and writing, but at the same time I have the distinct impression that, on this point as on many others, he is not a modern man. That is to say I don't think the promotion of women in civil or professional life interests him terribly. And despite the opinion of a certain number of important theologians and laymen, who say 'after all, why not women priests?' – to that there is an absolute 'niet'. It is an absolute 'niet' because the pope is an essentially traditional pope.

The whole issue of women in the church has, of course, hotted up since 1980, and we returned to it later in another programme with the somewhat mischievous title 'Revolting Sisters' of which I tell the story in the next chapter. For the moment, however, I would like simply to set out some thoughts on the workings of the synod itself.

When bishops criticise the Roman synods they seem to do so on the following grounds:

1. *There is no freedom to introduce relevant issues*

The freedom of the bishops during the 1980 synod was to a great extent preempted by the pope in a series of talks at public audiences, from September 1979 onwards, which outlined his own views on marriage, the family and human sexuality. I attended one of the audiences which attracted press attention because the pope spoke about the possibility of a man committing adultery with his wife! I must confess that the heavy Polish accent coming over the loudspeakers repeating the same text over and over again in different languages, with words like 'concupiscence' and 'sexuality' recognisable in every version, seemed to me out of place in the hubbub of a public audience in St Peter's Square. However maybe I am squeamish. Anyway nobody seemed to be listening – which seems the norm with many of John Paul's public discourses where people come to enjoy the occasion rather than listen to instruction. He never seems to notice

– or maybe he doesn't mind, because they are written more for the record than for the average audience of pilgrims.

At the synod itself, Archbishop Quinn of San Francisco, President of the US Bishops Conference, proposed that the birth control issue should be discussed. His suggestion was brushed aside, and when the media portrayed him as challenging the pope he backtracked and fell into silence.

Cardinal Hume, fresh from the National Pastoral Conference in Liverpool, was also under pressure from his constituency to raise the matter at the synod. He steeled himself to do so before coming to Rome, but in the end he got nowhere. An anonymous American bishop, striding out of the Synod Hall, was reportedly asked whether there would be any discussion on birth control, and replied over his shoulder as he fled, 'Not in the lifetime of this Polack!'

The Tablet summed up the concluding remarks made by Pope John Paul at the synod as 'little more than an echo of what were foregone conclusions virtually imposed on a so-called consultative body'.

In 1990, after several other synods, Cardinal Aloisio Lorscheider of Fortaleza in Brazil, said simply that the original hope that the synod would be a decision-making body realising collegiality in the spirit of the Second Vatican Council had failed.

2. *Bishops have no say in the organisation of the synods*

After the first synod, the organisation was gradually taken over by the Roman curia. Pope John Paul put Archbishop Tomko, a fellow Slav, in charge of the 1980 Synod on the Family. Central control is exercised in four ways: by strategic appointments of members and officers, by imposing secrecy, by censoring the material that supposedly comes out of the deliberations, and by writing the final document.

Take the appointments: the pope appoints the permanent Secretary General of the synod who appoints the staff to service the synods. Opus Dei is said to be currently well represented. Presumably on the advice of the secretariat, the pope also nominates up to 15% of the bishops who attend any synod. More importantly he appoints the three co-presidents and two synod secretaries. Pretty well all his appointments must be rated 'conservative'.

The two co-presidents appointed to the 1987 Synod on the Laity were the Vietnamese Cardinal Joseph Marie Trinh van Can of Hanoi and the Ukrainian Cardinal Myroslav Lubachivsky. One reputable source said it would have been hard to find two men in the world more isolated from the stream of Catholic life. I don't know about the Ukrainian, but I do know something about the Archbishop of Hanoi – I was in his cathedral in May 1990, the day he was buried. Men sat on one side of the church and the women sat on the other, and if anyone of the clergy had heard of Vatican II they kept quiet about it. The cardinal had not left his diocese for twenty-something years, and in the end declined to come to the synod.

The laity appointed to attend the Synod on the Laity were also streamed in a predictable way. A member of the Legion of Mary was invited to represent the Irish Laity – Cardinal Ó Fiaich was not consulted and had to be introduced to his own country's representative!

3. *The bishops have no say in drawing up the final report*

The views expressed at the synod go through a curial sieve which eliminates anything which the Holy Father might not agree with. The pope writes his own report which appears some months later when the enthusiasm aroused by the meeting has all but disappeared.

According to *The Tablet,* the synod of 1980 was a particular disappointment:

> The bishops came to Rome and voiced the concerns of their people in an exhilarating spirit of freedom and honesty. Yet the pope's concluding address seemed to take little account of their deliberations, and a year later the papal document *Familiaris Consortio* contained no allusion to a number of recommendations the bishops had made.

Reviewing the situation in 1990, Cardinal Lorscheider voiced deep dissatisfaction with the way the synod is organised. The opening week of general discussion, he said, provided a 'rich panorama' of what was going on in the church. The discussions in different language groups were excellent. The trouble started at the next stage when the replies from the discussion groups were 'processed' by the curia, so that many bishops didn't recognise anything they said in the final propositions.

4. *The synod is weighed down by imposed secrecy*

The Synod on the Laity in 1987 provided a case-history of determined, but largely unsuccessful attempts to impose secrecy.

Many conferences of bishops around the world took trouble to consult the laity before making their submissions to the synod. However, they were forbidden to show that submission to their flocks! *The Tablet* was particularly scathing:

> It is lamentable that the human right to proper information – which Vatican II earned praise by vindicating – is not taken in Rome to stretch to this modest instance. Just when Gorbachev has discovered that a system cannot run effectively without openness, Rome decides that the laity are to know nothing of what the world's bishops are thinking and saying about their role in the church. It is hoped that this procedure is not designed to protect Roman bureaucrats who have already decided what the synod should say, and would not wish publication of the bishops' submissions to betray a divergence.

Episcopal delegates to the synod were told not to give press conferences, apart from the official (and non-informative) conferences organised by the secretariat.

After the discussions, the bishops were warned that to show the final documents to anyone, even to the lay people attending the synod, or even to photocopy them would be a 'grave sin'! The documents were the personal property of the Holy Father, and if they were published it would not leave the pope free to write his own document in six or eight months time!

Needless to say, some bishop or other must have had different views about what was or was not 'a grave sin' because copies of the documents did reach the better known journalists. And by a process of comparing first draft with final documents, they did expose the curial manipulation. For instance, the first version said that the ministry of serving at the altar and reading the lessons at Mass should be open to women. But everyone knows the pope doesn't like to see women on the altar, so this was cut out of the final document.

The reporting of the synod is manipulated

Fr F.X. Murphy ('Xavier Rynné'), who is credited with one of the important books on the Vatican Council, was one of the theologians we interviewed on film. 'The material the Press Office gives out,' he said, 'is very definitely censored. They have censored some of the speeches of the fathers of the synod for example. You cannot blame the press office for that – that comes from curial control.'

We came across an example of curial control in regard to a speech by Archbishop Hurley of Durban. Hurley made a speech at the synod designed to help find a way out of the problems raised by the church teaching that contraception was intrinsically evil. He told us about his ideas a day or two later in an interview:

> According to the moral theology that I was reared on, the taking of human life is not intrinsically evil. A human life can be taken in self defence, in the so-called just war situation, and in countries where capital punishment for murder or for some other heinous crime is permitted. So the taking of human life is not intrinsically evil. Yet people will say that the exercise of one vital faculty like human reproduction, if that is artificially limited, is intrinsically evil. So there seems to be a lack of balance between these two applications of the idea of intrinsically evil.

This idea was considered by the bishops present to be a significant contribution, at least to the extent that Archbishop William Barden spoke about it in the Irish Dominican house in Rome where we were staying, thus alerting us to the intervention. We looked up the report of the synod in the *Osservatore Romano*, the Vatican's newspaper, the following day. There was no mention of any intervention by Archbishop Hurley. So we went to the Vatican Press Office to ask for a copy of the speech. They had no record of any speech by Hurley. So we asked the archbishop himself when we later met him. He had only a few notes, because he had handed in his text to the Press Office so they would have an accurate copy! That is what is called news management.

While on the subject of the *Osservatore*, it's worth mentioning what Pope Paul VI thought about it. 'This newspaper,' he said 'does not present what happens, but what it would like to happen.' Peter Hebblethwaite, another of our interviewees, was a little stronger in his comments:

All its polemical articles, its editorial articles, always defend the most conservative positions. I mean – even being generous about how one defines 'conservative'. It is as though there were no other voices in the church except one sort of voice, and that all the others were made up by longhaired, irresponsible, probably sexually deviant intellectuals – this is the world picture you get reading *Osservatore's* editorial articles.

The future of the synod

Most bishops seem unhappy in private about the synods and would like to see the structure re-organised. However, they try to be optimistic in public, and when they report to their flocks they usually find something edifying to say. Archbishop Chiasson of Moncton in Canada, however, if one is to judge by a report in the *Toronto Star* 30 October 1987, was one of the few to tell his flock what he really thought:

The synod, he said, produced nothing of significance for Canada's eleven million Catholics. He felt deceived, he said, by a system that made dialogue impossible: Bishops were lectured instead by the Vatican bureaucracy. The group of sixty non-voting lay auditors was packed with directors of right-wing groups who neither challenged nor questioned the bishops. The synod's message to the world was paternalistic and full of platitudes. Proposals accepted in the working group of which he was a member were omitted from the final draft. And so on.

A postscript on the Synod on the Family

One amusing side issue in the Synod on the Family arose when Cardinal Palazzini, the man then in charge of canonising saints, was asked why the list of the sanctified included so few married people.

An endless list of founders and foundresses of religious orders clog the calendar. And even a brief analysis clearly shows that it was always a great advantage for a candidate to be Italian, Spanish, or French, and in recent years, Polish. Palazzini replied:

It is true that few married lay people have been canonised in the past, but today that situation is changing; and it is useful to be reminded of all those saints who, without being mothers or fathers, worked for the spiritual and material good of the family.

This comment caused a certain amount of merriment among the bishops. But Palazzini wasn't fazed at all . 'Even if there weren't very many married saints,' he said, 'some of the servants of God he was considering canonising had been widows or widowers before they entered religious life,' and – clinching the argument – 'ultimately every saint comes from a family'.

And there wasn't even a twinkle in his eye!

14
REVOLTING SISTERS
About the sin of patriarchy – and women priests

It was 1985 and the National Assembly of Religious Women (NARW for short) was having its annual conference in Los Angeles, California. We arrived during a session – four men – and stood uncertainly at the back of the conference hall waiting for it to finish. After ten minutes a woman came over to us.

'If you'd tell me who you are, it would help me control my feelings of aggression.' Not the best start, but things improved after that!

Around the back of the hall there were tables displaying conference literature. One of these caught my eye – it had a box of paper money. St Thérèse of the Child Jesus might be a bit surprised to find herself replacing George Washington on a fake dollar bill, but that indeed is who it was. To the side of her portrait we read that St Thérèse was the patroness of equality for women in ministry. 'She felt called to be a priest in a church that would not test her call. She prayed for death at twenty-four, the age of ordination, so she could celebrate in heaven at the age men could celebrate the eucharist on earth.' News to me, although I wouldn't have expected to find that in the pious biography given to me as a child.

The bogus bank note is issued by the Women's Ordination Conference (WOC). This name was thought preferable to 'Council for the Ordination of Women' (COW) one of the committee members explained with a tiny smile!

The currency is meant to be used. Catholic feminists are encouraged to drop the note on the plate during the Sunday collection. This gesture is intended to let the local priest know that some in his congregation want to protest at the dominant role of men in Catholicism and the exclusion of women from church life – including ordination to the priesthood.

NARW boasts that most of the participants are drawn from the 'grassroots' level of church membership. So the nuns that spoke were unlikely to be Reverend Mothers, (and maybe unlikely to ever become Reverend Mothers), while the lay women were unlikely to be leading lights in traditional parish councils. That did nothing to prevent a lively, sometimes strident, but always good humoured conference.

The theme was 'The politics of the struggle against patriarchy in the church'. Patriarchy was, as the Americans would say, the 'buzz word' at NARW. Maureen Fiedler explained:

> Patriarchy is the tendency of men to want to make decisions for women rather than operating on an equal basis with them, and equal participation in decision-making in their lives. And that's the fundamental problem. And we define it as sin – frankly.
>
> We believe it's the very first kind of domination that the world experienced, and it's the one on which all other kinds of domination are modelled – whether it's the white race over the black race or the first world over the third world, whatever kind of domination there is has been modelled on this.
>
> The members of 'Priests for Equality' – close on 2,000 priests – have endorsed equality, and want to be part of the struggle, and just as I for example, even though I am not black, want to end apartheid in South Africa and want to do what I can, so they want to be a part of the struggle for women in the church too. I think that women who are developing a feminist theology and are trying to understand their oppression are in many ways closer in touch with the message of Jesus, who I think was really sent, as he said in Luke, to set the captives free.

Over the past twenty years or so, the American bishops have been increasingly jolted by the outspoken views of American women. So in 1982, they decided to take the bull (!) by the horns and write a pastoral letter on 'Women'. Some of the women attending the conference had been meeting the bishops about the pastoral.

Ruth Fitzpatrick described herself as a housewife with three children and a split level house in Virginia. She drives a station wagon, has a family dog, and a husband retired from the military. Both come from an Irish Catholic background. She was one of the women delegates who met the bishops.

We felt really good because we had come up with a strategy that was different from what they expected. We decided that rather than a group of three women sitting and testifying at the end of one long table with all the bishops at the other end, we would break up into one woman, one bishop. We moved round the room very fast so they had to talk one-to-one. We told them our stories, woman to man – so they couldn't sit back and smoke their cigars, they couldn't leave the room to go to the men's room, they had to relate to us one to one.

What did you tell them?

I told them that I had observed that only now when there were Hispanic and black bishops, was the bishop's pastoral on racism able to say that racism is a sin. But there is no woman bishop who can get up there and say 'you must realise and you must say sexism is a sin'. And until they have women who are bishops, for them to write a pastoral on women I said was the utmost arrogance.

We were told we were supposed to talk to the bishops about questions within the teachings of the Catholic Church. Now they did invite the Women's Ordination Conference, and talked with them on the issues of ordination. They did not however invite people to come and talk to them about the issue of birth control and other sexuality issues in the Catholic Church.

Women were lectors at Mass in one parish in Virginia and the Pastor said, 'No woman can read at Mass.' And they said, 'Well, we'll put on some choir robes.' And the priest said, 'No, because the men in the pews will still be imagining what's under those choir robes.' Now our comment was: 'Well what does he say about all the women when the pastor is up there with his chasuble on?' That's the kind of mentality – you just can't win on some things.

Marge Tuite was a big-boned Dominican sister with a deep resonant laugh you could hear at the other end of the room.

The bishops in the US have written two other pastorals. One is on racism. They did not write on black people, they wrote on racism. They wrote another one on the economy. They did not write on poor people, they wrote on the issue of economic justice. Why in the world are the bishops in the United States writing on women and the lives of women instead of on the issues of sexism and patriarchy?

Dolly Cominsky wasn't one to hide her light under a bushel.

It is possible for a woman to become pope. A lay person can become pope. Therefore it is possible for a lay woman to become pope. I can foresee that possibility – definitely. I would run for the office of pope. Now that doesn't quite sound right, but we can call it an office, and yes I am interested in running. I think I would do a better job than Pope John Paul.

Kay Eaton is a mother with twelve children. Her husband had retired recently so she is in what she calls a reverse role marriage – where it is his turn now to cook and look after the family. We asked her what she wanted of the clergy:

I want to join them. And I want them to look at themselves and see where they may have been part of this sexism in the church that we are addressing here. The priests in my own parish know that I support women's ordination. And one of my own priests said, 'Well Kay, do you really want to get up at two in the morning and go to the hospital on a sick call?' And I said to him, 'Father, I've been getting up at two in the morning with baby's bottles for many years, so day or night doesn't make much difference to me. I've got the practice!'

Pauline Turner was one of the many women present who seemed unhappy with their parish liturgies.

It's always presided over by a person who is not someone that the community has chosen as its president – it is someone appointed again from above – no matter what we would wish. And this person more often than not will use non-inclusive language from which we women, as daughters of the same Father/Mother God, feel excluded.

The subsequent history of the pastoral on women

Archbishop Thomas Kelly, of Louisville, Kentucky, said about the bishops' pastoral on women, 'I don't recommend being an American man trying to interpret American women to Roman men'.

The fourth draft of the pastoral finally died in 1992 – the first time a pastoral theme was abandoned by the US hierarchy. The pastoral became a dead letter when it changed from being about women's concerns to being about what the Vatican would permit the US hierarchy to say about women's concerns. By the time all questions related to sexual ethics and participation in ministry were removed from consideration, there wasn't that much left to write about.

Most of the time the majority of American bishops themselves didn't know what was going on – they knew there were criticisms by the Vatican of the second and third drafts, but they had no idea what these criticisms were. It seems the small drafting committee was forbidden by Rome to talk even to the other bishops about the Vatican criticisms of their proposed pastoral!

A feminist liturgy

As part of our programme, we were allowed to film a feminist liturgy. It was held in a large canteen, draped with embroidered hangings which some of the participants had made specially for the meeting. People sat at small tables for most of the service, but at times they stood up and joined hands and sang. The liturgy had a structure similar to a Mass, although only similar – there was no attempt to pretend it was a full eucharist. However, there was the blessing and breaking and sharing of bread, with readings and intercessions and a kind of Eucharistic Prayer.

The blessing prayer was read by one woman at each table.

> The hope is in women everywhere, who break bread together without benefit of clergy – confident that God will indeed send the Spirit to make holy the bread of affliction, transforming it into the bread of affirmation; and to sanctify the cause of their suffering, transforming it into the cup of salvation – the hope is

in our incarnation of God herself in the resurrection of our very bodies here and now.

On Jesus's last night with his friends, he took bread and giving thanks he broke it and gave it to them saying: this is my body given for you, do this in remembrance of me.

Since the time of Jesus, many women have shed their blood and given their bodies for their acts of courage, from women of the early Christian era to women of South Africa and Central America today. In sharing this bread we are in covenant with them. We will continue their work as voices for justice. In sharing this bread we remember the radical nature of the life of Jesus. We take sustenance and celebrate the boldness of building a community of hope.

One interesting statistic which we discovered in the making of the programme was that, when it came to academic qualifications, America's 100,000 nuns were academically far ahead of not only the priests but also the American bishops. 25% of nuns held doctorates, while only 10% of bishops were similarly qualified. Which leads to an interesting situation. A priest who has never been to college may freely preach sermons. A woman with a double doctorate in theology may not preach – because she is a woman. She could, I suppose, write a book of sermons to help the less well educated clergy.

Women and ministry

The Vatican and women

Pope John Paul invited Fr Joseph Fessio of San Francisco to the 1987 Synod on the Laity, so he must think well of him. The pope normally invites bishops, not priests. More than that, Fr Fessio was made a theological assistant responsible for furthering the theme of women in the synodal discussions – together with a West German gentleman, said to be a member of Opus Dei.

Fr Fessio circulated informally a seven page paper which he wrote in reply to recommendations made by some synod delegates that certain non-ordained ministries should be open to women.

'Doctrinal grounds exist which argue against women being admitted to the exercise of those ministries most directly concerned with the sacrifice of the altar,' Fr Fessio wrote. 'The acolyte or altar server, for instance, becomes as it were the hands of the priest.' For a woman to act as acolyte would 'be in serious disharmony with the very nature and character of the whole order of grace and redemption.' If the re-evaluation of the Sacred Word is thought through to its conclusion, he said, 'it would raise questions about the appropriateness even of women exercising the role of reader'. There is, he believed a logical progression 'from altar boy to acolyte to lector to priest'. If women were admitted to any of these offices, 'it may give them false hope of becoming priests. Allowing them on the altar is unfair to women because it can only end in frustration for them'. Any change would be interpreted by feminists as a sign of weakness on the part of the church. 'Besides', he said, it would 'create an identity problem for a girl and affect vocations, since many boys would not want to be servers if girls were too.'

Very interesting!

Fr. Fessio was naturally confused and upset when the Vatican reversed its position on girl servers in 1994.

The arguments against women priests

1. Christ chose only men as his apostles. He must have done this deliberately, and we have no right to question his action because that would be to question his authority.

Response: Leaving aside the nuances that might be introduced by scripture scholars concerning the subject of apostles, one can fairly point out that Christ challenged the general attitude to women in his time, and even caused eyebrows to be raised among his own followers, to say nothing of the Jewish leaders. But the customs and attitudes of the times made it difficult to appoint women as apostles. To have women leave their homes and roam the world preaching, founding, and governing churches was not a real option in the circumstances of the time. But times have changed.

2. The church, in fidelity to the example of the Lord, does not consider herself authorised to admit women to priestly ordination. In other words, there is an unbroken tradition of 2,000 years. And that must say something.

Response: This argument is negative and inconclusive. The position of women is now very different from what it was at any time during that 2,000 years. So the question didn't arise before. Now it has arisen. And there would need to be better arguments against it. (Women didn't have the vote for a long time either!)

3. The priest acts *in persona Christi*, an expression used by St Paul in 2nd Corinthians. Therefore he has to be male.

Response: The priest at the altar addresses Christ, and therefore must be acting on behalf of the church, which includes male and female. Christ himself in taking flesh had to take one form, but was in solidarity with all humankind, male and female.

4. The church is entitled to say that, in accordance with its under-standing of its mandate from the Lord, one ministry is closed to women. Ministry follows on a calling by Christ. It is not anybody's right.

Response: Women feel called by Christ to the priesthood, just as men do. So one must ask the question: Could the church not have misunderstood its mandate in excluding women from answering this call?

5. The character conferred by the sacrament implies maleness in the priest.

Response: Who says so? Why should Holy Orders have a single sex character and baptism have a character applicable to both? Women can become prophets and saints and mystics and spiritual directors and abbesses and engage in ministry. Why not priests?

In addition there are of course other positive arguments or shades of arguments. The supporters of the ordination of women always quote Galatians 3:28 which speaks of there being neither male nor female, but all are one in Christ. Ordaining women would highlight this truth that God includes within himself the fullness of what it means to be male and female. And maybe help to communicate more of the feminine side of divine love.

The decision of the Churches of Ireland and England to ordain women

The present papal administration has shown no inclination to accept Anglican orders as valid – though some Catholic theologians in the 1970s were predicting a change. However, the Vatican still sticks by the hundred-year-old encyclical, *Apostolicae Curae,* which denies the validity of their ordination. Oddly enough, this intransigence probably encouraged the Anglicans to move on the question of the ordination of women, for some among them said that if the Roman church refuses to accept the validity of the male Anglican priesthood, what odds if they reject the female priesthood as well!

Could the ordination of women ever come about in the Roman church?

The ordination of women could only begin to be considered if a pope were elected who was sympathetic to the idea. It certainly won't happen under John Paul II, who by conviction is totally opposed to it. In that belief he joins some unusual company. Yves Congar, one of the great liberal theologians at Vatican II, tells us in his book, *Conversations,* that he personally subscribes to the Roman document against the ordination of women to presbyterate and episcopate – so opposition crosses the liberal/conservative divide. In the longer term, change might become more likely if future popes were to come to terms with a collegial church. The bishops in council or synod might be more sympathetic to considering change than the Roman curia.

Authority and ministry

I think the exclusion of women from participation in decision-making in the church is much more significant than exclusion from ministry, and might prove a less controversial area to begin to bring about change.

The *Annuario Pontificio,* which I have beside me, contains, I estimate, about 23,000 names in the index. Approximately 1% are women, mostly consultors to unimportant commissions. In the case of religious orders of men, some of whom have as few as seven members, the name of the superior is always given in the *Annuario.* In the case of orders of women, some of which have up to 10,000 members, the name of the superior is never given. One cynic suggested that this must be on the principle that since one never needs to discuss anything with women, there is no need to know their names.

There seems no reason why a woman couldn't be a cardinal, although without ordination it's difficult to see how she could be pope (because by definition the pope is successor of St Peter as Bishop of Rome). When somebody once said to the late Frank Sheed, the lay theologian and publisher (who with his wife Maisie Ward, founded Sheed and Ward), that he might be made a cardinal, he replied that there would be no Frank Cardinal Sheed without Maisie Cardinal Ward: which may be why there was no Cardinal Sheed!

There seems to be reasonable evidence that St Brigid of Kildare and her successors as abbesses exercised jurisdiction similar to that of a bishop, and appointed priests and even bishops to carry out the sacramental ministry. Other examples, like St Hilda of Whitby, suggest that this practice was not unusual in the Celtic church. So it appears that ministry – that is baptising, confirming and ordaining – was once separated from ruling and administration. And that some women, without ordination, still exercised considerable power in our ancestral church.

This separation of jurisdiction and ministry is, after all, a perfectly ordinary arrangement in other areas of life. Hospitals are set up and run by government officials and administrators – people without the skills to cure the sick by surgery or medicine. Medical doctors, surgeons and nurses are employed for that purpose. One doesn't need medical qualifications to make a good Minister of Health. Why should one need ordination to share in the exercise of authority in the church?

Women will always have a genuine grievance so long as they have no say in decision-making in the church. So this issue won't go away and must sometime be settled. And the sooner the better. But so far as admission to the ministerial priesthood is concerned, I think this is a much less serious concern. And where it raises so many problems – not least of which is the ecumenical question vis-à-vis the Orthodox Church – then I think the matter should be set aside for the immediate future. St Brigid was content, it seems, to have had some say in the appointment of priests and bishops, without trying to become one herself.

15

LIKE JEREMIAH,
I AM A VERY RELUCTANT PROPHET

Fr Albert Nolan reflects on God in the context of
South Africa, while the Vatican reflects on Fr Nolan

Albert Nolan is fourth generation Irish, and the most widely-read theologian ever to come out of South Africa. He went to school with Irish Dominican sisters, and became a Dominican priest. Ivory tower theology never interested him – his life-work has been devoted to the study of theology in context, his own context, which is the struggle against oppression in South Africa. He lectures, and writes books, and his writings are interesting enough to be picked up by international publishers and translated into many different languages, including Chinese.

Fr Nolan became Provincial of the Dominican Order in South Africa, and in that capacity attended the Chapter in 1983 which was due to elect a Master General for the entire Order, with its seven thousand members.

Most of the assembled Provincials would have known Albert only from his writings, but clearly they were impressed because they chose him to be their next Master General. He asked to be allowed to decline the nomination – the first time anybody could remember that happening in the history of the Dominican Order. So they chose an Irishman, Fr Damian Byrne instead. And why did he turn it down, so important a position?

I argued that there was very important work to be done in South Africa. There were not very many of us to do that work. It was a work that has significance, I think, far beyond South Africa because there was a form of oppression and racism that was being carried out in the name of Christianity and it had therefore to be contradicted by Christianity. Every single one of us Dominicans who were in a position to do that, and who understood the situation and could do it, should be there doing it, while other people could be master generals of religious orders. It's not a career thing, it's not a question of status, it's a question of where can each of us most effectively preach the gospel. When this was explained, the Chapter agreed. I am quite convinced that Damian Byrne, who was then elected, has done far more good than I could ever have done in those circumstances.

I don't think our film portrait of Albert Nolan was a great cinematic success, or that it made very popular viewing. But people who still like to hear interesting ideas were not, I think, disappointed. Some morsels from which to pick and choose.

Crucifixion today

The instrument that is used to make other people suffer, to control them, to keep them down as it were, is not crucifixion today – not like the cross was in Roman times. Today they would use tear gas, they would use rubber bullets, they would use chains to put people in prison, and now in more recent times they use even more subtle methods. They will get people to kill one another, organise that this one will be angry with that one and they'll starting fighting one another, so you don't even have to go in and crucify them, you get them to crucify one another. So there are different instruments of torture and oppression today – different from the cross.

Jesus and apartheid

Everybody suffers in some measure, but some people's suffering is so great, is so deep, is so continuing that I think the rest of us who don't suffer anything like that cannot even imagine what their kind of life is like. So what happens in fact is that the people of power, the people of money, don't want to even look at such horrific suffering. They don't know what to do about it, don't want to think about it – so what they do is hide it away. And South Africa did that very effectively with the system called 'apartheid' where you divided the sufferers from the people who had a lot of

228

money and luxury, so one didn't even see the suffering, it didn't have to be a problem for you.

On sitting on the fence

Now some people think you should sit on the fence and be neutral, but you can't be neutral in circumstances like this. When one person is sinning against another person it's impossible for a Christian to be neutral, and if you try to be neutral you are enabling the sin to continue. Therefore I am saying we must be against the sin and the sinner and the sin of the sinner, and on the side of the victim of the sin.

Romanticising the poor

Gustavo Gutiérrez has said that what he's learned most of all from the poor is their joy. And I think that is true. But I don't think one should romanticise the poor, or romanticise this way of life in the South African townships. It's certainly true that people in crisis situation like this – and every day is a crisis here – are able to love one another, to help one another, to sacrifice for one another, and one sees heroism of that kind here. But the whole way of life does dehumanise you. And the result is that sometimes people do very bad things as well in these circumstances. There's nothing romantic about this. This is the result of sin. This is wrong. This must be removed. This must be changed.

The gospel as good news

The gospel – as the very word itself says – is supposed to be good news. And one of the things that I've been very concerned about is that it doesn't often come across as good news. In fact it comes across very frequently as bad news, it comes across as something you have to accept, the kind of wet blanket, as they often say, preventing you from doing the things that you would like to do, and promising you hell if you do them – that sort of thing. And what we've been trying to do is to recover this element of good news in the gospel so it is something that people can receive joyfully and be pleased about, something that gives them hope. I suppose we're more aware of that need because there are people in our country who are desperately in need of the good news – they're desperately in need of some hopeful message.

The bible is by and about oppressed people

The bible, to a very large extent, was written by oppressed people; the bible, to a very large extent, is about the suffering of oppressed people. There are twenty different root words in Hebrew that are used throughout the bible for oppression. Now any group of people who have twenty root words for the same thing must talk a great deal about it, it must be a topic that's very close to their hearts. This was not noticed in recent centuries and it was not noticed because the people who were reading the bible didn't share that experience.

Since Constantine, most of the people who have studied the bible, who have written about the bible, interpreted the bible and translated the bible have not been oppressed people. They have been, to a very large extent, the oppressors in fact. They didn't understand that a whole people can feel crushed because they had no experience of being crushed in that way. And especially if we think about European colonialism, which brought Christianity to most of the world, it was people who either had no experience of oppression at all or very little, or were oppressors, or when they were oppressed had no idea they were oppressed – just took it for granted that life was like that. It's only the people who most of all felt oppressed who began to become conscious of that oppression and began to see that the bible was originally written from that point of view, and has a great deal to say about oppression. But it isn't scholarship as such that enables one to see that, but having something of a similar experience, or at least being in close contact with that kind of experience, that enables you to understand what the very words are saying.

Riches

Almost always, throughout the bible, the rich are regarded as the sinners. The bible takes things that are typical of rich people and uses that to describe what sinning is all about. For example, the great sin of pride and arrogance is described as the attitude that rich people have – this feeling of being superior to others, and so forth. And that becomes the way in which that sin is described for ever. Similarly with violence, it's taken for granted that the violent people are rich people. Robbing again – that is understood as what rich people do all the time and you mustn't imitate them. So sins are the characteristics of the rich. And then, on the other side, virtues are the characteristics of the poor. So for example, in Hebrew the word for poor and the word for humble or lowly are the same word. So to be humble is to be like the poor people.

The institutional church

I am not against institutions, nor am I saying that there shouldn't be an institutional church. I am speaking about one's attitude to institutions as institutions – whatever they are. And if one's attitude to the institution, church or whatever, is that it becomes for you more important than people, then you've got a problem. Then you are not following Jesus Christ. When the laws of the church, when the institutions of the church become more important than people, so that these are used in a way that is not for the benefit of the people and crushes people, in fact, then no matter how holy that institution is, it's not following Jesus Christ. Jesus gave us the example of the Sabbath. He was not against the Sabbath, of course not; but when the Sabbath becomes the master and we become the slaves who have to worship that law, then we have misused the Sabbath, then we have misunderstood it. But if the Sabbath is there and we understand it in such a way that it is at our service, it's there to help us as human beings, then the Sabbath is fine. The same with the church.

Obedience and disobedience

Jesus himself was disobedient. He disobeyed many of the laws in the traditional customs of his time. And he had to disobey them in order to obey God. So there are times when the only way to obey God is to disobey some authority that is unjust and that is asking you to do something that's different and contrary to what God is asking. So disobedience is not the problem in that sense. Any idea that to be a Christian you must always be obedient to whatever authority there is, and wherever that authority is, is totally false because Jesus was not like that.

Anger

Anger is another thing that we can see in Jesus himself. And we have a great deal of evidence in the bible that God gets angry. Now there are two kinds of anger, there is anger that's selfish, anger that is destructive, and so forth, and there's an anger that is what's sometimes called a justifiable anger, or indignation, or something like that, which is the opposite side of the coin of compassion. If I am concerned about people, and I see that others are being cruel to people, then I must be angry about that, and must be concerned, and I must express that emotionally. To come along politely and say I don't think you should be so cruel, or I don't think you should torture or kill that person, simply indicates you don't have love for the person being tortured or killed or hurt.

Oppression in the first world

If you ask me where are the victims of any particular society in Europe, I would say they are in other countries, they're in the Third World. The victims of injustice don't have to be in the same country. Economics goes far beyond any national boundary so the people that you're exploiting in Europe are generally in the Third World. But there are poor people in European countries as well, migrant workers for example, Travelling People in Ireland, Blacks, Hispanics who are discriminated against. Then, in almost all our Western European countries, there's the discrimination against women. So you find women are oppressed. Oppression, discrimination, that kind of sin exists in all countries but it takes different forms.

The honorary degree that never was

The University of Fribourg in Switzerland was having a centenary celebration in 1990, and the theological faculty decided that they would like to honour five people with degrees because of their outstanding contribution to theology. Albert Nolan was one of the five. Because Fribourg was a Pontifical University, the nominations had to be approved by the Congregation for Religious Education in Rome. Rome turned down three nominations, Archbishop Rembert Weakland of Milwaukee, (without informing him or giving any reason – for which they had to apologise), a woman theologian and

Albert, neither of whom would have expected to be informed. When we questioned him about it, Albert commented:

The University of Fribourg was very angry, and protested about it, rightly I think. However, I'm a soccer ball in all this. I cannot go to Rome and argue that I ought to get an honorary degree and deserve one; it would be daft for me to do such a thing. So I had to sit and say to the University of Fribourg, OK, you think I ought to get a degree, they think I ought not to get the honorary degree, you'd better fight it out. And that's what they did.

In the end the University decided to honour nobody.

Why don't they like him in Rome?

It's difficult to say why they don't like me. I suppose my manner of doing theology is not the same as their manner of doing theology in Rome. I think whenever you come up with new ideas, questioning, being creative, not only today but throughout the history of the church, there's a tension between the institution and people who are being creative – that has frequently happened before to people like Congar and de Lubac who once upon a time were not in favour, later on are in favour. That's the way the whole thing proceeds. Even in biblical times, one finds those who maintain and preserve the institution and those who are being creative; and either side can be wrong and either side can be right at any particular time. The tension is not a bad one, it's a creative one. Of course, sometimes people on either side do things that clearly are not the will of God, but that kind of creative tension is inevitable, not a problem for me.

If I look into my heart of hearts, I would prefer a peaceful relationship with authority, it makes life so much easier. If sometimes I speak up, I assure you it's not because I like being a rebel, but because I feel that is what I must do, that is what God is calling me to do. And if there's any sense in which that is prophetic, then like Jeremiah I'm a very reluctant prophet, and I wish to God that I didn't have to do it.

The rumour in Rome is that Fr Albert is 'up for the chop'. While apartheid was a big issue, the Holy Office left him alone lest they be accused of abetting the right wing white minority, with whom Albert was distinctly unpopular. But now that apartheid has ended, it should be safe to proceed.

What the inquisition will be about it is a bit early to say. I suspect it will zero in on one of Fr Albert's books, *Jesus before Christianity*. They are taking on a tough man in Albert!

For readers who don't know what I am talking about, I should perhaps explain that the Roman church has an office whose task is to guard the purity of the faith. It used to be called the *Holy Office,* but since the name was associated with disreputable persecution in the past, Paul VI changed it to the *Sacred Congregation for the Doctrine of the Faith.* Lately people have begun to call it the Holy Office again because it is easier to say, and anyway it doesn't seem to have changed that much after all.

Within its portals, curial clerics receive letters of complaint from all around the world about errors in preaching and lectures and articles and books. It is their task then to examine the complaints or the articles or books, and if they judge that there indeed are errors that must be corrected then a process begins. In the case of a priest theologian, it may involve his superior and/or bishop. Superior Generals of religious orders in Rome have told me that nowadays they spend a lot of time and energy going back and forth to the Holy Office dealing with cases relating to their members who are under suspicion of doctrinal aberrations.

Cardinal Ratzinger's apologia

Cardinal Ratzinger is head of the Holy Office. Speaking in Canada in 1986, the Cardinal said that the main task of the church was 'the care for the faith of the simple.' Because a teaching theologian teaches on behalf of the church, 'believers have confidence in the church's word, and so naturally transfer that confidence to those that teach in her name.' Abuse was committed by a teacher who exploited his students by using a position given to him by the church 'to encourage them to accept positions which are opposed to the teaching of the church.'

The penalty of dissent

When the Holy Office takes exception to the views of a theologian holding a teaching chair in a university or faculty controlled by the church, then the theologian either publicly retracts his erring views as specified by the Holy Office, or foregoes his chair. Hans Küng was the first to go in recent times in this way. A more recent *cause célèbre* was that of an American, Fr Charles Curran, who also lost his tenured teaching position at Catholic University in Washington.

Hans Küng made his name at the Vatican Council. He got on well with Paul VI, and according to the *National Catholic Reporter,* Paul minuted Küng's file no 399/57i in the Holy Office archives, 'Treat this man with charity'. (How did NCR know the number?) Curran's case being the more recent, is perhaps the more interesting to dwell on.

The saga of Fr Charles Curran

Curran has always stressed that he did not disagree with any dogmas or defined truths of the Catholic faith. At the same time, he said that he believed it was at times legitimate to dissent in theory and in practice from non-infallible church teaching. He claimed that other respectable American theologians whom he named, shared his view.

As so often nowadays, *Humanae Vitae*, the encyclical on birth control is close to the heart of the problem. In 1968 Fr Curran was the leader of a group of 127 theologians at Catholic University of America who wrote a statement dissenting from the encyclical, which was eventually signed by 1,000 other theologians. He was a marked man after that.

This time (1985-6) when Curran was brought in for inquisition, 739 theologians, including 60 Presidents or heads of departments of Catholic universities signed a petition addressed to the Vatican supporting him. A second petition, with nearly 18,000 signatures, followed from 'The Friends of American Catholic Theology'. The case aroused a lot of anger at the time. (A wealthy American friend of mine, who is not a Catholic and who never heard of Curran, told me recently that she was so annoyed by reading about the case that she made a substantial contribution to his defence fund.) Curran's bishop, Matthew Clark of Rochester, also issued a strong statement in support. Curran's personal life, the bishop said, was exemplary, and his theology was very much of the centre, not of the fringe of the Catholic experience.

Since sexual ethics was the problem, Cardinal Bernadin of Chicago supported a proposal that would allow Curran to retain his tenured position in exchange for an agreement that he would never teach in the area of sexual ethics (a course that anyway he hadn't taught for fifteen years). But the Vatican refused all petitions and compromises. He had to go.

Curran related some of what happened at his two hour meeting with Cardinal Ratzinger in the Holy Office. At one point Ratzinger said that a theologian cannot dissent. Curran spoke in reply about the many other theologians who held similar positions to his own. Ratzinger asked who they were. Curran gave several names including German theologians. Ratzinger replied, 'Well Father, would you want to accuse these people? The Congregation will look into it.' 'Your Eminence, I am here to accuse no one ...'

Although Küng and Curran lost their jobs in Catholic universities, it is important to be clear that they remain priests in good standing. They were not 'defrocked' or anything like that, and both got other jobs outside the Catholic system.

Disquiet about implications in the area of justice and human rights
The encyclical letter, *Pacem in Terris* (Peace on Earth), was in a sense John XXIII's last will and testament. He wrote it when he knew he had only a short time to live. One of its fundamental ideas is that respect for human dignity should provide the basis for much of morality. And while error may have no rights, people who err, do.

John brought about a considerable change in church thinking and policy when, for instance, he said that 'Every human being has the right to worship God in accordance with his own conscience, and to profess his religion both in private and in public'. In saying that, he was flatly contradicting his predecessor Pius IX who proposed the opposite view just one hundred years before. Furthermore, John saw respect for human rights as fundamental to the preaching of the gospel, because the act of believing must be free. And whereas Pius wanted the state to support Catholicism and suppress heresy, John supported the idea of a pluralist democratic society.

But if the church's teaching changed, the actual procedure of the Roman curia does not seem to have kept pace with the change. And here the Holy Office is the worst offender.

1. Normally, in a society where justice is taken seriously, the judge and prosecuting authority are distinct. Not, however, in the Holy Office where the same authority investigates, produces evidence at the trial, appoints defence counsel and prosecutor, judges, and then confirms the sentence.

2. When a case is being prepared against a theologian, the accused is only informed when the process has already been through thirteen stages of the procedure.

3. The accused person not only has no choice as to who is to defend him, but, by the rules, he is never to be informed of his defender's identity.

4. The accused is forbidden access to all documents relating to the charges.

5. Those taking part in the trial are bound to secrecy.

6. There is no right of appeal.

The time the great moral theologian, Bernard Häring, was brought before the Holy Office, he was dangerously ill with throat cancer which necessitated several operations. 'The terrible thing', he said, 'was that they did not stop persecuting me even when I was near death. I believe this to be shameful.' During the war he had been brought before a German military court, but this experience of the Vatican judicial system, he said, was much worse.

Theologians hide in the long grass

One of my abiding memories of Dr Gerry Mitchell, our professor of Dogma in Maynooth way back in the 1950s, was the emotion that came into his voice when he spoke of the Maynooth he knew as a young man, where the whole institution was gripped with fear as a result of the so called anti-modernist oath imposed by Pope Pius X.

The superior of a world-wide religious order told me recently that it was becoming harder nowadays to get bright students to take up the serious study of theology. Why court a life of danger, angst, and distress in the prevailing atmosphere while there were safer things to study which might still be relevant – anthropology or psychology for instance? Furthermore, a study commissioned by Catholic scholarly societies in the US in 1988 reported that Catholic scholars feel alienated from the church and are abandoning research and publication in controversial areas. So whither theology?

In a public statement issued on 11 October 1988, the Association of German-speaking Catholic Dogmatic and Fundamental Theologians complained that the *nihil obstat* necessary for appointment to Catholic faculties of theology had often been refused without those affected being accused of actual divergence from Catholic teaching, or the procedure which led to rejection ever being made clear.

Encouraging a witch-hunt atmosphere

The Cardinal Prefect of the Congregation of Religious is reported as having written to the President of the Union of Superior Generals of Religious Orders saying that the congregation was astonished that in their writing and teaching, religious priests and sisters distanced themselves from the teaching authority of the church without their superiors intervening. The superiors were reminded of their serious responsibility to keep a watching brief on all articles, interviews, journals and books published by their members.

When the Holy Office approached the Superior of the Claretian fathers in 1987, complaining about their Spanish magazine as having a negative view of the church and an anti-institutional bias, the editor was removed, and joint priest-editors put in his place. In November 1988, the joint priest-editors were called in and learned 'with amazement' of their dismissal and replacement by a committee. The editor of the Jesuit equivalent, *Vida Nueva,* was also dismissed in 1987. Three senior journalists then resigned, attributing the changes to pressure from the papal nuncio and Opus Dei, which was criticised in the journal. Three theologians were also removed from their teaching posts at Granada because of their theological views. One could tell many similar stories from other European countries.

A report in *The Tablet,* in October, 1987, stated that Vatican attempts to stifle theological expression are now causing major concern to publishers. One target was a major series on liberation theology. The Italian publishing house (owned by a lay institute) were told they could not publish. In Spain the Paulist *Ediciones Paulinas* were twice summoned to Rome by Cardinal Ratzinger about the same matter.

In January 1990, Pope John Paul II exhorted writers and editors of the respected Jesuit fortnightly, *Civilta Cattolica,* to express Vatican policies and opinions even at the sacrifice of their personal judgement. He assured them that the sacrifices they made in obedience to the pope would not be lacking in spiritual fruits.

The Instruction for Catholic Writers and Publishers, signed by Cardinal Ratzinger and published in 1992, says that religious superiors, even though they are not 'authentic teachers of the faith', have the responsibility of giving permission for the publication of religious material. The superior should not give permission unless he has the 'prior judgement of at least one censor he considers reliable.'

I am old enough to remember this censorial mentality back in the 1950s and 60s, when I was responsible for a magazine which had to be censored every month by a priest appointed by the Dublin Archdiocese. But the practice died in Dublin with the passing of Archbishop John Charles McQuaid. Hopefully it is not on its way back again.

Repeating the mistakes of history

Fr Marie Dominique Chenu was the theological adviser to the French-speaking African bishops at Vatican II. When Pope John XXIII opened the Vatican Council and said that a distinction must be drawn between the substance of the faith, which couldn't change, and its expression, which must change, he could have been quoting from a book written by Chenu – which the Holy Office had put on the Index of forbidden books only twenty years before. At this period, Chenu lost his teaching post, was transferred to Paris, got into trouble again with Rome and was exiled for a few years to Rouen.

In 1962, Pope John XXIII named the German theologian Karl Rahner a Vatican Council *peritus* (expert) – one of seven whose task was to formulate some of the most important draft texts for the council. Six months before his appointment by the pope, the Prefect of the Holy Office had informed Rahner that in future everything he wrote must be submitted to Roman censorship before being published.

One could quote many similar stories: Frs Yves Congar, John Courtney Murray and Henri de Lubac were also casualties of the Holy Office who were rehabilitated only when the bishops at the Vatican Council recognised their worth.

Putting the guns into position

The concerted attempt to corral the theologians has gained momentum in recent years with a number of special measures.

1. Roman rules for Catholic institutes of higher learning

In 1986, Rome prepared norms to govern the work of Catholic institutes of higher learning.

Fr Theodore M. Hesburgh, President of Notre Dame University for many years, and friend of Paul VI and US Presidents, said the proposed document 'might have made sense in a particular Communist or Hitler-dominated scene, but never in a country where freedom is respected and cherished'. According to press reports, the presidents of all the larger Catholic universities in the US and Canada agreed.

2. A new Oath of Fidelity and Profession of Faith

In 1989, Rome introduced a new profession of faith in four parts:

a) The Nicene Creed which we say at Mass every Sunday.

b) A statement of belief in all truths divinely revealed and solemnly defined.

c) A commitment to firmly embrace and retain all and everything which is definitively proposed either about faith or morals by the church.

d) Submission to the teachings which either the Roman Pontiff or the college of bishops enunciate when they exercise the authentic magisterium, even if they proclaim those teachings in an act that is not definitive.

In addition to re-writing the Oath, the Holy Office extended the obligation of taking it to office holders below the episcopate, such as pastors, deans, teachers of faith and morals in universities and others. In the Oath the candidates must swear that they will observe all the laws of the church contained in the Code of Canon Law or in any other official document.

Those who question the need for this new profession of faith point to some of the strange teachings that the scrupulous might feel bound by this profession of faith to submit to. For instance: truths previously declared 'divinely revealed and solemnly defined' include the truth a) that sacramental confession is by divine law necessary for salvation, and b) that anyone who doubts the efficacy of indulgences is automatically excommunicated. So don't expect to find any Protestants in heaven!

As to truths 'definitively proposed' by the church, these would include awkward truths like 'Bishops must be elected by the other bishops from the same Province' (the Council of Nicaea). And 'Slavery is not at all contrary to the Natural Law' (Lateran II and several popes).

Submission to the 'authentic magisterium' would include acceptance of the ruling that clerics who receive interest on any funds should be deposed, that torture must be used against those suspected of heresy, and that democracy and religious toleration are anti-Christian.

Or otherwise cultivate a short memory when it comes to what the authentic magisterium used to teach.

Theologians scrutinise the oath

In a report on the Profession of Faith and the Oath of Fidelity, the Catholic Theological Society of America noted that none of the bishops were consulted on either document, although both were in preparation for five years.

The report refers to the witch hunts of the McCarthy era as helping to explain why many Americans are reticent about taking oaths imposed from above. Such oaths may 'foster not union but resentment, not partnership but divisions and alienation.' The report is in no doubt that the present relationship between Vatican offices and many theologians 'can unfortunately be characterised as one of distrust'. It contrasts this attitude with the pledge given by Pope Paul

VI to the International Theological Commission in 1969 'to respect that freedom of expression which belongs to theological science and not to limit or restrict the broad range of your studies.'

3. The Instruction on the Ecclesial Vocation of the Theologian, June 1990

The instruction divides theologians into two classes– good ones and bad ones.

The good ones believe what has been infallibly proclaimed. They embrace what has been definitively stated. They receive, with submission of mind and will, what is affirmed even if not defined. They submit loyally to warnings about dangerous opinions. They are aware that, even if some pronouncements of the teaching authority in the past contained deficiencies, these pronouncements were justified at the time they were issued. They are aware that to disagree with teachings, even those which might sometime be changed, could not be justified if it were based solely on the fact that the truth of the teaching isn't evident, or upon the opinion that the opposite position would be more probable. They understand above all that what they must never do is to go near the media, which manipulate public opinion (and which are never mentioned in the document except with expressions of muted hate).

The bad theologians are the other ones.

A German response to the Instruction

One of the more comprehensive responses to the Instruction was prepared by a group of twenty-two theologians in Germany which came to be called 'The Tübingen Declaration'. The theologians criticised the Instruction on the following grounds:

It attempts to suppress pluralism in theological opinion.

It attempts to stop the legitimate association of Catholic theologians at national and international levels.

It seeks to control public opinion in the church and mass media so that only the Roman voice will be heard.

The document is an attack on the freedom of theology and therefore an attack on the whole people of God.

They also appended the following declaration 'for the freedom of theologians and theology' signed in 1968 by 1,360 theologians, including Josef Ratzinger, now responsible for the present instruction:

> In complete, genuine and unambiguous loyalty to the Catholic Church, the undersigned theologians feel compelled in real and sober earnest to point out publicly: the freedom of theologians and theology in the service of the church, regained by Vatican II, must not now be jeopardised again. We are fully aware that we theologians can err in our theology. We are convinced however that erroneous theological conceptions cannot be rooted out by force. In our world they can only be put right and corrected by free and unimpeded objective argument and debate among scholars, in which the truth can gain the victory through and by itself. We firmly uphold and affirm a teaching office [magisterium] of the pope and bishops ... Any form of inquisition, however subtly, not only harms the development of a sound theology, it also causes irreparable damage to the credibility of the church as community in the modern world.

What is that saying about poachers becoming gamekeepers?

4. The Universal Catechism

The universal catechism arose from a suggestion of Cardinal Law of Boston at the 1985 Extraordinary session of the synod, which was presumed to have been inspired by Law's good friend John Paul II, and which was received enthusiastically by the synod secretariat. Knowing the kind of catechism they were likely to get, the majority of theologians, and possibly bishops, were less than enthusiastic about supporting the proposal.

Cardinal Ratzinger of the Holy Office chaired the commission which sent out a draft to the bishops in 1990 and asked for amendments and suggestions. The request for amendments implied that the draft was fundamentally correct in content and method. Some, however, believed it was seriously flawed and should have been rejected like the curial documents presented to the Vatican Council. However, this option was not on offer.

The catechism has since been published for good or ill. It is described as 'an exposition of the essential and fundamental topics of Catholic doctrine, in continuity with the preceding tradition, and in the light of the Second Vatican Council'. At the time of writing, the English language version of the catechism has not yet appeared because of differences of opinion about the translation. So it is difficult to comment on it. But the kinds of points made by critics of the draft version were as follows:

The text is not a catechism but a treatise of a certain conservative theological school.

Apart from the statutory references to Vatican II, the catechism takes no account of theological progress, and could as well have been written sixty years ago.

The catechism makes little distinction between myth and history. The story of Noah is presented on a par with the story of Jesus.

There is no provision for adaptation to national culture.

There is no attempt to distinguish what is essential from what is less important. The impression given is that the church teaching about angels is on equal footing with teaching about the Holy Trinity.

Someone who did read the final text reported that there are 145 citations from Pope John Paul II, but only a handful from Pope John XXIII; that no theologian is quoted after Cardinal Newman, who was born in 1801; while the few women who get a mention have all been in their graves for at least 350 years.

5. The Instruction on Catholic Media

On 9 June 1992, the Holy Office issued an Instruction laying out rules governing publishing by Catholic media.

The Instruction was considered at a meeting of UCIP, the International Catholic Union of the Press in Brazil. UCIP is the official Catholic international organisation for the press, and its officers are only appointed with Vatican approval. The meeting passed a resolution, 57 votes to 9, regretting the emphasis in this Instruction on legality, and the absence of any positive encouragement, and noted that the Instruction had 'threats of punishment woven through it like a red thread.'

The encirclement of theologians now seems complete. There is a blank cheque oath of loyalty, a new Profession of Faith, the various Instructions on what can be said and not said, and what can and can not be published – capped by the universal catechism, which says everything anyway.

Protests by theologians

The 1980s saw an extraordinary proliferation of protests by groups of theologians which relate broadly to the following issues: over-emphasis on some aspects of sexual morality, appointment of unsuitable bishops, decision-making without dialogue, creeping infallibility, proliferation of oaths of belief and loyalty, use of power so as to contradict the church's own goals, endangering ecumenical progress and reversing the openness of the Second Vatican Council.

Such a mass protest by theologians is unique in the history of the church.

In estimating the significance of protests one must bear in mind that any theologian who would sign such a document would by that very fact exclude himself from any promotion in which Rome had a say, and especially exclude him from ever becoming a bishop. So the cost of signing in career terms can be very high. In the case of the so-called Cologne Declaration, the organising committee said that in addition to the 163 who signed, many others replied to say that they were fully in agreement with the declaration but did not feel able to sign 'for reasons which are contained in the declaration itself.'

I once made the point at a meeting of the Irish Theological Association when there was some talk of making an Irish declaration, that if this was done, no theologian under a certain age, say fifty or fifty-five, should be asked to sign. Because that way we might lose some good potential bishops.

The Cologne Declaration was issued on 27 January 1989 and dealt with three issues: the recent appointment of unwanted bishops; Roman interference in the appointment of theologians; and the attempts to establish the pope's doctrinal competence in an inadmissible way. The Vatican Press office dismissed the declaration as a local phenomenon having no significance for the universal church.

In March 1989, fifty-two persons, representing the theological elite of Belgium, signed the declaration. They said that the Cologne Declaration cannot be dismissed as a local phenomenon, but in fact affects the whole Catholic community. 130 French theologians then added their voice, with another group from Spain. In June, 63 Italian theologians joined in, including the President of the Italian Theological Association and the President of the Moral Theologians Association. In July, 200 Brazilian theologians signed a letter expressing concern about the state of the church.

So much for the local phenomenon without significance.

How did the Vatican reply?

There was no reply. There were indirect comments, however, about rocking the boat. 'Rocking the boat,' *The Tablet* rejoined, 'may be the only way to get the barque of Peter off the mud-flats.' Another Roman comment was that it only creates scandal to have such matters aired in the press. The reply to that was, 'If Rome won't listen, where else do you air them?'

When the Italian theologians joined in, the pope eventually commented. 'Bishops,' he declared, 'are the real teachers of the faith.' 'Yes,' the theologians countered, 'But where do the bishops get their theology to teach with?' From theologians – there is no other way.

And how did the Holy Office eventually react to the Cologne Declaration?

Cardinal Ratzinger wrote to the bishops and religious superiors of those who supported the document. 'The Congregation thinks it opportune for bishops and superiors to make contact personally with the signatories to find out their motive for signing and their general orientation in the field of doctrine.' Replies from these investigations were to be sent to the Holy Office.

Ecumenical impact

One doesn't have to be an ecumenist to guess that the ecumenical impact of much of the activity of the Holy Office as outlined above is negative to the degree of about 100%.

Vatican II proclaimed that there is room in the Catholic communion for 'differences in theological expression of doctrine' and for 'different methods and approaches in understanding and proclaiming divine things.' That room seems to have disappeared. The image of the Roman church outside Catholicism used to be that of the enemy of intellect and personal conscience. Vatican II did much to change that. Now many feel the change was only temporary.

All this swearing and professing is one response to a problem which other churches recognise as well. The church has authority to teach. There is need for intellectual order if the church is not to split into countless factions. On the other hand, the lesson of history, time and time again, is that in the effort to impose uniformity rather than cultivate unity, people are crushed, the freedom of the children of God sacrificed, theological progress halted, and often in the end, only material error preserved.

The true mind of the church has to be expressed, not the mind of one faction – as many observers say is happening today. Much of the great teachings of popes and councils were unfamiliar and surprising in their day. Untidiness is inevitable on the path toward ultimate truth.

The Holy Office has tried with great vigour, during the reign of Pope John Paul II, to impose uniformity and outlaw dissent. Many would argue that in doing so it has done an immense amount of harm to the credibility of the church, and provoked disunity and dissent.

One of the effects of authoritarianism is to radicalise people, often in a way quite surprising to themselves. Before *Humanae Vitae*, I could never have imagined that most of the major theologians in Europe, and in North and South America would be protesting publicly and vigorously at the direction the church was taking, often at the cost of their future careers.

Nor could I have imagined myself, when in knowledgeable and critical company, so unable to retain my honesty and defend my beloved church.

16

SCIENCE IS FULL OF SURPRISES

Thoughts about God, creation, and the universe

There does seem to be a marvellous fittingness between our minds within and the physical world without. The two fit together in a way that is quite surprising and I think very significant. Einstein once said that the only incomprehensible thing about the universe is that it is comprehensible.

— John Polkinghorne, President of Queens' College, Cambridge

Explosions and stinks

I must have been about twelve when I learnt how to make an unusual explosive. It was made of iodine crystals and ... better not say in case any twelve year old should come across the recipe. It has to be handled in the wet stage – when dry it explodes to the touch. One can paint it on the door, in which case the door handle explodes when anyone tries to open it. I never had the heart to try that one on the teacher, but I did one day sprinkle a little around the classroom floor.

There are various methods of disrupting a class, but this way, I suggest, is by far the most effective. Every time the teacher moved from his podium, the stuff kept exploding under his feet. The poor man sent for the Dean, a portly man, who carried his weight with a majestic air. But when he walked into the room setting off a chain of small explosions, his customary composure rapidly disappeared. We were all threatened and kept in after school, but what more could be done when everyone looked so innocent and no one owned up?

From as early as I can remember, my favourite shop was called Lennox Chemicals in Leinster Street – round by the back of Trinity College, Dublin. There was usually nothing in the window, and nothing much on view inside either. But somewhere in the back they had glass bottles with ground glass stoppers, rubber corks with holes in them, glass tubes one could heat in the Bunsen burner and bend and blow into interesting shapes; and, loveliest of all, the glass retorts with long swanlike necks for distilling exotic liquids. Lennox also had, as their name implied, a large range of chemicals with sonorous names, like mercuric oxide and potassium permanganate. I must be one of the few people who has actually eaten potassium permanganate. For some reason it found its way into a brown paper bag which was used to pack my school lunch, and for some other reason I began to eat hungrily without checking the contents. Apart from being poisonous, it has a horrible taste.

Science at school

Science at home was much better fun than science at school. But certain triumphs and failures had an emotional impact which engraved them on the memory. I think it was at the end of fourth year that we had to chose between physics and chemistry. I decided to do physics because I felt I knew all I wanted to know about chemistry. I had done well in maths in the Intermediate exams, so physics shouldn't prove too difficult. Besides, Dan Morrissy, the chemistry teacher, had the reputation of being nice but dull. The physics teacher, on the other hand, had the opposite reputation which suggested his classes might be more interesting. Known to one and all as Henry X, he had a moustache like Hitler, spoke in a distinctive whiney voice which was easy to imitate, often lost his temper, threw wooden dusters at boys who fell asleep, and when he got his sums wrong on the board, said the answer was 'as near as doesn't matter'. All in all, he seemed to be a more interesting proposition.

But to come to my triumph story. One day Henry X was absent, and, there being no substitute, the whole class was sent into chemistry, parked at the back of the laboratory and told to keep quiet while the class continued. Dan Morrissy was doing revision on atomic theory – the position of elements in the table, their weights and so on, and making heavy weather of it. Chemistry had been my hobby so I knew most of the answers, while his pupils who were supposed to have studied it didn't seem to know any. Could nobody give Dan some correct answers? I put up my hand at the back and gave the required information. And then again for the next question, and again, until

Dan gave up and rounded on his own class in untypical anger and frustration. It was a cruel thing for me to do, but schoolchildren are cruel, as I found out later in life when I had to stand at the teacher's podium myself.

The nature of the physical world

Being interested from childhood in the natural as well the as physical sciences, I read widely in both fields when I had a relatively free seventh school year. The works of J. H. Fabre, in which he uncovers the mysteriously intelligent activity of manure beetles and hunting wasps, were a particular delight. But the book which stands out in my memory, and which I read several times was *The Nature of the Physical World* by Sir Arthur Eddington. It had a very elegant type-style and a black cover. I never understood it all, but quite enough to bore others with my superior knowledge of the wonders of Einstein's thinking on relativity, the mysteries of the quantum world, and the Second Law of Thermodynamics. (At that stage one-upmanship began to creep in.)

Such reading might have had a different effect on another person, but in my case it helped to strengthen my belief in God, the Intelligent Creator. It wasn't that I ever had a crisis of faith, or that I was looking for something to support my beliefs. It was rather an aesthetic delight in finding out how beautifully the world around us was designed and made, and how everything in it bore the mark of intelligence. I didn't find any need to try and tie this down in philosophical principles, or formally accept or reject any formulation of an argument for the existence of God. The universe seemed to me, even as a schoolboy, to require a Maker. The idea that such perfect planning and intelligent activity could have come about by chance, that is to say, without a mind behind it, never seemed to me a tenable option. And it wasn't that I particularly wanted to believe in God – because of the restricted, rather pessimistic view of religion that was part of my upbringing, I think I might have preferred at the time to believe God did not exist.

Science and religious belief

Fred Hoyle was a young physicist beginning to write popular science works when I was a boy, and I read some of them. I presumed he was an atheist. Forty years later I picked up and read a more recent book by Hoyle (now Sir Fred) which belonged to a young relative. It was called *The Intelligent Universe*. It seemed a different writer to the Fred Hoyle I vaguely remembered.

Hoyle now says that, whereas the entire structure of orthodox biology still seems to hold that life arose at random, it has become clearer and clearer to him that the chances of life originating by accident are so minute as to be completely ruled out of consideration.

His book is particularly critical of Darwinism, and evolution by natural – as opposed to intelligent – selection. And part of his gift as a popular writer is his ability to find vivid analogies to illumine his conclusions.

The intelligent universe

The idea that life could have arisen spontaneously is described by Hoyle as 'the junkyard mentality'. A junkyard contains all the bits and pieces of a Boeing 747 dismembered. A whirlwind blows through the yard and you have a Jumbo Jet ready to fly.

Another vivid example of his involves solving the Rubic cube. If a blindfolded person were to make one random move every second, it would take, he says, on average 1,350 billion years (or three hundred times the age of the earth) to solve the cube. If, on the other hand, somebody who knew the solution watched the blindfolded man make his random moves, and said 'No' every time an unproductive move was made, the blind man could solve the cube within two hours. That is the difference that intelligence makes.

The odds against solving the cube by chance moves are roughly the same as for the random creation of one protein. Human beings use about 200,000 different kinds of proteins, each of which performs a very specific and necessary task. Hoyle estimates that the odds against producing all the 2,000 enzymes that the body needs by chance are the same as throwing an uninterrupted series of 50,000 sixes with unbiased dice.

Whatever reading I have done in recent years in the science field suggests that since my younger days there has been a significant change in the attitude of many scientists to the larger questions which are the concern of religion. The old bogus tensions between theology and science seem no longer so persistent. Both disciplines have learnt to be more humble in their pronouncements about truth. It is now not only possible, but in certain quarters fashionable, to be both a professional scientist and a religious believer.

Looking for a scientist

In 1989 we began talking in Radharc about doing a short series of film portraits of interesting people – to include at least one scientist. Fred Hoyle declined on grounds of family illness. Neil Porter, Professor in the Department of Experimental Physics in UCD, recommended John Polkinghorne, President of Queens' College, Cambridge, who was coming over shortly to lecture at Trinity.

The Polkinghorne lecture was an unusual affair. It seems that the former Taoiseach, Garret FitzGerald, and Professor Enda Mc Donagh of Maynooth, are guiding lights among a group of academics who meet periodically to discuss matters of scientific and theological interest. Polkinghorne spoke to them about science and cosmology. About thirty people were present. We arranged with him then and there to visit him in Cambridge and work together on a programme.

The Reverend President

John Polkinghorne is a mathematician, former lecturer and later Professor of Quantum Physics in Cambridge, where he supervised a large research team. While he enjoyed this work, he knew that most innovative work in the scientific field is done by young people. Einstein made his major contribution to science before his thirtieth birthday. So at the age of fifty, John decided to use his talents in another way and become an Anglican priest. Fortunately his wife approved of the idea as well.

After serving as curate in Bristol and vicar in Kent, he was asked to come back as Dean of Trinity Hall in Cambridge, and accepted. Later again, he was elected President of Queens' College, Cambridge, where he now lives and works in a splendid baronial setting. The long hall where we interviewed him was built in the sixteenth century. His present position in academia allows him to pursue his two loves, science and theology. In the past few years he has produced a series of books which crystallise his thinking in this area. Wonder, he says, is an experience which is common to science and religion.

In each case I believe, of course, that we are encountering an aspect of God – the orderliness of his creation in science, his own presence in religion. Indeed it is the mind of God the creator that we are observing, and our wonder is, in fact, a response to God's presence.

It's a very remarkable fact that we can understand the physical world as well as we do. Take for example the quantum world, the sub-atomic world where if you know where something is you don't know what it's doing; if you know what it's doing you don't know where it is. That world is unpicturable, but is not unintelligible and it turns out that mathematics – which is a sort of free creation of the human mind – is the key to understanding it.

In mathematics one looks for equations that are beautiful and elegant, in the expectation that they will describe the world. That's a very profound fact, I think. The greatest theoretical physicist I ever knew was Paul Dirak, a professor here in Cambridge. He once said it was more important to have beauty in your equations than to have them fit experiments. For if they didn't fit the experiments, then maybe the experiments were wrong; whereas if the equations were ugly, they just couldn't be right.

John Polkinghorne gives several reasons why science today is more hospitable, more encouraging to a religious point of view. The first is the realisation that the world is not mechanical or predictable to the extent that Isaac Newton and his Victorian admirers once thought. It is a far more complex and interesting world, open to the possibility of the exercise of human freedom, and the possibility of God's action within it. Another reason is that the real world, while increasingly intelligible, is at the same time more complex and mysterious than was once thought. So called 'common sense' is not always a good guide to the way things really are.

If you have two electrons, once they've interacted with each other, then they will attain a power to influence each other however far they separate. So if one stays behind here and the other goes beyond the moon, and if I do something to the one that stays here, it will have an immediate effect on the one beyond the moon. That's a most astonishing discovery which has been verified experimentally. So there is a sort of togetherness in separation in the physical world that's very strange and surprising but part of the rich story.

Another recent realisation in science is that we live in a universe which is unique in the sense that if one were to change anything about it to the smallest degree, the human race could not exist.

Our universe started fifteen billion years ago as an expanding ball of energy – one can't get anything much simpler than that. But the rate of expansion had to be precise to an almost unimaginable degree. If it were too fast, stars like the sun could never have formed. If it were too slow, it would have come to a halt and collapsed long before life could come into existence. The speed of expansion had to be accurate to a parameter of one part in 10 to the power of minus 60. That is (I think) a millionth part of a millionth part of a millionth part of a millionth part of a millionth part of a millionth part of a millionth part of a millionth part of a millionth part of a millionth part of 1.

Since the beginning, which now everyone knows as 'the big bang', the expanding universe has become more and more complex under the action of a number of constants: examples are the force of gravity, the so called 'strong force' which helps bind atoms together, or 'the weak force', responsible for radioactive decay. Again if any of these were different to a tiny degree, the human race could not have come to be. If the weak force, for instance, was slightly stronger, one would not have had enough helium in the universe either to make up the heavier elements necessary for human life, or to unlock and distribute these elements through the medium of supernovae explosions.

Questions, answers and mysteries
Dipping again, for the second time in my life, into the story of the world as seen by the physical sciences, I found that several questions from the past were answered.

Why, for instance, did the universe exist so long before the coming of the human race? And why was it seemingly so over-designed, with countless billions of stars spread throughout space? Given present understanding of the laws governing the development of the universe, it seems it had to exist for fifteen billion years, and it has to be as large as it is, to permit the emergence of complex living organisms such as plants, animals and finally the human race.

I sometimes say to people who talk about the Blessed Trinity as a mystery, that I don't find it unusually mysterious: because everything for me is mysterious. How does a seed grow? Why do atoms and molecules act in so tightly organised ways? How does a body rally to protect itself against disease? It's all a mystery. One may describe to some extent what happens, but understand – never.

For some eternity is a mystery, for me the more difficult mystery is time. For some an immaterial spirit outside space is a mystery. For me the mystery is matter, and the space which matter inhabits.

The present generally-accepted theory of the origin of the universe posits that the whole universe began fifteen billion years ago as a speck of matter, unimaginably small. And now that speck has grown into billions and billions of great galaxies. Is that less mysterious than the presence of Christ in the eucharist? It now seems possible that our understanding of the material universe will eventually be expressed in terms of positive and negative fields of force – which in sum cancel each other out! Is that less mysterious than creation out of nothing? In the end the only things we are in direct contact with are our thoughts and our desires, which are not material and not spatial, even when we think of matter and space.

The real world is the world of the spirit.

17

A CHURCH FACING EXILE

*Division in the church after the Vatican Council
which first came to a head in Holland*

In the nineteen sixties, when the result of the Second Vatican
Council was working through to the people, the bishops in Holland
were extremely popular. They were very credible. Everyone
listened to the bishops and what the bishops said they believed was
right. There was a bond between the bishop and his flock. Then
they started replacing moderate bishops by reactionary bishops
and what happened? One million after another left the church.
That is what happened. In fact this is what they, in Rome, believed
would happen, I think. Because about three years ago the bishop
who was in charge of the synod in Rome said to one of my
colleagues that what happened in Holland was that they had
already written off two or three generations of Catholics. Now
this is what we see here – the Catholics are leaving the church by
the hundreds of thousands.

— Rex Breco, a Dutch journalist who writes on church affairs

The Dutch Catholic Church yesterday and today

Slightly less than half of the fifteen million Dutch are, or used to be,
Roman Catholics. Up to the 1950s and 60s they claimed to send more
missionary priests overseas than any other country in the world,
including Ireland. Up to the 1970s they were a close knit community,
sharing the same facilities – Catholic hospitals, schools, churches –
they even had their own radio and television station and newspapers.

In 1955, 97% of Catholics subscribed to a Catholic newspaper, 98%
to the Catholic Broadcasting system (KRO), 90% were members of
a Catholic Trade Union and, in 1959, 84% voted for the Catholic
party.

Mass attendance was, as in Ireland, 80% to 90%. Now Mass attendance in the diocese of Haarlem, which includes Amsterdam, is close to 14% – less than one in every seven adults. So presuming churches were built to fulfil the needs of the early sixties, there is now about six times as much space in the pews as is currently needed. At the same time the overheads – upkeep, heating, servicing, including the servicing by clergy – all cost the same.

In 1987 we filmed in Leeuwarden in the diocese of Groningen, Northern Holland. In Leeuwarden there used to be six Roman Catholic churches. One has been sold to the community as a social centre, another has been handed over to the evangelicals, the other four are run as one parish by a parish team. Two of these four churches are relatively new, built in the period of expansion of Leeuwarden after the Second World War.

Catholic boarding schools in Holland have virtually disappeared. We stayed in a large convent in Ter Eem near Amersfoort: the nuns have not had a vocation since the 1960s, so they have given up the school, turned some of their quarters into a conference centre, and the rest into a home for ageing sisters. All but one or two were over fifty. The picture with regard to clergy is not much better.

The death of Christianity?

I spoke once with the producer of an important BBC religious programme. In his considered view, Christianity is dying. It has lasted as a force in the world somewhat longer than other forms of religious faith, and has made an important contribution to European culture, but now it too is dying. It will be replaced, he believes, by a different faith more suited to the needs of modern man. The Catholic Church, in his view, was always totalitarian in nature, and has to remain such to be true to itself. The Second Vatican Council with its *Declaration on Religious Liberty* and emphasis on collegiality was a temporary aberration, and indeed an indication of decline; as was the growth of liberation theology, and the emphases put on secular questions of justice and peace.

Just as the Welsh Methodist Churches moved from having prayer meetings to having prayer meetings which were also trade union meetings, to having trade union meetings which were no longer prayer meetings, so the movement to social concern in the Catholic Church had Christian motivation in the beginning; now it finds it doesn't need the Christian motivation. Indeed the church institutional framework has come to be seen as a barrier in the way of achieving desirable goals. This came about when the church authorities, as is their wont, began to get worried about innovations in thinking, and to move against some of its leaders. Under this kind of reaction, Christians begin to wonder whether their Christianity adds anything to their social concern. The social concern remains. The Christian motivation begins to fade.

It was a cold assessment which at the time pulled me up with rather a shock. It's an interesting point of view, but I suppose if I agreed with it I wouldn't be writing this book. And if you agreed with it you probably wouldn't be reading it.

So if we reject the notion that Christianity is just a passing phase, then we're left with one of two alternative theories about the causes of the present decline.

Two theories about the current decline

1. A crisis of authority brought about by the media

According to one theory, people have become self centred, selfish, self indulgent, and unwilling to accept authority from any other human being, even though that human being may be delegated by God. This canker in Christianity has grown largely through the influence of the broadcast media which snipe away at Christian values, refuse to accept the authority of church leaders, and question everything in an effort to destroy all certainties.

In this view, the fall in belief and church attendance among Catholics also results from the excesses of a liberal element who gained a large measure of procedural control at the Second Vatican Council, and have since claimed its decrees and decisions as favouring their own libertarian attitudes. To survive in this situation, the church needs firm strong bishops who will lay down the law and the limits of the law, and demand that Catholics who wish to remain Catholics, accept and obey, or get out.

This point of view was expressed to us by Mr Jan Laugs, a concerned Dutch layman:

> There is a crisis of authority in the church. Every Dutchman thinks he is a very qualified man and a kind of pope of his own. Our bishops are noble men, noble priests. They are really holy men. But they are not trained to lead the kind of battle going on here. The laity no longer obey their bishops, and it is very difficult for the bishops to handle that.

So, in this view, the fault is with the people, not the church.

2. The church has failed to come to terms with a changed society

The alternative view is that men and women have changed, and society – which is the structure of inter-relations between persons – has changed as well. The church is in decline because she has not responded to these changes. So the fault is with the church, not the people. Political and social life, on the other hand, have to a large extent kept in tune with these changes. Absolute monarchies, where absolute authority passed from father to son, were once accepted as divinely ordained. Nowadays they are no longer tolerated.

The human race is acquiring knowledge at an ever-increasing rate, and through mass education makes much of this knowledge available to all. So the average person – in the developed world at least – is much better equipped to control his or her own destiny, and to share in the decision-making process which determines it. This has happened in a relatively short time – I remember when the majority of people in Ireland had only primary education. So dictatorships and authoritarian forms of government are out. Participation in decision-making by informed citizens is in.

Taking these two areas, one can see immediately that the Roman church has not responded to changes. The papacy is still a monarchy, the only real one left in Europe. Participation in church affairs by bishops has been reduced in recent years rather than increased. Participation by the laity is still a matter of talk rather than substance. So in this alternative view, the church is losing ground because the church is seen by modern men and women to be unwilling to adapt to a changed society, particularly in its unwillingness to widen participation in decision making.

Bishop Niënhaus, Auxiliary in Utrecht, was one of the few bishops left on the liberal wing of the Dutch church whom we could get to interview. (The retired Cardinal Alfrink refused.)

> I am convinced that in the long run the church will become very different to the medieval church which we have had since the Council of Trent. At present bishops are appointed who are not at all wanted by the local people, and I think that is in contrast to the right way of doing things. One of the church Fathers said, 'No bishop should be appointed against the wishes of the local people'. The bishop should serve the people, not just in name but in reality. And I think servants should listen to people, otherwise they can't serve.

A Dominican priest, Andrew Lascaris, put it more strongly: 'The bishops are exiles in their own country.'

Today in Holland there is little ground between these two views. And so there is a conservative church, and a radical church, and confused people in the middle who drift away from practice, and ultimately – one must fear – from belief.

The history of the crisis

The Pastoral Council

The Dutch crisis first came to a head in 1968 when, in accordance with their understanding of the spirit of Vatican II, the Dutch hierarchy organised a Pastoral Council where representatives of Dutch clergy, laity, and bishops met to discuss the great issues facing the church in the second half of the twentieth century. Preparations for the meetings took two years, and involved the whole of the laity, young and old, from all social classes. 15,000 discussion groups were recruited from Holland's 1,800 parishes and met regularly. The principal debates in the plenary sessions were broadcast on radio and television, and were closely followed by Dutch people. Complicated issues of dogma and discipline were hotly debated in public. Perhaps for the first time since the Reformation, theology became a subject for popular discussion.

The conclusions and recommendations of the Pastoral Council were sent to Rome where they disappeared, never to surface again. The

Dutch bishops were summoned to Rome in 1970, and given a stiff talking to. Roman thinking was further revealed when the papacy disregarded the candidates recommended to fill the vacancy of the important city of Rotterdam, and appointed Chaplain Adrian Simonis instead. Simonis had been the strongest conservative voice at the Pastoral Council. Thus Rome announced its opposition to the council and everything it stood for in strong and uncompromising fashion.

Bishop Simonis

Much of what the Dutch liberal church had seen as progress up to that point had been possible under the leadership of Cardinal Alfrink. Alfrink at first refused to ordain Simonis as bishop, and the Dutch people cheered him for his resistance. However, under pressure from Rome, he relented – provided Simonis would agree to work with the other Dutch bishops. That was in 1971. Many feel that the capitulation of Cardinal Alfrink at the time of Simonis's appointment was a very critical weakness on his part at a time when Rome might have been forced to relent and not pursue the tough policy which, once it succeeded, was pursued relentlessly.

Bishop Gÿssen

The next Roman appointment after Simonis was an even more conservative candidate. When Jan Matthijs Gÿssen was appointed to the diocese of Roermund, he was director of a convent of nuns, and had no experience of working in a parish. He had such difficulty in communicating with other people as a young man that some had opposed his ordination to the priesthood. The Cathedral Chapter, the Diocesan Council, the Chiefs of Services and the Theological School all openly declared their disapproval of his appointment via press radio and TV. It was quite an extraordinary situation. So Gÿssen was brought to Rome for ordination as bishop to avoid possible demonstrations against him. On his return, he founded a new traditional seminary with a very strict regime, refused to co-operate with the other bishops in common activity – for example on behalf of Third World issues – and from time to time made strange statements which shocked many Christians and non-Christians in Holland. Gÿssen resigned in 1993 after several major scandals rocked his diocese.

Bishop Bär

When a vacancy occurred in Utrecht, the most prestigious diocese, Simonis was transferred there and later made cardinal. Bishop Ronald Philippe Bär, a Benedictine, conservative, but with a human face, then went to Rotterdam. Bishop Bär also resigned, suddenly and mysteriously, in April 1993 – under pressure from Simonis, according to a Dutch newspaper report.

Bishop Bomers

Another strange appointment took place in Haarlem. Bishop Zwartkruis was a kind and gentle cleric who used spend his holidays in West Cork, and was well known to many friends in Ireland as 'Teddy'. With retirement imminent, Zwartkruis tried to find out who his successor might be. He was not given the advance notice that a bishop, out of the normal courtesies, might expect. In fact he only heard the announcement on the same day as everybody else. His successor was to be Henrik Bomers, a missionary in Ethiopia, who had not been in Holland for twenty years! That same evening Bishop Zwartkruis had a heart attack and died.

In May 1993, many priests of the Haarlem diocese publically asked Bishop Bomers to step down. 'We are ashamed of the way he frustrates and discourages the diocese,' they said. 'He has proved incapable of giving guidance as a bishop.'

Bishop ter Schure

Rome's next appointment was to the diocese of Hertegenbosch. When the Canons of the diocese heard who was appointed, they met the next day and voted to reject the appointment, informing the pope of their decision. They were ordered to accept and obey. Bishop ter Schure had been an Assistant General in the Salesian order, and spent much of his life in Poland and Rome. We were told that the first four priests he asked to be Vicar General refused. The fifth accepted and was ostracised by the other priests. This was a quite unparalleled situation in the European church at that time – though a similar kind of boycott took place more recently in Chur, Switzerland.

In an opinion poll in the late 70s, a majority of Dutch Catholics said they had no confidence in their bishops.

According to what I was told, it was normal in Holland for three names to be proposed from a diocese to Rome, and in the past one of these three was invariably appointed. However, between 1971 and 1993, no person recommended by a diocese for a Dutch bishopric has been appointed. Rome has always chosen outside and apart from the local recommendation. The first exception appears to be the appointment of a replacement for Bishop Bär.

One must remember, of course, that the conservative thrust of the bishops is to a great extent softened by the lower clergy who staff the various offices of the dioceses, and have to implement policy. Experienced qualified personnel cannot be changed overnight, and pass from one regime to another. Like any civil service, they can easily thwart the wishes of their minister.

Protest and resistance

1. Talking to the pope

Some of the Dutch clergy did try and make their strong views known in Rome. One priest told me that he had an opportunity to get near Pope John Paul II and tell him that the Dutch people as a whole did not like the men he was appointing as bishops. 'Maybe they will get to like them,' the pope replied.

There is little evidence that Pope John Paul II enjoys hearing views expressed in public which differ from his own. So when he visited Holland in 1985, the Dutch hierarchy were anxious to avoid any manifestation of anything except unanimity. Catharina Halkes, Professor of Theology at Nÿmegen, would have been a natural choice to include in a panel of speakers – she was spokesperson for the women's organisations. Archbishop Simonis banned her, however, as he felt she might make provocative remarks. However, one fish did escape through the screening net – Ms Hedwig Wasser was chosen to address the pope about the Dutch contribution to the foreign mission. Towards the end of her address she departed from the official text. She spoke of 'Shepherds on high thrones wagging their finger,' and added:

> Are we preaching the liberating gospel in a credible way if we lay down the law rather than extend a helping hand? ... Are we credible in performing the pastoral work of Christ if bishops show

themselves above us instead of among us and in our midst? Developments in the church in recent times have forced many of us, because of our faith, and in obedience to Christ, to be critical and disobedient towards the church.

As she spoke, the lay members of the audience gave her a surprised applause and a cheer. Cardinal Casaroli, Papal Secretary of State, looked up from the script he was reading and gave an amused smile in the direction of Archbishop Simonis. The interpreter who was translating quietly into the pope's ear worked overtime while the pope gently waved the script from side to side and looked unamused.

Minutes later, when the speech was over, the general audience gave Ms Wasser an enthusiastic ovation, Cardinal Casaroli and the interpreter gave a modest clap, Archbishop Simonis looked at the ground and the pope looked straight ahead. The pope mustn't have blamed Simonis for this embarrassment, because he made him a cardinal three weeks later.

2. Showing another face of the church

On 8 May 1985, three days before the pope arrived on a visit to Holland, the liberal wing of the Dutch church – they would say the real Dutch church – met in the Hague, about 15,000 of them. Their purpose was to remind the world press, who had come to Holland for the papal visit, that there was another Roman Catholic Church in addition to the one the pope was being allowed to see. The Hague was so successful that the organisers held another meeting one year later in Den Bosch, and the following year in Zwolle.

Radharc looked in on the meeting in Zwolle – with about 12,000 others. The crowds came in cars and coaches and met in a truly enormous building – at other times a cattle mart. The main hall with about 10,000 seats was surrounded by smaller halls, tents and open spaces available for multiple manifestations – concerts, lectures, dramas and exhibitions. It was very much a family occasion, with something of interest for all ages. There were a group of musicians who played Irish airs for our benefit. There was a Hyde Park corner where anyone who wished was free to set up his or her soap box and look for an audience. Elsewhere one could join community hymn-singing in the open air, natter in the bars or cafes, or collect literature from the seemingly endless numbers of organisations catering for some aspect or other of Christian concern.

There was so much going on, we could only sample activities of unusual interest. We looked in on a marionette show. One of the marionettes had grey hair and a long beard, and looked like God; the other was a naked woman who spoke in Dutch which God presumably understood, but we unfortunately didn't. Elsewhere a drama cum poetry reading on sexuality concluded with skeins of unravelling ribbon being thrown around so that the whole audience was tied together in some kind of symbolic net.

Perhaps the main artistic feature was the presentation of a large number of tapestry banners designed by religious groups from all over the country to express some religious theme. One reflected local concern with American involvement in Nicaragua, another showed a young man clasping another young man and carried some message about homosexuality. Democracy in the church – or the lack of it – was another prominent theme.

Holland is a very democratic country, one of the first to have students elected to the university boards, and to have a trade union for soldiers (and to allow them grow their hair long). 8th of May Dutch Catholics, as they call themselves, emancipated by education and economic prosperity, tend to be critical of what they see as slavish obedience to clerical authority. They invite the Dutch bishops to their annual meeting, but they don't worry when invariably they don't turn up. At least that is what they say, but deep down I think they would love them to come.

One of the side-shows in the interval between speeches in the main hall was a busking act. A man dressed as a bishop with mitre paraded around with a bit of wire holding a mirror in front of his face. A woman dressed as a nun had an inverted megaphone covering her face. The general tenor of the message in each case was not too hard to decipher! Which reminds me of one of the interesting facts about the 8th of May Movement – the chairperson is always a woman. This is policy, in so far as the organisers maintain that women are never listened to in the church, and that it is symbolically important for women to be seen to lead.

It makes me sad to think of that meeting in Zwolle. All those thousands of earnest Catholics giving up their weekend, full of enthusiasm and, in spite of certain excesses by fringe groups, a strong commitment to Christ, still hoping that someday Rome and the bishops will take notice of them and listen. What they are not prepared to admit may be nearer the truth – that Rome has already abandoned them. Maybe some of their antics are a bit outrageous. Like youngsters pushed out of the family because of some misdemeanour, they become defiant. But they are the concerned and idealistic wing of Catholicism, and it is a tragedy that they should feel unwanted, cast away.

Dutch Christians, Catholic and Protestant, favour public discussion of all the great liberal issues – celibacy, women's rights, divorce, etc, etc. The Vatican favours its own authoritative teaching to anything that might come out of dialogue or argument. So it chooses to impose a type of bishop who will oppose dialogue with the majority on all these issues.

I say 'oppose the majority' for liberal elements seem to be the majority and conservative elements the minority in the Dutch church. A study as far back as 1979 revealed that less than one in ten Dutch Catholics wanted a stricter church; only one in ten wanted the church to condemn divorce in all circumstances; only one in fourteen wanted it to condemn the use of contraceptives.

The essential problem: Participation

When one analyses the problems of the Dutch church, one finds that they all revolve around one central issue: whether members of the church, other than the pope and his curia, have any right to participate in decision-making that affects their Christian lives. Or even if they have no right, whether better decisions might be made if they were allowed to participate.

In the history of the world up almost to this century, most of its inhabitants have had little say in the laws that govern them, or in the appointment of those whose task it was to see the laws were obeyed. In most areas of life, in the developed world at least, that has now changed. The instrument of that change has been relatively equal opportunities of education for all citizens.

It is said that the main effect of education is to increase one's choices in life. One acquires the ability and confidence to weigh alternatives and come to personal decisions. The uneducated lack both the ability and confidence to handle complex decision-making, and have in the past tended to leave that to their 'betters'.

A television programme about the servant/nobility relationship in Edwardian England in the early part of this century, reminded me recently how this part of the authoritarian structure in society, which had lasted so many thousands of years, so suddenly crumbled in my lifetime. We had a 'live in' maid when I was a child who was treated as if she had no mind of her own, and was paid £30 a year. And if she wanted to leave there were plenty to take her place.

Decision making in the work place is changing

Most people spend half their day at work. So fundamental changes in attitude in the workplace spill over into the rest of their lives.

General Electric is a multinational with nearly 300,000 employees and $60 billion sales. A company with such muscle has an enormous influence on management strategies world-wide. One of their new strategies is called 'Work-Out', a massive programme to let workers in on decision-making. Work-Out means setting up meetings throughout the company whereby workers can air their ideas on how to improve and simplify their work. The bosses are then brought in, and under Work-Out rules must respond immediately and concretely to proposals developed by teams of workers. Tens of thousands of GE Workers have already taken part in these sometimes confrontational sessions.

Half the population of the world – women – were totally excluded from political decision making until well into this century. In retrospect that fact seems incredible. But it is true.

Throughout this century, kingdoms, oligarchies, and dictatorships have continued to wane and die, and some form of electoral democracy has taken their place. And this process is by no means finished. A democracy, for instance, where only relatively wealthy minorities have access to power and where a candidate has to spend many millions of dollars to become president is certainly ripe for further development .

Representative democracy as we know it today has great merit. But it was designed in an era when people and information travelled at the speed of a horse. Now people can travel at 1,500 miles an hour, and information travels at the speed of light. More importantly, representative democracy was designed in an era when education was limited to a small minority. Universal education now means that on average the voters are probably as wise as those they vote for, and in certain specialist areas, much wiser.

The final stage of democratic development

Participation in democracy in its final form may come with the aid of the home services computer which is now part of every home in certain areas of France and the US, and which in ten or twenty years will be part of most homes in the developed world – just like the telephone is today. With such an instrument a proposal or referendum on any issue can be put to the whole population and an answer produced within seconds of the closure of whatever period is allowed to people to key in their decision.

The growth of referenda, even in Ireland where the system is clumsy and costly, is manifest. But it is even more widespread elsewhere. In the United States referenda are often attached to other voting procedures, and they are proliferating. Politicians themselves are not likely to push for this fundamental change because it will reduce their own power and importance. Nevertheless the natural desire of human beings to share in the control of their own destiny will mean that when the voters fully realise that the technology is there to make greater participation possible, they may well demand that it be used more often.

Can people seek participation in decision making in their ordinary lives, and not seek it in their religious lives? Will they not demand to be consulted about social questions before the church speaks in their name? Will they accept complex directions in their moral life, knowing that the formulation has been arrived at without consultation?

The answer seems to be they don't and they won't. And Holland is only significant in recent church history in so far as it was the first place that the Roman church ran head on into this authority problem.

Even if Christ designed a church where the Holy Spirit only spoke in the final analysis through the pope and his staff, it could still help in having the pope's decisions accepted if those affected by his decisions could feel they were sometimes allowed to share in the decision-making process as a matter of courtesy, if not of right.

But the more acceptable theological position, supported by the most recent council of the church, is that the Holy Spirit also speaks through 'The People of God'. If so, then consultation with and participation by the ordinary members of the church is not just a public relations exercise, but something required of the process – something that is necessary.

À la carte Catholicism

One of the criticisms often made of the 8th of May Movement is that it is à la carte Catholicism. In other words the customer picks and chooses what he is prepared to accept, whereas Catholicism is about a body of truth which one either accepts as a whole package, or not at all. Traditional Catholicism, in this analogy, is table d'hôte, where the menu is decided by the head chef.

How good an analogy is it? Well first of all very few restaurants would dare offer only table d'hôte. And if they did they would be wise to consult the customers first. The chef who decides on his own what everybody is going to eat, may end up with no clientele. The other question is whether the chef is the only person with the ability to decide what may be best for his clients to eat. Some of his clients may be food nutritionists, health experts and even cordon bleu chefs themselves.

The Vatican ethos, which the present pope seems to share, is that decision-making in the church rests with the pope and the curia – the latter, in theory anyway, always acts on his behalf. A more liberal ethos sees the Holy Spirit working through the church as a whole. The *Constitution on the Church* in Vatican II chose to treat the church as the community of God's people rather than something committed by God to the absolute control of an officer corps.

The church is not a democracy

'The church is not a democracy' is a phrase one often hears. Well if it's not some kind of democracy it must be either an oligarchy, an elected monarchy or a dictatorship. And if it's not an oligarchy, monarchy or dictatorship, (or if one decides it shouldn't be, because none of them seem to fit well with the teaching and example of Christ), then it must be some kind of democracy – or should I say, ought to be in the light of Christ's instructions. 'You know that among the pagans the rulers lord it over them, and their great men make their authority felt. This is not to happen among you.'

In his recent encyclical, *Centesimus Annus,* Pope John Paul II tells us that 'the church values the democratic system.' Among the reasons given by the pope are that democracy leads to greater participation of citizens in society, makes the elected accountable, prevents small groups from seizing power, and ensures an orderly changeover of government. If these are the values to be admired in civil society, one wonders why they should not be desirable in the church as well. The only possible reason would be that they are unnecessary. But to presume they are unnecessary in any institution run by human beings presumes a degree of daily divine intervention which few if any would dare to say is there, and which anyway the whole human history of the Vatican contradicts.

The great and continuing appeal of John Henry Cardinal Newman is his ability to see what is important in a timeless way. Which is why many of his observations have a relevance outside his own era. Newman applauded the church of the fifth century for welcoming the interest of all the people in its deliberation in the Council of Ephesus. He went on to deplore the situation in his own age when ordinary Catholics were expected to practice an unparticipatory and uncritical faith which 'in the educated classes will terminate in indifference, and in the poorer classes in superstition.'

I sometimes feel that the Vatican is cushioned against accepting the obsolescence of its structures by what it sees as growth in membership in the developing world. What isn't taken into account is that, apart from population increase, the church is only growing in relatively uneducated or traditionally authoritarian societies – like parts of Africa or Korea. But even these societies are changing and becoming more democratic. And the same authority problems will arise there in time as they have in Europe and America.

Collegiality and communication

The lifeblood of any organisation is efficient communication.

A pyramidal system, such as the one that operates in the Roman church, has few if any provisions for authentic communication between different levels of the system. Ecumenical Councils meet only when decreed by the Bishop of Rome. When they do meet they're only attended by bishops and a handful of religious superiors. The bishops in synod can only submit suggestions and conclusions for the pope's consideration, leaving him complete freedom to accept or ignore them in the preparation of a final synod document, which he writes after everybody else has gone home.

After Vatican II, for a brief moment, the doctrine of collegiality looked as if it might be taken with real seriousness, and be expressed in structures like the synod which would actively encourage participation, openness and genuine communication. What has happened to that inspiring vision? Edmund Hill put the matter bluntly in *Ministry and Authority:* 'The proposers and supporters of collegiality were naïve enough to hand over its implementation to its most committed opponents, who being anything but naïve have done their best to neutralise it ever since.'

I cannot bring myself to see the church as a pyramid where God speaks only to the apex and the base eventually gets the message. Surely it's a community where God communicates with every member who is prepared to listen, and where every insight and conviction is potentially important for the whole body. Communication which is open and free is the life blood of any healthy functioning organisation in human society. The real trouble with authoritarianism is less the misuse of powers than the blocking off of possible channels of grace and inspiration and the denial of opportunity to people to belong and contribute to the church body of which, according to St Paul, they are living members.

Freedom to leave

Some say, 'If you don't like the way the church is run by the pope and his ministers, you are quite free to leave.' That's as much as saying, if you have criticisms of the captain or crew of your ship, jump overboard! Instead of jumping off, one should have an opportunity to dialogue with the captain and crew to see if there is another and better way to run the ship. Especially so if it seems clear that the majority of the passengers share the same critical views.

When it comes to facing criticism, churchmen do have armour which it is very difficult to pierce. Your conservative churchman who is subjected to public criticism, invariably identifies with the suffering Christ who was despised and rejected. 'You will be hated by all men on account of my name'. So the criticism becomes a mark of election – proof that one stands with Christ rather than (as I suspect is more often the reality) stands against him.

Lessons from history

I know I will be accused of gross simplification, but be that as it may, there is a point to be made about theological controversy which probably can't be made without simplification!

In the great upheavals in the Christian church – like the break with the East, and the sixteenth century Reformation – the primary irritant and factor for change was dissatisfaction with the authority exercised by the pope and the curia rather than the actual reforming issues, many of which, in the beginning anyway, only concerned matters of church law – the vernacular in the liturgy, permission to read the bible, clerical celibacy, the sale of indulgences and so on. It was usually only after the imposition of discipline through condemnations and excommunications that rigid theological differences began to emerge. People at odds with each other have to rationalise their positions; and one way to do this is through creative theology. In retrospect many of the theological differences may now seem largely a matter of words and how you interpret them, but at the time they helped to copper-fasten the divisions. In the sixteenth century Reformation, Christianity was split in two, and there was enormous damage to the ideal of a truly Christian Europe. It took the trauma of two world wars, where Christians of all sorts were thrown together in suffering, to put the differences between Christians in a better perspective. At the Second Vatican Council, the Roman church faced the disciplinary issues raised by the Reformation and gave in on most of them. The curia was of course horrified by this betrayal, and while paying lip service to the council, has tried to row back ever since.

Just as the sixteenth century upheaval in the church followed hot on the proliferation of the printing press, so today there is a new liberal threat to a conservative church brought about by the arrival of radio and television broadcasting. That threat first came clearly to a head in the Netherlands. It has been and will be temporarily contained. But in this contemporary second reformation, the split in the church is fundamentally different. People who have become dissatisfied with Catholicism of the Roman kind no longer establish themselves as new sects, or even join existing ones. They retain loyalty to Christ, but simply drift from any formal attachment to an institution. They still want to be Catholics, and still consider themselves Catholic, and refuse to consider themselves as having left the (real) church.

Whether belief in Christ and his gospel can pass on from generation to generation without institutional attachment is something which only the future can tell us. At one moment I feel it can't. But then I remember that religion runs deep in man, and that other persistent religions, like Hinduism, carry on from generation to generation with little formal structure. Perhaps people can be faithful to Catholicism and yet reject the institution. As an officer of that institution, however, I would prefer that it didn't happen that way, and that we could change the institution to the extent that modern men and women, creatures of this new broadcasting age, would not feel unwanted or alienated.

18

ASKING THE BRITISH TO SAY 'SORRY'

The Bishop of Salisbury's views on the Irish Question

Repentance and forgiveness

Acknowledging guilt in Russia

Having met many Polish communities in different parts of the world, I have come to realise the enormous emotional significance for Poles of the one word 'Katyn'. Every Polish church has its shrine to Katyn. I see in my mind's eye for instance, a modern church in Melbourne dominated by an enormous cross with the simple inscription 'Katyn'.

One of the many great wrongs perpetrated against the Polish people was the massacre in cold blood of the flower of the Polish army at Katyn forest in 1940. The Russians blamed the Germans. And even set up a kind of bogus commission to establish their claim. But all along the evidence pointed the other way. When President Gorbachev withdrew his troops from Poland, there remained this one obstacle to renewing friendship between the two peoples – Katyn.

In April 1990, fifty years after the event, General Wojciech Jaruzelski, then President of Poland, went to Moscow. There in the Kremlin, Gorbachev publicly acknowledged the Russian people's guilt for the wartime massacre of 15,000 Polish officers. And he expressed his deep regret to the Polish people. The following day General Jaruzelski visited Katyn. The government in Warsaw said the Polish authorities were very satisfied at the lifting of a burden that weighed not only on relations between the two States, but also between two peoples.

Acknowledging guilt in Germany

In April 1990 when the then East German Volkskammer met to swear in the first elected government, the East German President read out a remarkable and unprecedented apology in the name of all the political parties, acknowledging the immeasurable suffering that Germany had inflicted on the people of the world, and the genocide resulting from nationalism and racial madness.

Acknowledging guilt in Japan

Fifty years ago, Korea was subjected to a brutal occupation by the Japanese. Korean cultural artefacts were destroyed, property expropriated and Koreans moved to labour camps in Japan. By 1990 commercial factors were pushing towards reconciliation. But before Korea would enter into collaboration with Japan, its government demanded a public apology. And so at a public reception for South Korean President Roh Tae Woo, the Japanese Emperor Akihito expressed 'his sincere remorse and honest apologies for Japanese actions that inflicted unbearable sufferings and sorrow on the people of the Korean peninsula.'

Acknowledging guilt in Ireland

In 800 years of attempts to control Ireland and protect its flank from hostile invasion, Britain has pursued policies which assured the Irish people of a sad history, and even at times brought the race to near extinction. In the long drawn out struggle, Ireland lost its language, its laws, and much of its culture. Yet there never has been any admission of responsibility or expression of sorrow on the part of Britain, not to mention any thought of asking for forgiveness.

Fr Denis Faul, the first person to publish documentation proclaiming the innocence of the Guildford Four and the Birmingham Six, once spoke about repentance in another Radharc film called "British Justice in Northern Ireland."

> The British think this old colonial torture and thumping and internment and violation of the law right left and centre will succeed, but we're not fools, we can read it and until they repent of what they have done and make amends for what they have done, there'll never be peace here.

Apart from Fr Faul there are others who think that relations between Britain and Ireland may never come finally right until somebody, like a King or a Queen or a Prime Minister, can bring themselves to say on behalf of the British people, 'we have done terrible things to

Ireland, acting in our own selfish interest. We are responsible for the divisions leading to all the troubles, past and present, and now we want to say we are sorry.'

Could that ever happen? It could, because the British are a fair minded people. But as of the present, with one or two exceptions, they don't see themselves as having responsibility. The prevailing notion in Britain is that the Irish are always fighting each other and the best that Britain can do is to help keep them apart. We need to help change that view, and to acknowledge those who, like Bishop John Baker, see the Irish problem in another way. What marks the bishop out among members of the British establishment is that he is not afraid to accept British responsibility for some of Ireland's woes. Which is why we found ourselves spending a week in Salisbury in the summer of 1991.

Salisbury Cathedral is familiar to most people through the famous series of paintings by the British artist John Constable. It is a glorious building inside and out, although the external aspect was somewhat spoiled for us by the current renovation work on the famous spire, costing in the region of £6 million.

The bishop lives with his wife Jill in a comfortable house in the Cathedral Close called 'The South Canonry'. He has responsibility for one of the largest and most active dioceses in England. He is a member of the House of Lords, and takes a serious interest in its activity. Before coming to Salisbury, he was chaplain to the Speaker of the House of Commons at Westminster, and had time to reflect on what theology might have to say about politics.

I believe it is perfectly right for Englishmen — as I and some of my friends have done — to go over to Ireland and say, 'Look I am sorry.' Not just we are sorry, but I am sorry for what we have done to bring about the problems you now face. And I believe that it would be an enormous step forward in the whole situation if our own political leaders, preferably the Prime Minister — I tried this on when Margaret Thatcher was in power — were actually to say something like that in a speech. Not to say we think that everything we're doing at the moment is wicked or anything like that, but to accept responsibility for having brought the situation or contributed to bringing the situation to where it now is. And that in itself is very important. You can't make other people forgive you, but you can at least say 'we need to be forgiven', and I think that is a very important Christian insight.

Bishop Baker is no maverick, but a respected member of the British establishment. The former Northern Secretary, Peter Brooke, and the bishop were at school together. Salisbury Plain, the traditional training ground of the British Army, is within his diocese and the GOC is stationed there. The former Prime Minister, Edward Heath, is a friend and near neighbour, living within the cathedral close. Perhaps the only thing that is unexpected about Bishop Baker are his views about Ireland.

The Nationalist community have a perfectly justifiable objective and aim and it's one with which I happen to sympathise, because I would love to see a united Ireland, I make no bones about that. What I think has been one of the greatest difficulties is that the aspiration for a united Ireland has not been allowed to be politically legitimate. If it was on the table as part of the agenda all these years, and had been pursued by normal democratic discussion, I think we would be a lot further forward.

The island of Ireland in the past was not a political unity in the sense in which we understand that now, but it makes sense as a human unity: it is an island of manageable size, where people certainly now are interrelated. It was recognised as a natural unity when the Act of Union joined it to Great Britain and it is only the differences that have arisen since then between communities which have made the idea of dividing it seem the accepted thing. Now I myself believe that there would be an enormous gain to everybody and indeed to the world if Ireland could again come together as one community, because I think the richness of the community which contains very different elements is far greater and that those elements themselves, the Protestants and the Catholics, the nationalists and the loyalists, would actually find themselves in a humanly more creative situation if they were to live together.

The common English stereotype of the Irish is that they are always fighting each other, and that a British presence is needed to keep the factions apart. What may be overlooked is the origins of these divisions in Ireland, and who bears the main responsibility for creating them.

I believe Britain made a very substantial contribution to these divisions in Ireland. The strategic and political reason was that Ireland was a vulnerable front, as far as Britain was concerned, and therefore it had to be taken over. That meant that people had to be planted there who were regarded as loyal to the British State, and so you get the settlements, not only in the North, but in the South as well. And then the terrible history of the 1641 Rebellion and of Cromwell, and these events, which are deeply embedded in the Irish consciousness, were all part of a programme of subjecting Ireland in the interests of British security.

Then later on the business of Wolfe Tone – the very dangerous possibility, so far as the British were concerned, of an alliance with the French Revolution and Napoleon, which led directly to the Act of Union, and the whole business of the land problem and also the fact that the penalties and restrictions placed on Catholics went on much longer in Ireland than they did in England – all these things created a tradition and a background which is still active in the present, and there has been a lot of suffering. Both communities in Ireland have suffered at the hands of each other and also at the hands of the British.

Moral responsibility

One of Bishop Baker's sayings which sometimes shocks people is: 'We must accept that the things our enemies do are in a way justified.' This is not of course an attempt to justify physical violence or murder, as he is quick to point out. No one, no matter what their grievance, has a licence to kill. What he does say however is that along with our moral responsibility not to render evil for evil, we have a companion duty to recognise that our own evil may have given grounds for the evil done to us. We are rarely in the position of sinless martyrs turning the other cheek. Our enemies' anger, if not their actions, may well be the result of just grievances. In his own words:

An idea that has come to mean very much to me – because of feeling and trying to understand the Irish situation – is that of corporate responsibility. This really means that the individual accepts moral responsibility or shared moral responsibility for what his country or church or whatever it is has done. Now some people are not very happy with this because they say, 'Well I have never done anything to hurt an Irishman or a black man or a Jew or anybody, so why should I be blamed?' But the fact is that the way communities behave, and the way we English behave, is the result of the values and attitudes in our community, which we all support and bolster up. We all have them in ourselves, we inherit them, or at least we receive them in our education.

Old attitudes still control many of the ways in which we behave towards Ireland. And one of these is this awful English superiority. Other countries don't actually know anything and don't know how to run anything. And in the case of Ireland, because of generations of comic Irishmen portrayed in Punch, there's a general idea that Ireland is a pretty good mess and that they don't know how to run anything. Also it is really very very angry-making when you talk to somebody and they end up saying, 'Oh well, Irishmen like fighting each other – there's nothing you can do about it.' These things, which it is possible to laugh about or regard as trivial, are not trivial because they are part of the attitude.

There is also in England – though it is dying out thank God – a very latent anti-Catholicism, and it still bursts out from time to time. When I was teaching at Oxford University I went into lunch one day and there was a young colleague, a brilliant chap – went off to America, some frightfully high paid job. But he was a complete atheist – virulent militant atheist. Archbishop Fisher, of the Church of England, had just been to visit the pope and this chap rounded on me at luncheon and said, 'I think it's the most disgraceful thing I've ever heard.' I said to him, I said, 'Gerald, what can it matter to you – they're both talking nonsense according to you.' 'It does matter, no Englishman ought to have anything to do with the pope.' Now here was an enlightened young man, a brilliant academic and where did he get it from? He got it from his culture – and as long as a culture carries values like that, then nobody in that culture can escape responsibility.

Jingoistic history lessons at school, the popular media and even our family values are often blamed for reinforcing our cultural prejudices. But there's surprisingly little examination and analysis of such negative attitudes, and even less attempts at reversing them.

Some of us have been over to Ireland and we have said, not just we are sorry, but I am sorry: sorry that as an Englishman I've been part of this story, the story that included the Famine, that included the fact that while people were dying in Ireland in the nineteenth century there was grain, corn being exported from Dublin and Cork and other places, and all the things which we have contributed to the present situation. And I think the most wonderful thing in a way that could happen would be if one of our own leaders, preferably the Prime Minister – I tried this out on Mrs Thatcher, as I've said, and didn't get anywhere – would actually make an important public speech in which he or she would recognise this.

I think the contribution that Britain made to the situation in Ireland has been a serious wrong, and if people still feel hurt by it, then of course there's nothing wicked in feeling anger about that. Justice is always angry that things have gone wrong. But it's when you can feel that anger, which is a righteous anger, and actually go on and say, 'No, we're going to put that behind us in order to start a new relationship.' But that can't be done until the other person says, 'We were wrong.'

One of the things I would want to stress about the problem of Ireland, after having tried to think and feel about it, is this: that it is one of those problems you sometimes get in human history where all the rational discussion in the world and all the goodwill cannot actually provide a solution that will do justice to everybody's interests. Somebody has to give. Somebody has actually to lose what they have laid on the table as their prime requirement.

One of the great moments of illumination for me came while watching a television programme where Brian Faulkner was walking up the steps of Stormont and Paisley shouted at him the one word 'Lundy'. I don't need to explain that word to an Irish audience! [At James II's siege of Londonderry in 1689 the Protestant soldier in command of the garrison, Lt Col Robert Lundy was in favour of surrendering and the subsequent outrage of the citizens forced him to flee the city. Today the name of Lundy is still used as a term of abuse in Northern Ireland for any Protestant who weakens on his radical fervour for the Protestant cause.] But history – you cannot just cut history out. Let's take an example from England. When I came to this diocese there was a local school where the children all sent me a wonderful scrapbook to welcome me. And one boy had written a story about adventures in space that he had with his dog. He ended up with hostile spaceships coming in blazing their laser guns and he only got himself out if it by the device of waking up and realising it was all a nightmare. But the significant thing about the story was that the spaceships were French! Not German, not Japanese, not Russian, but French. The French are the hereditary enemies of the English – for 900 years you see! And where that boy got it from I cannot think, but he'd imbibed it with his culture somehow; when he had to think of the enemy, it was France! You cannot get away from history.

One cannot get away from history – true – but one can try to understand it, and share one's understanding with others. Bishop Baker has thought deeply about Ireland and its difficult history, and shared his thoughts with others in an influential sector of British society. For that we in Ireland owe him a debt of gratitude. Is there no way we can acknowledge it?

19

'SOMETIMES I HAVE TO BE
A TROUBLEMAKER'

*A Portrait of Bernard Häring, perhaps the greatest
moral theologian of the twentieth century*

And so I can say with Leonardo Boff, and Charles Curran, and Gustavo Gutiérrez who came and prayed with me during their time of procedure – that all loved the church; and that they loved the church more than those who claimed the right to have a monopoly of doctrine. And I think study proves that those theologians – and it's a long long list – who were under procedure as I was, that they are men of church. I remember especially John Henry Newman, who was surely not treated better than I was, and how did this man love the church?

— Bernard Häring, speaking of the Congregation for the Doctrine of the Faith which held inquisitions on him and many other theologians throughout the 1980s

I first heard the name Bernard Häring nearly forty years ago. Even then it was mentioned with some reverence by Enda Mc Donagh, a friend and classmate in Maynooth, who had gone on to study moral theology in Rome and Tübingen.

Journalists like Louis MacRedmond, Sean MacRéamoinn, and John Horgan, reporting from Rome during the Second Vatican Council, spoke of Häring with enormous respect. Raphael Gallagher, Professor of Moral Theology at the Redemptorist house in Dublin, said of him more recently, 'he is my hero.'

Seventy-two works of Häring have been published in English so far, and the full list of the books he has written runs to about twice that number. Put in perspective, that is more than two books a year for sixty years of adult life. So it was with some little trepidation that we drove up to the foothills of the Bavarian Alps to meet the great man.

Most of Häring's adult life was spent teaching at the Alphonsianum, the Redemptorist university in Rome. Now officially retired, he lives in the monastery at Gars, near Munich. But we had chosen to meet him in his home town of Böttingen where he spends one month of the year, says the parish Masses, and allows the local priest to go off on a holiday.

Böttingen is a small village, and it wasn't marked on our map – nor could we find it on any other. In the end we had to phone him for instructions. And when we reached the outskirts of the town an elderly man was waiting on a street corner waving his walking stick at us, his coat blowing in a cold alpine wind. It was Häring himself, come out to meet us lest we have trouble finding the house.

The Härings have lived in Böttingen for many generations. Nowadays Bernard stays with his niece, but the old family home is just around the corner and down the hill. His father owned a horse driven taxi/transport service, and must have done well because he built a fine house for his family of ten surviving children. The house is still there, as is his grandfather's house, now a small hotel. And the family is still very much part of village life – one nephew owns the sawmills, another farms deer.

Böttingen was built among gentle hills. The streets roll up and down so that the town looks different from every new point of view. Under a blue sky in the freshness of a late spring, it looked almost too perfect – a Christmas card picture waiting for a dusting of snow. We got to know that village well in our four days there, for even at seventy-nine years Bernard is a fast and committed walker who likes to show friends his different haunts as a child, and the slopes where he first learnt to ski. He also brought us to the highest point of the town where masses of brown-gold violas surround some hundreds of wooden crosses laid out in rows with military precision. Members of Häring's family died in both wars and are buried there, while Bernard himself escaped death by a whisker in World War Two. The experience of that war proved to be the most formative influence in his personal life.

Stupid obedience

Already a Redemptorist priest pursuing further studies when war broke out, Häring was conscripted into the German army – as a medical orderly in deference to his religious vocation. Conscripted priests were forbidden to say Mass publicly and the penalty was stiff – ten years in prison. Häring was with the German army in France, in Poland, and ministered to the injured, the dying and the dead all though the chaotic horror of the Russian campaign. At Stalingrad he led 300 men to safety through the encircling cordon of Russian armour. For that he was condemned to die as a traitor by the German military establishment. He is only alive today because the Russian advance came before the sentence could be carried out.

One of the first hard lessons he learned from the war was what he called 'the stubborn stupid obedience of Christians towards cruel orders'.

I've seen people do the most terrible things justifying it by obedience. One of the soldiers of my regiment came to me after shooting 10,000 Jewish people in Cracow, Poland. He was crazy. He told me that he had prayed while he shot down innocent Jews! So it was clear for me that the churches, both Catholic and Protestant, had not done their job, and especially moralists had not done their job educating people for discernment, for responsibility.

On another occasion a general who was a friend of mine and a good man told me that he had once put the question to an officer to try him out.

'Have you men who are willing to shoot down the partisans that we have captured?'

and the officer said,

'Of course, everyone will do it.'

And the general was furious about that.

Seeing people doing the most terrible things and justifying it by obedience was a hard lesson for Häring who had been brought up in a church tradition which laid great emphasis on keeping the rules.

That whole kind of blind obedience, stupid obedience of Christians of all churches made me extremely angry and I told them 'if ever after the war I have to teach moral theology, this will not be based on the concept of obedience but on the concept of responsibility and discernment: a discerning obedience and a virtuous disobedience.' As I all the time had to disobey law in order to fulfil my priestly vocation.

One law that Häring most often disobeyed during his time in the army was the law forbidding him to say Mass. Sometimes there was collusion with sympathetic military officers, but often too he was in trouble. On one occasion he was called in by a colonel.

'Is it true that you once conducted a service for Polish people in the church? Is this true?'

'No, not once but at least five times.'

'Have you anything to say for your defence?'

'No. I knew the law.'

'So you have nothing to say in your defence.'

'Well perhaps I do have something to say. There is the example of one of your officers whose case I think should be treated with mine. (Häring was aware that this officer was the one who had denounced him.) This officer is known to have been drinking alcohol on occasion with Polish prostitutes. I suggest to you, Colonel, that to get drunk and fraternise with Polish prostitutes is a rather more serious question that to pray with Polish people!'

The German army were only the first to learn that it wasn't that easy to take on Bernard Häring when it came to matters of unquestioning obedience. Many Vatican officials had to learn the same lesson in more recent years.

'In Fr Häring I find my own soul . . .'

Having lived in Häring's company for a few days one comes to recognise some of his great strengths. First of all he is a man who, despite his great erudition, can express himself simply. And even when he offers new and strange concepts, he does so in a way that makes people say to themselves 'that makes sense'. Pope John XXIII recognised this when he remarked once to Fr Capovilla, his secretary, 'In Fr Häring I find my own soul, my own attitudes.'

It is obvious too that Häring's life and thought are informed with the love of God revealed through Jesus Christ. It is a state that many Christians aspire to, and some try to pretend that they have reached, but not many achieve. Those who do, find a serenity that cannot be easily hidden.

Another strength is his sense of humour. He may not tell a lot of jokes, but an engaging, welcoming, sometimes mischievous smile is never far from his face. 'If anyone cannot smile,' he said to us one day, 'then he doesn't know he is redeemed.'

The young priest's ecumenical attitudes were moulded on the battlefield. When death was near, differences between Christians tended to disappear. On the evening before the Russian campaign was to begin, he held a eucharistic service with absolution for the whole regiment. Catholics and Protestants all attended and all received Communion. In Russia, when Orthodox priests were not available, he said Mass for the Orthodox, and baptised their children.

It was from this background that Häring came to teach moral theology in Rome. His predecessor presented him with the standard textbook – a kind of slide rule to measure venial and mortal sins. He tried to use the book, but it was too distasteful and his students encouraged him to throw it away. So he did throw it away and started to propose 'the good news', not just the law, 'and it was my concern that moral theology too must be thoroughly good news, not "you must", not a thousand temptations around the corner; but God gives you great trust, God gives you great dignity, God offers you tremendous chances – an encouraging and healing moral theology.'

Under pressure from his students, Häring published his 'notes'. There were so many of them that it took three volumes. Five thousand copies – a whole first edition disappeared in three months – an astonishing success for a serious theological work. It was eventually translated into fourteen languages including Japanese and Chinese – the Chinese version is used today with government permission in all Christian seminaries in China.

Needless to say, *The Law of Christ* was not well received by more conservative theologians. His superior received many critical letters. More importantly, copies were sent to the Holy Office and Häring knew from the ecclesiastical grapevine that the clouds were gathering and that he would soon be in serious trouble. But then his Superior General received a beautiful letter from Pope John XXIII, congratulating him and Fr Häring on the book which the pope said he had read with great interest. Later on Pope Paul VI echoed the same sentiments and of course, with such papal recommendations, Häring was armour-plated for the time being against the inquisitorial cast of mind.

Vatican Council years

Häring made a prominent contribution to the Second Vatican Council. Many of the Fathers had read some of his written works and were influenced by them. Pope John invited him to take part in the preparations, and during the sessions themselves many bishops sought his help and advice.

He told us that the first among his main concerns at the time was religious liberty. The Roman thesis was that wherever Catholics had a majority the state should support Catholicism, and so far as possible outlaw other religions because only truth has rights. On the other hand, wherever Catholics were in a minority and where they could not hold sway, then they must argue for religious liberty. So clearly the church's position was inconsistent and not credible. Häring helped to change it. In the end, one of the most important documents to come from the council, the constitution known as *The Church in the Modern World,* was in fact drafted by Häring.

But it was on questions like marriage and the family, and particularly birth control and contraception, that Häring's name first appeared in the headlines of the international press. Before the council, the church's attitude on artificial means of contraception was set out clearly in an Encyclical of Pius XI, *Casti Connubii.* But opinion at the council began to develop into a clear criticism of *Casti Connubii,* and many argued for a change in the church's teaching on contraception. Conservative forces rallied to organise a holding operation and prevent any hasty decision being taken. Pope Paul was persuaded

287

to reserve to himself the decision about any change in church teaching.

And so a special commission on the regulation of conception was set up to advise the pope. Häring was appointed to the Commission, against the wishes of the curia – one liberal voice among twenty mostly conservative theologians opposed to change.

The Birth Control Commission

According to Häring, as the meetings continued and the bishops and theologians listened to the lay members, in particular people like the American couple, Mr & Mrs Crowley of the Christian Family Movement, almost all moved from their 'no change' conservative position. The exceptions were Fr De Lestapis SJ who was pretty near to change but didn't quite get there. Fr Visser, Redemptorist, who was in favour of a change – not in essence but only in pastoral practice. And two Jesuits – Fr Ford, an American, and Fr Zalba, a Spaniard, who felt change was impossible.

The Commission having presented its report, most of the members went home. But the Holy Office remained. Cardinal Ottaviani summoned the few remaining conservative members of the Commission. A Franciscan, Fr Lio, who was an advisor of Cardinal Ottaviani told some of his confreres (who later told Häring) 'that two audiences with the pope organised by Ottaviani were sufficient to reconvert the pope, who had already been seduced by the Commission'.

Häring, as one of the members living in Rome, knew that the conservative forces were lobbying Pope Paul. He himself tried to see the pope. Each time the reply was, 'We will let you know'. In the end none of the men and women of the majority of the commission were allowed to see the pope.

Häring's witness helps one understand the conservative thinking which made change for them inconceivable. The arguments for and against the use of artificial means of contraception had very little to do with it. The real problem was the teaching authority of the church. The Lord Jesus had promised Peter that whatever he would bind on earth would be bound also in heaven: Pius XI had taught that it was seriously sinful to use artificial contraceptives. He had condemned other Christians who had changed their attitude. How could this teaching be wrong thirty years later? Infallibility in its majesty might not be at stake, but certainly the teaching authority of the church would be much weakened and open to ridicule. Artificial contraception must be wrong because otherwise, to put it crudely, God would be making a fool of his own church!

Häring well understood the problem at the time and he pointed out that there were many papal encyclicals in favour of burning witches, even of torture, while others condemned the charging of interest on loaned money.

> But the church has changed and everyone was happy that the church changed. If the church would only say to people, 'We are learners, we did our best at the time; but we have got to realise that we have to listen to those competent in the human sciences, listen to ordinary people,' then I think everyone would have been ready to give the pope peace, and he would have gained tremendously in stature. And so it is an unfortunate fact that by holding on to this one point of sexual morality, young people and not so young people in great parts of the world are now unwilling to listen to the magisterium of the pope and this is a great pity, because we need guidance in sexual matters.

Fr. Häring first received a draft copy of *Humanae Vitae* from *Time/Life* who when questioned, admitted they had purchased it from a Roman monsignor for a couple of thousand dollars. They asked Häring for an interview but he refused. He kept the copy of the text, however, and read it over and over looking for the best possible interpretation. He also hid himself, giving his address only to his superiors, for he had, he says now, firmly decided to be silent.

Then someone disclosed his telephone number. 'It was ringing day and night', he told us. 'I leave the church, famous theologians said, I leave the church'. A priest called him to say that Cardinal Felici had written in the Vatican newspaper that whoever does not fully accept this teaching, thereby makes a decision to leave the church. With these thoughts in mind he prayed through the night. Eventually, moved by the spectacle of many people leaving the church, he resolved to write an article for *Commonweal,* an American Catholic magazine. Briefly the message was that if, after serious thought and prayer, any individual or couple find that they cannot in conscience accept the teaching on birth control, they should follow their own conscience, and nobody should feel themselves to be a bad Catholic because the encyclical does not convince them. The international press reprinted this message in headline terms. 'Fr Häring tells people no reason to leave the church: Follow your conscience: But try to form your conscience carefully.'

Afterwards a number of Bishops Conferences followed with public statements more or less in the same vein. But Häring was the first to open an escape valve and prevent an explosion of dissent and disbelief which could have led to a full schism.

Obiter dicta

The professor is an elderly man now, but his mind is young, and he has interesting views on everything: he is eminently quotable even in English – which for him is a foreign language. The following are some more snippets from the interviews recorded for the Radharc programme.

On Pope John Paul II

I think I do understand him. He was under Cardinal Wyszynski, primate of Poland. Like among African chiefs, the paramount chief does not speak against the highest chief. It was a rough time in Poland and they needed a leader like Wyszynski. He was a model for the present pope. But not all the church is an embattled church as the Polish church then was.

On socialism

I think it's a pity that many people can only think of that kind of socialism of Stalin, and that oppressive Communism he imposed on Eastern Germany, Poland, Romania, Bulgaria. It's a pity, because Karl Marx was wrong in many issues, but not on all.

On Teilhard de Chardin

I was inspired by his words, 'the world belongs to those who offer the greatest hope.' And that is what we Christians should do. That is what I try to do in my own modest way. Sometimes people say I'm the greatest optimist, and I always say I'm not an optimist, I'm a realist, but I believe in God's power. I believe in God's grace. Teilhard was a bearer of hope, an inspiration of hope, and that is what we need.

On women priests

How interesting the council Fathers did not think at all about women in the church, and yet they said in the draft document on bishops that the most noble and highest office of bishop is to proclaim the resurrection of the Lord, to be witness to the death and resurrection of the Lord. If this is true then women are qualified. (It was women who brought the first news of Christ's resurrection to the apostles). It will come. But I do not press the thought of ordaining women. The Orthodox Church is not at all ready. So we must go slowly.

On married clergy

An African bishop asked my advice: he intended to ordain his best married catechist as priest because the parish had 30 or 40 outstations and the priest could only reach them once or twice a year. I said, 'Don't do that, the pope will never condone it. Make something better. Have a solemn, very solemn ritual of mission for the catechists. Work it out with the neighbouring bishops. Define well what they can do besides the service of the word of God. Rome cannot control these things. You can work out a genuine African liturgy; and a genuine African service of communion; and sometime in Rome somebody will understand.' But why should these catechists travel hundreds of miles to get consecrated hosts, why should they not be ordained? Things are changing. Young people will see it. So I have a message of hope.

I have been at dinner with so many Protestant, Anglican and Orthodox priests and their families, and so I know what wonderful family lives they live. So I cannot see the fact that a holy man has a holy wife should be an obstacle for priestly ministry. Otherwise Jesus would not have called Peter, and as Paul instructs us, Peter took his wife on his missionary trips. We do not want celibacy to be degraded, it's a wonderful gift of the Lord, wonderful! One should not say, as some churchmen do, 'If we do not make it an absolute condition in the law, we will have no one for celibacy.'

This is an offence for me, an offence against the Holy Spirit. The Spirit does not want to work only through one channel.

On collegiality in the church

Pope John Paul I said that 'collegiality is the decisive criterion of catholicity'. And this is very important. Since then, a cardinal, the head of the Congregation for Religious wrote to the Major Superiors of religious orders. 'We need more collegiality, and that means you put your questions to us and you can get your directions from us.' So they thought in Rome of one way collegiality, to make all the others a kind of altar boys!

On authority

The pope's authority depends on gathering all the wisdom, all the life experience of the church. But if too many documents come out, and there's a tendency to control too much, there will be a feeling of distaste, of anger, of disobedience.

On Christian unity

Christian unity, which is the concern of my prayers, my life, my activity, Christian unity is only possible with the successor of Peter, not without him. But it is possible with the successor of Peter if he is one of us, Christ Son of God translated into one of us; it is only possible if collegiality is the sign of his catholicity; and that means that we can learn also from other churches. However, the Roman magisterium then must again become more humble.

The appointment of bishops

In the first thousand years, bishops were not appointed by Rome. Pope Leo the Great emphatically said, 'Nobody should be bishop anywhere whom the people do not want as their bishop.' Things went to the bad during the exile of the popes in Avignon. There they had no financial resources, no money. The machinery of church government had to be paid for. They got resources by appointing monsignors and bishops, and so the newly appointed bishops had to pay a sum of money. So it's a late event which should be changed. I feel Rome can have a final control, a final say, but the normal procedure should be that bishops arise out of the dioceses. This will change very much the ecumenical situation. It will bring pressure on the church and there will be more creative bishops. It is unnatural, and, I would say, an institutionalised temptation if a small group of men can appoint 4000 bishops. This cannot happen without temptation of undue power.

On nuncios

Frequently apostolic delegates were appointing the man not wanted by anyone, and I know cases in which apostolic delegates accepted gifts, noticeable gifts, and that already tells me enough. When Archbishop Jadot was appointed apostolic delegate to the United States, he made a simple statement. 'I come from a wealthy family but I live as simply as I can and everyone should know that the apostolic delegate does not need and does not accept any gift.' And he appointed a magnificent number of good bishops in the United States. I think everyone can make his own commentary on this fact.

Häring had throat cancer fifteen years ago and his larynx was removed. He had to learn again to speak with his oesophagus, but even this handicap did not prevent him continuing his talks and lectures. His work will live on in his corpus of writings, which he is still adding to, but above all in the three thousand or so students who studied under him in Rome over a period of thirty-five years. They are the people who will carry on and develop his teaching into the twenty-first century.

20

CO-RESPONSIBILITY IN THE CHURCH

A Portrait of Léon-Joseph Cardinal Suenens,
one of the driving forces at the Vatican Council,
and outspoken critic of the Vatican curia

Cardinal Suenens is well known in Ireland for his support of the Charismatic Movement – he featured strongly in a film we made back in 1977 of the Charismatic Conference in the Royal Dublin Society. He is also a strong supporter of the Legion of Mary, and has written a book on the Legion envoy Edel Quinn. His major interest at present centres on 'Fiat', a movement to encourage family prayer.

So he doesn't exactly fit the image of a raging liberal.

Yet it seems to me that when the history of the church in this century comes to be written, three initiatives of his will put him head and shoulders over most of his episcopal contemporaries.

Initiative 1: Setting a liberal agenda for Vatican II

The Vatican Council was John XXIII's idea but, surrounded by a curia which deeply distrusted the whole concept, he needed some outsiders to help to bring it about. At John's request, Léon-Joseph Suenens devised the liberal agenda which made the whole Vatican II experience possible. History will thank him for that. If the curia had had its way the bishops would have assembled, rubber stamped some reactionary documents they had prepared, and gone home to their dioceses.

Initiative 2: A letter to the pope on the limits of papal authority

In 1968, when a statement on birth control seemed imminent, and Paul VI appeared to be setting aside the report and recommendations of his own Commission, Suenens wrote a letter to him which must be quoted if and when, as many seem to think, there will be a re-think of *Humanae Vitae*.

The letter, which Suenens publishes in his autobiography, is a moving document. The following short extract suggests the theme:

> Having prayed very intensely, I would like to put this problem before you, Holy Father, in the presence of Our Lord; for I believe that what is at stake here is the manner in which pontifical primacy is exercised – and thus the very future of the church.

> The sense of unease which surrounds this problem can be felt throughout the world. It arises with particular intensity in the context of two burning issues – that of birth control, which affects countless couples, and that of optional celibacy in the Latin church, which continues to trouble the clergy – and this despite the encyclical which should have brought it to an end ... The feeling of general unease, in my opinion, does not stem from any specific issue *per se*, but rather from the fact that Your Holiness has reserved for yourself the right to choose the appropriate solution, whatever it may be – thus foregoing the possibility of any collegial input or analysis by the bishops.

One of the few possible grounds for a dignified withdrawal of *Humanae Vitae* would be the acceptance by a future pope or council that Paul VI acted at least unwisely, if not *ultra vires*, in this matter, by taking upon himself, as Suenens says in his letter, 'the role of sole defender and guardian of the faith and of moral standards ... cut off from the college of bishops, from the clergy and from the world.'

Suenens sent a copy of this letter to Cardinal Villot, Vatican Secretary of State, who replied:

> The situation is complex. On the one hand there is the isolation of the Holy Father; I know that I am not the only one, among those in charge of various dicasteries (Vatican Offices) to be aware of the painful aspects of this isolation. There is also, however the absence of sustained communication and trusting dialogue with the bishops conferences. Personally, I believe that a synod that would bring together the presidents of these conferences would allow a new style of co-operation to develop.

Initiative 3: Focusing on the dominant theme of Vatican II –
Co-responsibility in the church

In 1968 Cardinal Suenens published a book called *Co-responsibility in the Church*. In his preface, he noted that within the vast complex of problems facing the church, some priorities can be discerned, 'and in these pages I have tried to draw out that which on the level of pastoral activity seems to be the dominating theme of the council: the co-responsibility of all Christians within the people of God.'

Paul himself expressed some anxiety about the book, but Cardinal Villot saw its importance when he acknowledged his copy.

> This is an extremely invigorating book, so clear-sighted that it should help us all to move forward at a time when fear might perhaps paralyse all efforts at renewal.

Co-responsibility in the Church was translated into several languages, but being a serious theological work, passed relatively unnoticed by the wider media. The following year however a French journal, *Informations Catholiques*, published an interview with Suenens on the same central thesis, and this was taken up by a wider press, and caused a tremendous stir. The key passage was the following.

> For ecumenical reasons, as well as for theological reasons, we must avoid presenting the role of the pope in a way that would isolate him from the college of bishops, whose head he is. When it is pointed out that the pope has the right to act and to speak 'alone', this word 'alone' never means 'separately' or 'in isolation.'

The curia was furious. Two French cardinals working in Rome disavowed the article in public. One said it was regrettable that Suenens made his views known to the press. Another asked him to retract. Cardinal Siri commented that Christ did not intend the church to be a democracy. (The rejoinder to which is, of course, Christ even more evidently didn't intend the church to be an autocracy!)

In the Vatican's newspaper, *Osservatore Romano*, Mgr (later Cardinal) Felici stated that Suenens wanted the pope's primacy 'to be subject to the control and approval of the bishops' – a claim that suggests Felici never read the document. Only one bishop in the world came out publicly in support – Cardinal Pellegrino of Turin, although many wrote to Suenens privately. Suenens quotes one letter from an African bishop in his biography:

We are not unaware that to speak aloud what many others think, but do not say, often requires great courage on your part. Only your profound love for the church can be the motive and the secret of such great courage.

Suenens said regretfully that most commentators did not see the main point of the interview, which was to 'note that the principle of collegiality proclaimed by the council has yet to be applied in practice.'

The 1969 Synod on Collegiality

From the very beginning of this synod, Suenens was under attack. Cardinal Heenan stated that bishops had the right and the obligation to criticise the pope – but only within the synod, never in interviews. Suenens replied with spirit:

We must be willing to recognise, with serenity and in a spirit of charity, the tension that exists within a common faith between a tendency that is known as 'monarchic' and one that is known as 'collegial'. Underlying this tension are two different theologies of the church. There is also a difference in approach, as well as a difference in sensitivity to the signs of the times, in a world in which participation in decision-making (rather than 'decision taking') is increasingly viewed as a normal exercise of co-responsibility and as the *sine qua non* condition for the correct use of authority, whatever its nature ... It would be far too easy to attempt to outdo one another in respect for the Sovereign Pontiff ... As I read the schema submitted to the synod for discussion I cannot help noting that its underlying theology exalts primacy to such an extent that bishops appear to be reduced to little more than attendants to the pontifical throne.

Speaking out

What makes Suenens unusual is not what he thinks – because many if not most bishops (at least before John Paul II began appointing them) think the same way as Suenens does. The difference was his willingness, as an active bishop, to say what he thought should be said when the need arose. I know very few other bishops in the world today who do the same.

I am continually amazed by the unwillingness of bishops to express even the slightest public criticism of either the curia or the pope in public. Yet in private where they trust the (generally clerical) company not to report them elsewhere, they will weep and tear their hair in frustration over Roman intransigence and machinations. One prominent bishop whom I much admire said, when asked why he was not at the Roman synod, 'I will go to Rome when there is some sense of reality there.' We need more bishops who will say that sort of thing in public.

I once said to a member of the Irish hierarchy, 'You are a bishop, successor of the apostles. You can't be put out of your diocese, or silenced the way a priest so easily can. You have probably gone as far in the hierarchy as you can go, and are unlikely to become a cardinal. So why don't you speak out? Why don't you say in public what you say at this dinner table?'

One has to remember of course that every bishop is chosen by the curia, and that the first requirement in the curial code is loyalty to the Holy See. I think that even if the Mother of God appeared to the commission for appointing bishops to vouch for a man's worthiness, even she wouldn't stand a chance of being heard if her candidate was ever on record as having criticised pope or curia! Those who pass this hurdle then have to take oaths of loyalty. So there is a lot of preconditioning to silence. And of course the curia have ways and means of making life difficult for those who stray.

The Vatican curia

I was once technically part of the curia with my name in the Annuario Pontificio, the Vatican Who's Who. In late 1965 I was appointed a consultor to the Pontifical Commission for the means of Social Communication. The appointment involved attending a number of meetings in Rome over a thirteen year period, so I got to know a little about the working of the Holy See. There was useful work to be done which made the experience worthwhile. The Vatican council

298

had issued a decree on communications known as *Inter Mirifica* – from the first words of the Latin text. However, many bishops were dissatisfied with the schema proposed for their approval, and only agreed to accept it on condition that a further 'pastoral instruction' be prepared after the council. Its purpose would be to fill out what was lacking in *Inter Mirifica,* and provide some guidance and inspiration for Christians working in the media.

I found it strange and quietly amusing to enter the Vatican for the first time as something more than a tourist. The Swiss guard seemed to recognise the difference – by a sort of sixth sense I presume. He clicked his heels and saluted me smartly – as befitted the dignity of a new member of the curia. And so up the side of St Peter's and through another archway – which brings one into an open space, mostly cobbled, but relieved by a little garden and a large fountain. To the left were the Vatican petrol pumps, where employees got their petrol for half nothing (they have since been moved), while in front, behind some cypress trees, stood the magnificent Palazzo San Carlo, where we held our meetings.

They say the Vatican is short of money, and I have no doubt that it is. But it couldn't have been short of money when, many years ago, it built and furnished these opulent offices. The Commission held its meetings in a fine *sala* with a balcony at one end – the perfect place to put a string quartet. But what struck me most about the Palazzo San Carlo were the pictures and *objets d'art* scattered through the offices which contributed to the ambience of quiet elegance. But let's be clear. The pope doesn't buy pictures or objets d'art, or not usually. Among artists it is a mark of honour to have one's work accepted by the Vatican, where hopefully someday it may be seen associating with Leonardos and Michelangelos. So many gifts arrive that only some can be shown publicly in the art gallery. Some of the rest find a home in places like the Communications Commission.

There were three cardinals, eleven bishops and thirty-five consultors on our Commission. Fortunately not everybody turned up. Marshall McLuhan was a consultor, but I never remember seeing him at a meeting. The President of the Westinghouse Broadcasting Corporation, Don McGannon came several times, and made an impression as a big tycoon, but I think he found the culture too strange and never contributed much to the proceedings.

My only contribution worth talking about was made during the first consultation. The Commission was presented with a text prepared in advance for our approval. It was soon clear that people with a feel for media were unhappy with it. I went to lunch with Agnellus Andrew, from the Religious Department of the BBC, and Pat Sullivan SJ, Director of the US Bishops' office for Radio and Television. There was much moaning about the draft. Agnellus informed us it was written by Fr Baragli, SJ who had also drafted the council document *Inter Mirifica*. (Which was ironic because dissatisfaction with *Inter Mirifica* was the reason why we had assembled to prepare a new document). Lunch over, the older men went for a siesta. I sat in the colonnade of St Peter's and prepared an intervention.

Early on in the afternoon session, I put my hand up and spoke briefly to three points: 1. The draft was an unsuitable basis for discussion, and this appeared to be the general view among consultors; 2. There was now a wide variety of experience among the consultors from which to pick a new drafting committee; 3. Anyone who had a part in drafting *Inter Mirifica* should be excluded. (Fr Baragli was sitting opposite to me at the table).

There was a shocked silence. Roman Commissions weren't used to doing business in that blunt way. And I was the youngest person present. However, it was soon clear that I had expressed the real wishes of the consultors and those wishes prevailed.

Agnellus Andrew savoured this moment, and made it into a good story which enhanced my reputation as a sort of *enfant terrible* in the Commission. But truth to tell, I made little enough contribution after that. I did once make an intervention about how money might be raised to pay for church initiatives in the media, and suggested – a little tongue in cheek – that perhaps the Vatican could sell a few works of art and solve all our problems.

I thought nothing more of it, but at the afternoon session the cardinal in charge of the Vatican fabric came unexpectedly to our meeting – especially it seems, to make a long speech explaining why the Vatican couldn't sell anything. I was amazed and amused, though I didn't argue with him.

This experience of one relatively insignificant part of the curia, was a great help to me to understand the culture, and its workings in larger and more important fields of the church. Cardinal Suenens has had a lot more experience of the curia. He talked of the first time he came up against it.

> I felt at once the human side of the church. I have never had trouble with that; because if you read history, well, the church is made of men and women, but we are bringing our treasures in very frail vessels.

The curia is a civil service, and perhaps the best way to understand it is to remind oneself of the popular BBC TV series, *Yes, (Prime) Minister!* This was a comedy programme, but a good comedy programme because the humour was rooted in a deep understanding of the particular foibles of human nature which emerge in the civil service situation.

Yes, Minister! 1. Manipulation and control

Governments come and go, civil servants remain – and manipulate their ministers so they can control, and generally oppose change. Popes and bishops come and go, the curia remains, and seeks control in order to oppose change. Take for instance, Cardinal Ottaviani.

Now everyone will tell you that Cardinal Ottaviani was a nice man and a good man – he ran a home for the homeless, which it seems was his only leisure activity. He was also pre-eminently the curial official, and head of the powerful Holy Office. Suenens has written of Ottaviani: 'Ottaviani was too sure that the Holy Office had the truth in everything. When an Orthodox bishop came to Pope John, before starting the conversation he said, "Holy Father, I must tell you I am not a theologian." And Pope John answered, "Neither am I, but don't tell the Holy Office." '

In Ottaviani's view of things, Pope John was leading the church towards total disaster. The Holy Office – where he was virtual dictator – had in his not so humble opinion, a monopoly on authentic theology – that is to say, his theology. The Vatican Council, he believed, had no business discussing the seventy schemas which he had had prepared for it under his own instructions. They should approve them and go home. As a member of the council's central steering committee, Cardinal Suenens had to face him head on.

> I said to Ottaviani, 'No! No! The pope has approved seventy schemas as – matters to be discussed,' so there we had to fight. Also he didn't accept it when I proposed to put questions to the assembly without consulting him. He said, 'I only have the right to put questions, you have no right.'

In fact the seventy schemas were thrown out by the council. Ottaviani never recovered from seeing the council regulations applied to him on the same basis as other bishops. When he spoke for more than the allotted ten minutes, and was pulled up by the Assembly President, he got such a shock that he didn't appear at the council again for several days!

If you have seen *Yes, Minister!* and have a reasonable memory, you will recognise much of this behaviour.

There is one more story about Ottaviani which perhaps encapsulates the curial mind. Suenens felt that if one could have an international theological commission made up of theologians appointed by their bishops from different parts of the world, one could have a theology in Rome which was closer to reality than the theology of the curia. He wrote about the matter later.

> Finally the idea came through, and even Ottaviani was not opposed to the idea of an international theological commission, but he said, 'We will name them!' So there was no reason any more to have a commission!

Ottaviani is long dead, but his successor still appoints members of the theological commission, now largely an honorary position. It in no sense represents a cross section of Catholic theological opinion, as Suenens once hoped it might.

Yes Minister! 2: Civil and ecclesiastical sycophancy
Civil servants please or displease their ministers and thereby move up and down the promotional ladder. Curial officials please or

displease cardinals and popes, and move up and down the ecclesiastical tree.

I hate sycophancy, boot licking, call it what you will. 'Eminenza' and 'Eccelenza' and kissing rings and bowing and scraping – there's a lot of that in the Vatican. And if you don't enter into the game, there's no point in wasting time there. It's endemic in the civil service tradition. But there is one crucial difference between the curia and the normal civil service. Ministers in civil society are elected politicians from outside the service, who are in tension with it. More often than not ecclesiastical ministers, heads of Congregations, even a majority of popes, come from within the curial system itself. So that creative tension between elected politician and career civil servant, which is so important in civil society, does not exist in the church.

I don't think one needs to know much about human nature to realise that the most important of all processes in the Vatican open to manipulation is the election of the pope himself. The curial cardinals are in the best position to study form – it could be considered part of their job. The cardinals from busy dioceses around the world don't have all that much opportunity to get to know each other. And who has access to all the files to sow a bit of praise here and a bit of dirt there? Who indeed but the members of the curia. Sometimes they make mistakes but not often. John XXIII was a mistake. He was only supposed to be a caretaker keeping the seat warm for the former Under Secretary of State and Head of Ordinary Affairs, Giovanni Montini (later Paul VI). Pius XII had been annoyed with Montini, some have suggested, and deprived him of the cardinalate so he couldn't succeed him. True or not, the heir apparent wasn't a cardinal when Pius died, and therefore could take no part in the election. Then John went wild in curial terms and called the Second Vatican Council, but that was an aberration that no one could have foreseen.

Yes Minister! 3: Keeping in touch with reality

Despite the fact that they live in a very closed society (in the British model, bowler hats, umbrellas, and select London clubs) civil servants are quite happy to make decisions for the real world, which they often know very little about. The clerical version is no exception.

Dermot Ryan, Archbishop of Dublin, was appointed Prefect of the Congregation for the Evangelisation of Peoples in 1984. This is the biggest 'ministry' in the church, having responsibility for appointing bishops and providing most of the finance for over 800 dioceses in mission territories all over the world. One of the first things the archbishop did was to call his staff together for an information session. He was troubled to find that many of the senior officials who were dealing with the church in various parts of the world, had never even visited the countries for which they were responsible, and in whose interest they were regularly making decisions. To Dermot's credit he told them to make up the deficiency as soon as possible, and he would pay their airfares.

It seems to me that the kind of co-responsibility and collegiality that Cardinal Suenens would like to see is quite impossible without drastic controls being placed on the Roman curia. It's a brave man who will try it, and if such a person exists among the cardinals, the curia will naturally take all the steps necessary and within its power to see he is not elected. But then even the curia can make mistakes. And maybe the Holy Spirit will want them to make another big one.

Yes, Minister 4: Knowing better than the boss

Pope John had many problems with the curia. The one that irked him most perhaps was that they censored what he said. Speeches of popes are noted for posterity in the *Acts of the Holy See (AAS)*. Pope John found himself repeatedly and deliberately misquoted and misrepresented.

Take for instance his speech at the opening of the Vatican Council when John said: 'Christians and Catholics of apostolic spirit all the world over expect a leap forward in doctrinal insight ...'

The AAS do not mention any leap forward.

John added: 'But the authentic doctrine has to be studied and expanded in the light of the research methods and the language of modern thought.'

The AAS substituted: 'This certain and unchangeable doctrine to which faithful obedience is due, should be investigated in the way our age demands.'

John said: 'For the substance of the ancient deposit of faith is one thing, and the way in which it is presented is another.'

The AAS substituted: 'The deposit of faith itself, or the truths which are contained in our venerable doctrine is one thing, and the way in which it is expressed is another, retaining however the same sense and meaning.' (In other words, no change!)

At other times, the curia simply said 'No' to the pope. When against the advice of the Secretariat of State, John met Khrushchev's son-in-law in the Vatican, John asked that the account written at his request by the interpreter be published. The Secretariat of State refused to allow *Osservatore Romano* to do so.

John wrote a note for history about this episode. 'I deplore and pity those who, in these last few days, have lent themselves to unspeakable manoeuvres.' Then, good man that he was, he added typically, 'I forgive and forget'. Which is probably one of the reasons the curia knew they could get away with frustrating him.

I am indebted to *John XXIII, Pope of the Council*, by Peter Hebblethwaite for these details   (pp. 431-2)

The importance of monarchy

A big gallery of theologians – from the radical wing one must surmise – came together to celebrate twenty-five years of *Concilium*, a theological publication. It was just after the collapse of Eastern Europe, and some nameless theologian is reported to have observed, 'Now the pope is the only dictator left in Europe'.

I don't like the word 'dictator'. It's a pejorative word. But 'monarch' is not, or usen't to be. Monarchs are such by divine right, or so the theory once went; in other words God put them there. Apparently he doesn't want them there any more, except for a few figureheads, and of course the pope.

The fact that the Roman church is a form of absolute monarchy depresses many people. I hope it will change in the long run, but for the moment I find it a consolation. The fact that the pope is still a relatively absolute monarch means that the church has the capacity to be changed out of all recognition simply by papal decree, in a papal reign, a papal year, a week, even a day. (Although a long reign is probably needed because reforms have to be copper-fastened against one's successor, and that takes time.) John XXIII was one who changed the church very radically, but didn't live long enough to prevent his successors reversing the trend.

I wouldn't care much for being a bishop nowadays, but I'd find it hard to refuse if the Lord appeared to me and said he wanted me to be pope! There is so much good one could do. I would dismantle much of the curia, much like Yeltsin and Gorbachev dismantled the communist party; and of course abolish nuncios. I would move the Papal Court to St John Lateran, which is really the pope's proper church, and try and divorce the church someway from those triumphalistic buildings, artworks and museum that crown Vatican Hill. I would not cry at losing St Peter's. That building cost us the Reformation, and all the immeasurable suffering that religious division brought to the peoples of Europe.

I would admit women immediately to decision-making in church government. I would find some way of consulting the church as a whole on the vexing question of the ordination of women. Vexing because, for instance, a change in the practice would bring enormous ecumenical problems vis-à-vis the Orthodox Church. In the end, if after consultation it appeared that the Holy Spirit, speaking through the church at large, favoured the change, then I would perform the first ordinations. For all the conservative arguments against it must fail when I say it is to be done. Conservatives, by definition, believe in my infallibility, and therefore if I declare with my full authority that women can be ordained, then it must be so.

I would appoint a commission largely made up of lay people to examine the whole tortuous area of sexual morality, and trust that the Holy Spirit would speak through them. I would infallibly declare in the interests of Christian unity that the pope was not infallible – though not in the beginning, because it would be a useful tool in cutting the ground from under the reactionary elements who would be opposing with tooth and claw every move I made.

I would apologise for much that my church has said and done in the past. I would apologise for the Holy Office, now disguised under still another name, and suggest that Cardinal Ratzinger study Christianity in a German monastery. I would be an autocrat promoting a liberal agenda – which is probably a contradiction in reality as well as in terms!

It's easy to say all that, because I have as much chance of becoming pope as well ... name your favourite Hollywood star.

On a more serious note, however, the full power of the papacy as presently constituted is truly awesome in terms of the power a pope can wield. He is above church law – not above Divine Law of course, but then if he says something is not Divine Law, who is there to contradict? In practice popes are hemmed in, manipulated, frustrated by the curial officials around them. But that needn't be. The pope can fire everyone in the Vatican down to the most junior papal guard and appoint whomsoever he wills in their place: and fire all the replacements the following day.

Come, O Holy Spirit, fill the hearts of the cardinals at the next consistory – the time is ripe for a truly reforming pope.

Why the film portrait took more time to complete

But to come back to the programme about Cardinal Suenens, and why it wasn't completed. Suenens gave some useful interviews. But now that he is retired he is no longer willing to speak directly about the great controversial issues, but refers one to what he has said and written in the past. One must respect that decision. He spoke out when he was Archbishop of Malines: to speak out now might only embarrass his successor. Nor is he willing to comment on what is happening in the church today. 'Keep it in the past or keep it in the future,' he said when asked about collegiality, 'but I don't wish to enter into discussion of today'.

Suenens was on the famous birth control commission, and is known to have been one of the large majority who recommended a change in the church's position on artificial contraceptives. But again he would not talk about it directly.

It was a private secret commission so we cannot speak about it easily, but a book has been written by an American publisher. [*The Politics of Sex and Religion* by Robert Kaiser]. Well, I have to say that the story is true, what he says there, but I may not go into details, but you have it there, the essential story.

True! The story is there, and in great detail. And it is of considerable historical importance that Suenens should confirm its veracity. But for the purposes of our programme we would have preferred to have Suenens tell more of his story himself. The only way out is to use script to fill the gaps. That needs archive pictures from film libraries and they can take time and trouble and money to come by. But we are working on it!

EPILOGUE

I realise this book will have offended some who get this far, and I much regret that. I realise too that I am leaving myself open to a variety of criticisms, some valid, some off the mark. I hope I can face criticism the way I would expect others to do. But I foresee criticism in one area where I would like, as it were, to make a pre-emptive strike.

I have *not* a chip on my shoulder because any ecclesiastical authority ever dealt roughly with me. In nearly forty years of priesthood, I have received nothing but continuous encouragement and support from those in high places.

I have *not* a chip on my shoulder because I was never made a bishop – this is one of the commonest *argumenta ad hominem* used against any priest who publicly criticises church or hierarchy. If I had ever wanted to be a bishop, or even considered it as a remote possibility, then I was certainly very, very stupid – far too stupid to be a bishop. Because if anyone looks at my record they will see that, from the beginning, I did all the wrong things and made all the wrong choices (often deliberately). In fact, one reason, I sometimes thought, why I got on well with bishops was because they knew I had no ambition to join them.

I take no pleasure in the thought that some people who have no love for the church will find comfort in any of my criticisms. The Christian church has been the greatest humanising and civilising force in human history. But the church doesn't need people like me to catalogue that contribution. It does seem to me to need help to begin to come to terms with the idea of a loyal opposition.

In the course of the book, I quote Dr George Lindbeck, who was a Lutheran observer at the Second Vatican Council, speaking in 1989, some twenty-five years after the council. I want to quote him again because, in a sense, he encapsulates the reason which brought me to write much of this book.

One way of describing the limitations of the changes that have taken place in the Roman curia is to say that the Roman Catholic Church still has not learned to deal with a loyal opposition – it has not learned how to make a distinction between a loyal opposition and a disloyal one. And no church can, it seems to me, really have the kind of renewal that was projected by the Second Vatican Council unless it learns to live with those who, out of love for the church, for God, for Jesus Christ, criticise the church.

I would like to make that final sentence mine.

Index

DATE DUE